DATA ANALYSIS IN CRIMINAL JUSTICE AND CRIMINOLOGY

DATA ANALYSIS IN CRIMINAL JUSTICE AND CRIMINOLOGY

HISTORY, CONCEPT, AND APPLICATION

FIRST EDITION

PHILIP D. MCCORMACK AND ANGELA CALLAHAN

Bassim Hamadeh, CEO and Publisher

John Remington, Acquisitions Editor

Gem Rabanera, Project Editor

Alia Bales, Production Editor

Emely Villavicencio, Senior Graphic Designer

Trey Soto, Licensing Coordinator

Jennifer Redding, Interior Designer

Natalie Piccotti, Director of Marketing

Kassie Graves, Vice President of Editorial

Jamie Giganti, Director of Academic Publishing

Cover image: Copyright © 2017 iStockphoto LP/MicroStockHub.

Printed in the United States of America.

ISBN: 978-1-5165-1816-6 (pbk) / 978-1-5165-1817-3 (br) / 978-1-5165-4635-0 (al)

CONTENTS

This section of textbook introduces and provides a general discussion of why we use data analysis in criminal justice and criminology. The section will provide both historical and contemporary context to this discussion, providing you with the foundations and origins of data analysis in the fields of criminal justice and criminology. Further, a chronology of analytical developments will be discussed, specifically those which have brought the field (and the classroom) to where it is today. Each chapter herein introduces fundamental concepts of data and analysis needed before any computation can take place.

SECTION II: DESCRIPTIVE STATISTICS   75

This section provides a general discussion of samples (versus populations), as well as distributions (such as the assumption of the normal curve) and, briefly, the central limit theorem as it relates to data analysis. This section will provide you with the fundamental knowledge and skills needed to understand statistical concepts and perform rudimentary statistical calculations. Each chapter herein explains, with the use of examples and practical application, the components, uses, and most appropriate times to use particular descriptive statistics.

SECTION III: INFERENTIAL STATISTICS   131

This section provides a general discussion of the purpose of moving from statistical description to statistical inference and how sample statistics can be used in the estimation of population parameters. The section will build upon the previous section, explaining the utility of descriptive statistics and their importance in inferential statistics, and provide you with practical examples at each step. Each chapter herein explains, with the use of examples and practical application, the components, uses, and most appropriate times to use particular statistical tests and inferential statistics.

CHAPTER 6. TESTS OF EQUALITY   132

SECTION I

THE BASICS OF DATA IN CRIMINAL JUSTICE AND CRIMINOLOGY

This section of the textbook introduces and provides a general discussion of why we use data analysis in criminal justice and criminology. The section will provide both historical and contemporary context to this discussion, providing you with the foundations and origins of data analysis in the fields of criminal justice and criminology. Furthermore, a chronology of analytical developments will be discussed, specifically those which have brought the field (and the classroom) to where it is today. Each chapter herein introduces fundamental concepts of data and analysis needed before any computation can take place.

CHAPTER 1

ORIGIN OF THE DATA WE ANALYZE

INTRODUCTION: DATA ANALYSIS IN CRIMINAL JUSTICE AND CRIMINOLOGY

For the past half century there has been a great deal of discussion of the need for dependable facts relating to crime, criminals, and the administration of justice in the United States. ... But despite all of this work, there has not been produced in the United States any systematic collection of information on crime which furnishes the factual information desired, or which is comparable to the criminal statistics of many other countries. (Beattie, 1955, p. 178)

Despite the seemingly distant nature of Ronald H. Beattie's quote, the same words could be spoken today. The fields of criminal justice and criminology have developed exponentially in the last several decades, particularly in terms of quantitative methods, e.g., statistics and data analysis. These fields are relatively young in their genesis compared to other social sciences, such as sociology (from which criminology was born) and psychology, and are far more recent of a development than any physical science. What has helped bridge the gap in terms of progression of the fields has been the use of advanced analytical methods. While the social world functions differently than what can be controlled and measured in a laboratory, criminal justice and criminology can (and do) utilize the same methods to collect and analyze data. The sources of data are varied in scope, focus, content, and use. However, today, even if researchers may desire more and better data, those which are available are a far cry from those which were available just a few short decades ago.

Consider the following questions:

1. How many crimes are committed in the United States each year?

2. Which individual characteristics are associated with criminal victimization?

3. What are the staff levels and operating budgets of law enforcement agencies?

These questions can be answered without learning advanced research skills. In fact, most of the information related to, if not exactly, the answers to these questions are publicly available. This was not always the case. Not only were these data unavailable in the not-so-distant past, but the data that were available were limited in their dissemination. Due to advances in technology, specifically the Internet, these questions and many more can be answered simply by searching the web or visiting the webpage of your local law enforcement agency. The data are collected by different groups, such as individual researchers, law enforcement agencies, and federal offices. The data are also collected from different groups, such as agencies, institutions, households, and individuals. And, the data are collected for different reasons, such as description, explanation, administration, and prediction. This chapter examines the histories, characteristics, and uses of the various forms of criminal justice data collection instruments.

LEARNING OBJECTIVES

By the end of this chapter, students will be able to:
1: Identify the various forms of crime data collection
2: Discuss the history of each crime data collection instrument
3: Explain the purpose of each crime data collection instrument
4: Evaluate the strengths and contributions of each form of crime data collection
5: Assess the advantages and limitations of each form of crime data collection

KEY TERMS

ADMINISTRATIVE DATA

AGGREGATE

COHORT STUDIES

DARK FIGURE OF CRIME

INCIDENT-BASED REPORTING SYSTEM (IBRS)

INDEX CRIMES

OFFICIAL STATISTICS

OMNIBUS SURVEYS

SECONDARY DATA ANALYSIS

VICTIM SURVEYS

OFFICIAL STATISTICS

The fields of criminal justice and criminology often use official statistics to measure and analyze criminal phenomena. These data are the function of official bodies, such as law enforcement, courts, and correctional agencies collecting and aggregating information about incidents, individuals, and cases processed within their respective systems. Perhaps the most commonly cited official statistics relating to crime are those gathered and produced by United States law enforcement agencies.

UNIFORM CRIME REPORTS (UCR)

The Uniform Crime Reports (UCR) have the distinction of being the oldest and most expansive, in terms of population and geographic coverage, sources of crime data in the United States. Interestingly, despite legislative approval, it took 60 years until the initial national collection of crime statistics. In 1870, Congress authorized the collection of crime statistics, but neither the development nor the implementation of any national data collection instrument was realized. This was also the year in which the agency responsible for this data collection, the Department of Justice, was established. What was the impetus for the implementation of the UCR? The lobbying of police executives initiated the collection of crime data. In 1893 the International Association of Chiefs of Police (IACP) was formed to:

> ... advance the science and area of police services; to develop and disseminate improved administrative, technical and operational practices and promote their use in police work; to foster police cooperation and the exchange of information and experience ... among police administrators throughout the world. (IACP, n.d.)

During the 1920s, there was widespread belief that crime was ever-present and on the rise. Highly publicized criminals such as Al Capone, John Dillinger, and Bonnie and Clyde helped to perpetuate this notion. What was there to refute these claims? In the vein of criminal statistics, there was nothing available. Only anecdotal or local information was available. As a result, the IACP began to lobby for the implementation of some form of a data collection program. Beginning in 1927, the UCR began to take shape. In 1927, the IACP created a group called the "Committee on Uniform Crime Records," which included the acting Bureau of Investigation (now the Federal Bureau of Investigation [FBI]) director, J. Edgar Hoover, to develop and oversee the data collection program. The Committee had several issues to deal with initially, including the source of funding, leadership and responsibility, and the setting of universal (*uniform*) definitions of crime. Which crimes were to be measured? How would these crimes be defined and classified? These questions needed to be answered before the instrument could be developed for use.

The question of what to include in crime reporting has been at the forefront of data collection for nearly 200 years. In his treatise, *France, Social, Literary, Political*, Henry Bulwer (1836) discussed the problem of using A) offenses known or B) offenses reported as measures of crime. He concluded that each were ripe with limitations but were still better than using C) convictions. Related, Morrison (1897) routinely critiqued criminal statistics, even those used in his own work. Perhaps his most notable contribution to criminology and statistics was his introductory paper in the *Journal of the Royal Statistical Society* (1897). He notes it would be a mistake to assume that official statistics, e.g., crimes known to and recorded by the police, were a complete index of yearly crime. Morrison divided criminal justice data into three categories: police, judicial, and prison statistics. He specifically stated that police statistics are the most comprehensive accounts of annual crime.

The IACP held this same belief. The most appropriate measure of crime would be those reported to police. The IACP identified what we now classify as Index, or Part I, crimes: murder, rape, robbery, aggravated assault, burglary, larceny/theft, and motor vehicle theft. Future reports would include the crime of arson as well, due to a 1978 Congressional mandate (Pub. L. No. 95–624). The IACP then adopted standardized offense definitions for these offenses. Agencies were to be guided on how to classify specific offenses in order to accurately document their occurrence. This ensured every agency was classifying offenses in a similar fashion. The IACP published the first Uniform Crime Reports bulletin in January 1930.

Figure 1.1 Uniform Crime Reports Logo

The first bulletin reported crime in 400 cities and 43 states, providing the nation with its first count of crime. Amazingly, the UCR was finalized just two months prior. The IACP was responsible for these bulletins until later that year, when they became federally managed. Congress had authorized the Bureau of Investigation to be responsible for the collection, compilation, and publication of crime data (28 U.S.C. § 534). The Bureau was to begin just three months later, providing its first report in September of 1930. The UCR has continually expanded, been refined, and experimented with the collection of different data elements, classifications, and definitions to keep up with the constant change in legal codes and police practices. Today, in addition to the Index crimes, the UCR also collects data on what is referred to as Part II crimes, providing only data pertaining to arrests for these offenses.

The latest publications of the UCR data show just how much this voluntary program has expanded. For example, in 2014, 18,500 unique reporting agencies submitted data via the UCR program, including city, state, federal, county, university, and tribal agencies (FBI, 2016). These data represent 97.7% of the United States population. Although the UCR is popular in its participation by

INDEX CRIMES:
The eight most serious offenses, as determined by the FBI, for which data are collected on reported crimes and arrests. There are four violent Index and four property Index crimes.

law enforcement agencies and in its use by media, researchers, and the populace alike, it is not without its flaws. One of the fundamental concerns has already been made clear by Bulwer. In addition to relying upon data only from law enforcement, the data that are collected are considered even more conservative

RETURN A - MONTHLY RETURN OF OFFENSES KNOWN TO THE POLICE
1-720a (Rev. 3-08-06)
OMB No. 1110-0001
Expires 01-30-10

This report is authorized by law Title 28, Section 534, U.S. Code. Your cooperation in completing this form will assist the FBI, in compiling timely, comprehensive, and accurate data. Please submit this form monthly, by the seventh day after the close of the month, and any questions to the FBI, Criminal Justice Information Services Division, Attention: Uniform Crime Reports/Module E-3, 1000 Custer Hollow Road, Clarksburg, West Virginia 26306; telephone 304-625-4830, facsimile 304-625-3566. Under the Paperwork Reduction Act, you are not required to complete this form unless it contains a valid OMB control number. The form takes approximately 10 minutes to complete. Instructions for preparing the form appear on the reverse side.

CLASSIFICATION OF OFFENSES	DATA ENTRY	2 — OFFENSES REPORTED OR KNOWN TO POLICE (INCLUDE "UNFOUNDED" AND ATTEMPTS)	3 — UNFOUNDED, I.E.	4 — NUMBER OF ACTUAL OFFENSES (INCLUDE ATTEMPTS)	5 — TOTAL OFFENSES CLEARED BY ARREST OR EXCEPTIONAL MEANS (INCLUDES COL. 6)	6 — NUMBER OF CLEARANCES INVOLVING ONLY PERSONS UNDER 18 YEARS OF AGE
1. CRIMINAL HOMICIDE						
a. MURDER AND NONNEGLIGENT HOMICIDE (Score attempts as aggravated assault) If homicide reported, submit Supplementary Homicide Report	11					
b. MANSLAUGHTER BY NEGLIGENCE	12					
2. FORCIBLE RAPE TOTAL	20					
a. Rape by Force	21					
b. Attempts to commit Forcible Rape	22					
3. ROBBERY TOTAL	30					
a. Firearm	31					
b. Knife or Cutting Instrument	32					
c. Other Dangerous Weapon	33					
d. Strong-Arm (Hands, Fists, Feet, Etc.)	34					
4. ASSAULT TOTAL	40					
a. Firearm	41					
b. Knife or Cutting Instrument	42					
c. Other Dangerous Weapon	43					
d. Hands, Fists, Feet, Etc. - Aggravated injury	44					
e. Other Assaults - Simple, Not Aggravated	45					
5. BURGLARY TOTAL	50					
a. Forcible Entry	51					
b. Unlawful Entry - No Force	52					
c. Attempted Forcible Entry	53					
6. LARCENY - THEFT TOTAL (Except Motor Vehicle Theft)	60					
7. MOTOR VEHICLE THEFT TOTAL	70					
a. Autos	71					
b. Trucks and Buses	72					
c. Other Vehicles	73					
GRAND TOTAL	77					

CHECKING ANY OF THE APPROPRIATE BLOCKS BELOW WILL ELIMINATE YOUR NEED TO SUBMIT REPORTS WHEN THE VALUES ARE ZERO. THIS WILL ALSO AID THE NATIONAL PROGRAM IN ITS QUALITY CONTROL EFFORTS.

☐ NO SUPPLEMENTARY HOMICIDE REPORT SUBMITTED SINCE NO MURDERS, JUSTIFIABLE HOMICIDES, OR MANSLAUGHTERS BY NEGLIGENCE OCCURRED IN THIS JURISDICTION DURING THE MONTH.

☐ NO SUPPLEMENT TO RETURN A REPORT SINCE NO CRIME OFFENSES OR RECOVERY OF PROPERTY REPORTED DURING THE MONTH.

☐ NO LAW ENFORCEMENT OFFICERS KILLED OR ASSAULTED REPORT SINCE NONE OF THE OFFICERS WERE ASSAULTED OR KILLED DURING THE MONTH.

☐ NO AGE, SEX, AND RACE OF PERSONS ARRESTED UNDER 18 YEARS OF AGE REPORT SINCE NO ARRESTS OF PERSONS WITHIN THIS AGE GROUP.

☐ NO AGE, SEX, AND RACE OF PERSONS ARRESTED 18 YEARS OF AGE AND OVER REPORT SINCE NO ARREST OF PERSONS WITHIN THIS AGE GROUP.

☐ NO MONTHLY RETURN OF ARSON OFFENSES KNOWN TO LAW ENFORCEMENT REPORT SINCE NO ARSONS OCCURRED.

DO NOT USE THIS SPACE

	INITIALS
RECORDED	
EDITED	
ENTERED	
ADJUSTED	
CORRES	

_____ Month and Year of Report

_____ Agency Identifier

_____ Population

_____ Prepared by

_____ Title

_____ Telephone Number

_____ Date

_____ Agency and State

_____ Chief, Sheriff, Superintendent, or Commanding Officer

Figure 1.2 Uniform Crime Reports Return A Form

in their crime estimates due to the hierarchy rule. Under this rule, only the single most serious crime is counted and reported for each criminal incident. Thus, if several crimes were committed as part of one event—such as a burglary, vandalism, and then aggravated assault—we would never know this as the UCR only counts one offense: in this case, the aggravated assault. The two property crimes would not be reported, only the violent crime.

Box 1.1 WHAT WE'VE LEARNED: Uniform Crime Reports

The Uniform Crime Reports (UCR) have provided the government, researchers, practitioners, and the general public with annually published crime totals, as well as rates to account for populations of varying size. Research has shown that varied circumstances, geographic and temporal, have influenced crime rates. Using the data provided by the UCR, research has shown that some factors have consistently been found to affect the frequency and rate of crime, such as population density, residential mobility, economic conditions, climate, and law enforcement size—to name just a few (FBI, 2010). Research has also shown the youth concentration of a jurisdiction, commuting patterns, education and religious characteristics, family conditions, and reporting practices of the public to be related to the frequency and rate of crime (FBI, 2017). The yearly collection of data also allows for the examination of crime patterns over time. For example, violent and property crime have significantly decreased since the mid-1990s. Between 1995 and 2015, the total violent crime rate in the United States decreased by 46.6%, with the largest reduction seen in robbery offenses. During that same period, the total property crime rate in the United States decreased by 43.4%, with the largest reduction seen in motor vehicle theft (FBI, 2015a).

NATIONAL INCIDENT-BASED REPORTING SYSTEM (NIBRS)

In an effort to address some of the shortcomings of the UCR, a joint task force composed of prominent members of both the FBI and the Bureau of Justice Statistics (BJS) was created. The task force was charged with conducting a three-phase initiative. The first phase began in the fall of 1982 when the UCR was examined from its development to the (then) present day. The task force studied the construction and implementation of the data collection instrument, as well as its evolution over time. The second phase of the project was to identify possible enhancements to the UCR. This phase resulted in recommendations to modify the UCR. As an extension and follow-up to these recommendations, the task force then used the recommendations to develop a new, revised system of crime data collection. This was initiated in 1988 (Roberts, 1997). The result was the National Incident-Based Reporting System (NIBRS) (Poggio, Kennedy, Chaiken, & Carlson, 1985).

NIBRS is a cross-sectional incident-based reporting system (IBRS) operated by the United States Department of Justice, FBI, just like the UCR. In fact, NIBRS can be thought of as an extension of the UCR. When data are reported using NIBRS, the agency nearly always also submits data through the UCR. Just like its predecessor, participating law enforcement agencies voluntarily report information on a monthly basis. These agencies operate at the municipal, county, and state levels. As an incident-based reporting system, data are collected for each criminal offense. The data provided by NIBRS are far more detailed than the previously developed summary reporting system—the UCR. The UCR contains summary data that only allow for analysis of aggregate data. NIBRS allows for the detailed examination of incident-level crime data. Specifically, the data available provide information

IBRS

on administrative, incident, property, victim, offender, and when applicable, arrestee characteristics. NIBRS contains data on each criminal incident within 23 offense categories that include 49 specific offenses (FBI, 2013). These crimes comprise Group A offenses. Group B offenses comprise 10 additional offenses that only provide arrest data. These groups are somewhat similar to the UCR's Part I and Part II crimes, since they were initially derived from them. However, over time, NIBRS has expanded to include far more offense types in its reporting.

After some years of development, a pilot program was conducted in South Carolina for seven months in 1987. After receiving feedback and further developing the instrument, the FBI began to collect crime data using NIBRS guidelines in 1989. However, it was not until 1991 that states began to meet certification standards in order to submit data to NIBRS. South Carolina was the first state. The initial year saw the participation of 663 law enforcement agencies, concentrated in just three states: Alabama, South Carolina, and North Dakota (Reaves, 1993). This first-year data represented only 3.3% coverage of the United States' population, vastly inferior to the UCR. As a voluntary and, perhaps more importantly, supplemental data collection instrument, NIBRS has clearly yet to reach the level of participation that the UCR has. To this point, data from 2014 show that participation has expanded to 6,520 law enforcement agencies, representing approximately 29% coverage of the United States' population (FBI, 2015b; McCormack, Pattavina, & Tracy, 2017). Not only is the coverage relatively low, but the agencies that participate are overwhelmingly smaller agencies (Addington, 2008). One can imagine the wealth of information that is unavailable to researchers—which is not reported by large cities.

Roberts (2009) has a widely cited summary of the utility and, perhaps more importantly, limitations of NIBRS since its inception. As a result of how young and expansive NIBRS is compared to the UCR, there are many generalizability issues. The data we gather and analyze from NIBRS may be best used at this time to describe smaller agencies. There are issues of regional representation as well. NIBRS is overrepresented by southern agencies and underrepresented by western agencies (Chilton & Regoeczi, 2007). As a result, we might think of NIBRS as being best used at this time to describe small, southern agencies and criminal incidents therefrom, rather than United States criminal incidents.

Despite its limitations, largely due to participation levels, the potential of NIBRS is incalculable. It is quite versatile in its application based on the vast amount of information that can be made available for each criminal incident. For Group A offenses, there can be up to 10 different offenses, 99 offenders, 999 victims, and six types of property loss recorded for each incident. For Group B offenses, there can be up to 99 arrestees recorded for each incident. With the potential for this much information, one might assume that what NIBRS can tell us about crime generally in the United States is far more than what the UCR can. In fact, there are only slight differences with respect to national estimates derived from each instrument. Research has examined what would happen to crime counts (and rates) if NIBRS was used instead of the UCR and the hierarchy rule. Both early and more recent findings suggest that the effect is minimal, specifically for the most severe crimes (Rantala & Edwards, 2000; FBI, 2015c).

Box 1.2: WHAT WE'VE LEARNED: National Incident-Based Reporting System

One of the most common ways the National Incident-Based Reporting System (NIBRS) is used is in the examination of arrest rates or the likelihood an incident will result in some form of a clearance-like outcome. Countless studies have examined the context in which these outcomes are observed, utilizing a variety of theoretical perspectives. Findings show that factors such as race, age, gender, weapon use, victim injury, and the presence of the offender affect the likelihood an incident will result in arrest (Hirschel & Buzawa, 2008). Hirschel and Buzawa (2008) examined the likelihood of arrest in intimate partner violence cases submitted through the 2000 NIBRS. The study found several significant relationships between jurisdiction, incident, offender, and victim variables and the likelihood an incident would result in an arrest. Significant factors included: population density, residential mobility, and racial composition of the jurisdiction; who reported the incident, the offense type, whether an injury occurred, if a weapon was used, and if a minor or offender was on scene; the gender and race of the victim; and the gender, race, age, of the offender and whether they used drugs (pp. 27–29). Results also showed that states with mandatory and preferred arrest laws had higher arrest rates than states with a discretionary arrest law.

NATIONAL CRIME STATISTICS EXCHANGE (NCS-X)

The National Crime Statistics Exchange (NCS-X) is currently in development to address the fact that NIBRS is not yet representative of the entire United States. As a joint project, including collaboration and insight from multiple organizations, the BJS is spearheading this attempt to make incident-based data generalizable. The NCS-X is an attempt to add to the current data submitted through NIBRS. In 2014, NIBRS included incident-level data from over 6,000 law enforcement agencies, compared to over 18,000 agencies represented in the UCR. The hope is that the participation of an additional, and strategically selected, sample of 400 law enforcement agencies will balance the small and southern agency skew the current data have (BJS, n.d.).

Figure 1.3 National Crime Statistics Exchange Logo

VICTIM SURVEYS

Victim surveys ask individuals about incidents in which they may have been a victim of a crime. These surveys are, generally, not purposive: individuals who were not victims of crime also participate. This has allowed for the comparison to officially recorded data from instruments such as the UCR to quantify the dark figure of crime. Such comparisons have yielded estimates that suggest only approximately half of all committed crime is reported to and then recorded by law enforcement. The first wide-scale criminal victim survey was conducted in 1967 by the National Opinion Research Center (NORC).

NATIONAL CRIME VICTIMIZATION SURVEY (NCVS)

Henry Bulwer, in his 1836 treatise on France, provided insight into the (appropriate) measurement of crime. He stated that to measure the volume of crime, it would be most appropriate to use recorded crime or that of the accused. It would be some time until a reliable instrument was developed to obtain data from victims. In the United States, that instrument was the National Crime Victimization Survey (NCVS). The NCVS is the most widely known and cited source of information regarding criminal victimization in the United States. The origin of the NCVS can be traced back to 1972 when the National Crime Survey (NCS) was initiated.

Responsible for the creation of the victimization survey was the President's Commission on Law Enforcement and Administration of Justice. Established in 1965 by President Lyndon B. Johnson, the Commission was charged with a variety of responsibilities, one of which was the determination of the causes and distribution of crime. As a result, the Commission was involved in several initiatives to measure victimization and attitudes toward crime. At the time, the UCR provided the only national measure of crime. However, it only described crimes that were made known to law enforcement and were recorded, not those unmeasured by official statistics. This discrepancy is commonly referred to as the dark figure of crime.

By 1969, federal agencies were working in a collaborative attempt to develop an appropriate, and accurate, instrument to measure victimization in the United States. For the next three years, the instrument was discussed, developed, and piloted across the United States. In July 1972, the National Crime Survey was launched. The survey varies in its respondent size when conducted. However, it always includes a large probability sample, initially including 72,000 households (and 15,000 businesses) while the most recent data from 2015 were collected from approximately 90,000 households (Rand, 2006; Truman & Morgan, 2016). When the NCS began, the sample was staggered in its data collection: one sixth of the initial sample began every six months. The households chosen for the sample are surveyed for three years. Every six months, the households that have been in the sample for the full three years are rotated out of the sample, and another group of households enters. This helps ensure representativeness. The rotating sample of households accurately reflects the changing characteristics of the United States.

The NCVS is a crime panel. Panels are repeated interviews that are conducted at regular intervals to provide a benchmark for reporting. The NCVS is conducted every six months for three years. The initial survey is conducted using a traditional face-to-face interview. An adult household member, usually the head of household, is interviewed. The primary survey takes approximately 30 minutes to complete. This includes screening questions and incident reports. Questions concerning personal victimization are asked of every household member 12 years or older. Subsequent interviews are obtained through a combination of personal and telephone interviews. In addition to the frequency of victimizations, the NCVS can provide much greater detail of incidents, such as victim–offender relationships, injury or loss suffered, characteristics of the incident, and characteristics of the offender.

Box 1.3: WHAT WE'VE LEARNED: National Crime Victimization Survey

The NCVS has been instrumental in providing a more complete description of crime in the United States. One of the strengths of the survey is its inherent ability, as a victimization survey, to provide data that law enforcement is unable to: that of unreported crime. Without the NCVS, we would not know that approximately half of all crimes go unreported to police. The NCVS has been able to provide more accurate measures of victimization in terms of demographics, crime types, locations, and the outcomes found therein—such as reporting behaviors (Truman & Morgan, 2016). Since the NCVS has been collecting data in its current form since 1993, crime trends can be examined. For example, like the UCR, the NCVS shows a significant decline in crime since the mid-1990s. From 1993 to 2015, the overall rate of victimization declined a staggering 76.7%. Despite this substantial decline over time, the data from 2015 suggest that approximately 1% (1 in 100) of all persons age 12 or older experience at least one instance of violent victimization, while 7.6% (1 in 13) of all households experience one or more property victimizations. The data suggest the decrease in victimization is not the result of reporting practices, as the percent of victimizations reported to police remained fairly stable from 1993 to 2015 (p. 5).

NATIONAL VIOLENCE AGAINST WOMEN SURVEY (NVAWS)

While the NCVS might be considered a general victimization survey that seeks information on a variety of offenses experienced by the population at large, several more surveys have been conducted with specialized foci. One of the most well-known and most cited of these specialized surveys is the National Violence Against Women Survey (NVAWS). Developed in the 1990s through a collaborative effort, NVAWS was administered in 1996 using telephone interviews to just over 16,000 adults (8,000 women and 8,005 men). Sponsored by the National Institute of Justice (NIJ), the National Center for Injury Prevention and Control, and the Centers for Disease Control and Prevention (CDC), the survey sought to obtain data from respondents based in six emerging themes:

(1) their general fear of violence; 2) emotional abuse they had experienced by marital or cohabitating partners; 3) physical assault they had experienced as children by adult caretakers; 4) physical assault they had experienced as adults by any type of perpetrator; 5) forcible rape or stalking they had experienced by any type of perpetrator and; 6) threatened violence they had experienced by any type of perpetrator. (CDC, 2016)

OMNIBUS SURVEY:
This type of data collection
instrument collects information
concerning a wide variety of
subjects and can be very
comprehensive.

The survey intended to isolate and collect data on violent victimizations. To screen for these particular incidents, the survey used questions discussing rape, physical assault, and stalking. When a victim was identified, victim–offender relationship information, victim characteristics, incident characteristics, and the outcomes and consequences of the violent acts were described. The data obtained provided researchers with knowledge concerning understudied (and underreported) acts of violence, specifically violence which concerns any supposed link between childhood victimization and adulthood victimization—and that which concerned minority women—and subsequent outcomes. Even though the survey is cross-sectional and was only conducted once, its impact cannot be denied, as it has been cited seemingly countless times and has spawned other specialized surveys, particularly surveys that examine intimate partner violence.

Box 1.4: WHAT WE'VE LEARNED: National Violence Against Women Survey

While the NCVS provides a substantial amount of information concerning victimization in the United States, the NVAWS was able to specifically focus on female victimization, which, despite researchers' attempts, is still largely underreported—particularly when discussing specific crime types such as rape, assault, and stalking. The NVAWS found that age and racial differences exist in both rape and physical assault victimization, and females are victimized by intimate partners significantly more than males. The survey suggests that individuals identifying as Asian/Pacific Islander report lower rates of intimate partner violence than individuals from any other minority group. Individuals identifying as African-American and American Indian/Alaska Native report the highest rates of intimate partner violence. In addition to increased frequency, females are also found to endure victimizations of physical assault of increased severity: females are more likely to be injured. There were also significant differences in experienced intimate partner violence based on the sex of the couple. The results of the survey suggest that same-sex male partners experience more intimate partner violence than males who live with a female partner. Conversely, same-sex female partners experience less intimate partner violence than females who live with a male partner (Tjaden & Thoennes, 2000).

OMNIBUS SURVEYS

Omnibus surveys, unlike the previously discussed examples of survey instruments, do not focus on one particular item or area. Instead, these surveys are comprised of several items or areas. These surveys seek to tap into several dimensions, since in social science research (e.g., criminal justice and criminology), phenomena such as crime are the result of several factors. As a result, research spans the spectrum of academic disciplines and, often, scholars from many different fields utilize the data gathered from a single instrument. However, despite the variety of information provided, the fact that these surveys are so varied does not avail them to detailed analysis, since they are not developed specifically by or for those interested in criminal justice or criminological outcomes.

NATIONAL LONGITUDINAL STUDY OF ADOLESCENT TO ADULT HEALTH (ADD HEALTH)

Perhaps the most widely cited and used omnibus survey in criminology is the National Longitudinal Study of Adolescent to Adult Health (Add Health). The various data, from inception to present day, have been used and cited in more than 5,000 individual pieces of research (ICPSR, 2016), with the study's internet homepage stating the number is more than 6,000 (CPC, 2016a). The study was created as a result of a congressional mandate to study adolescent health. The study was developed to obtain time-specific data, which changed as the participants involved grew and matured. The survey, despite its evolution over time, was developed to examine the development, and factors related to such development, of an individual based on social, behavior, and biomedical data collection.

Utilizing a longitudinal panel design, adolescents across the United States were randomly selected to become part of the study's sample. The initial year of data collection, 1994, involved a two-stage sampling technique to obtain respondents. Information was obtained from school administrators in the school setting and the adolescents and parents in the home setting. In addition, "biomarkers" were also collected to document physical qualities. To date, the study has consisted of five waves of data collection. Each wave of data collection includes different groups of individuals providing information, as well as changes in the information requested of participants. For example, the initial wave in 1994 left out the students and parents and instead collected data just from school administrators (for the school sample) and from adolescents (for the home sample). As the youth aged, additional physical and health data were obtained, and romantic partners were surveyed (wave three). While the subsequent waves have collected abundant information on participants, the first two waves show how expansive an omnibus survey it is. In both wave one and wave two, nearly 2,700 variables are available for study. It is no surprise, then, that there are thousands of studies spanning dozens of disciplines utilizing this dataset. These collection efforts continue to this day. Currently, the participants in the sample have aged to be at least thirty years old and the fifth wave is ongoing, scheduled to have completed sometime in 2018 (CPC, 2016b).

GENERAL SOCIAL SURVEY (GSS)

Another frequently cited omnibus survey is the General Social Survey (GSS). This survey has been in place since 1972, collecting data most years. The data are collected in a similar fashion to the Add Health survey, utilizing a longitudinal approach and collecting data at regular intervals. The GSS, however, has only recently begun to include a panel component. Previously, the survey was a repeated cross-sectional design. The panel implementation allows for individual respondents to be measured multiple times. In addition, the mode by which data are collected (via interviews) is often quite similar across collection periods. The data that are collected cover a variety of areas, including socioeconomic status, social mobility, social control, family characteristics, race and sex relations, and other social

---

Box 1.5: WHAT WE'VE LEARNED: National Longitudinal Study of Adolescent to Adult Health

Omnibus surveys, such as Add Health, provide us with information that criminal justice sources of data would not. As a result, researchers are able to ask broader questions and those perhaps more criminological in nature. Using data obtained through Add Health, researchers have found that child maltreatment increases the likelihood a child will engage in crime, as will access to a firearm and higher levels of alcohol consumption. Currie and Tekin (2012) sought to uncover the effects of maltreatment on crime. The researchers found that being a victim of child maltreatment increased the likelihood of being convicted of a crime as a juvenile. However, not all victims experience the same negative outcome. Results showed there were significant gender differences in the likelihood of engaging in crime after being a victim of maltreatment. Boys were more likely to engage in armed robbery or assault, while girls were more likely to engage in burglary and theft. The type of maltreatment was found to be important as well. For example, if a child was left alone when they should have been supervised, there was little effect in terms of future criminality. However, experiencing physical or sexual abuse significantly increased the risk of future offending. Thus, the severity of one's maltreatment may be proportionally related to one's criminal offending (p. 535).

---

characteristics and attitudes (NORC, n.d.). Of particular interest to criminal justice and criminology scholars are the data collected through the GSS that examine arrests and sanctions, attitudes toward the criminal justice system, fear of crime, fear and use of firearms, attitudes toward capital punishment, and victimization, among others (NORC, 2016).

Box 1.6: WHAT WE'VE LEARNED: General Social Survey

The GSS has provided attitudinal information from the United States citizenry about criminal justice-related matters. Recent data show that, over time (the last 20 years), there has been a decline in the percentage of the population that believes police use of force against citizens can be justified. The GSS is one of the primary ways in which attitudes toward topics, such as the death penalty, are measured. Results have been shown to be relatively stable in the last several years. Long-term trends suggest something different. Support for the death penalty (in cases of murder) reached an all-time high at two points in time: 1985 and 1994. In those years, it was estimated that 75% of the population favored the death penalty for murder. By 2016, that number had dropped to 58%—the lowest number since the initial collection of survey data in 1972 (53%). In addition, the GSS provides us with the knowledge that public support for increased law enforcement spending is at an all-time low and, generally, citizens believe courts are too lenient on offenders. The percentage of the population that believes local courts are too harsh has steadily increased since 1994. At that time, only three percent took this position. In each subsequent collection period, the GSS observed increases in this number. By 2015, the percentage of the population that believed local courts are too harsh had increased to 18% (NORC, 2015).

COHORT STUDIES

The first cohort study in criminology was conducted in Norway by Nils Christie as part of his doctoral dissertation, published in 1960 as (translated) *Young Norwegian Offenders*. Cohort studies involve the examination of groups of individuals with the common characteristics of shared experience. Cohorts are often constructed using birth year/age, school grade, or some other time-dependent marker. This allows researchers to measure groups over periods of time without the need to consider time-specific effects, e.g., different effects as the result of measuring individuals over different periods in time. Thus, any disparities are the result of individual differences, not group differences.

PHILADELPHIA COHORT STUDIES

The Philadelphia Birth Cohort study was the first longitudinal birth cohort study in the United States that was constructed and conducted with the purpose of measuring crime and delinquency on a large scale. In fact, there were two Philadelphia Birth Cohort studies. The seminal study is referred to as the 1945 Birth Cohort study, as the individuals studied were born in the city of Philadelphia in that year. In this first research endeavor, Marvin Wolfgang, Robert M. Figlio, and Thorsten Sellin (1972)—along with research associates and staff at the Center for Studies in Criminology and Criminal Law at the University of Pennsylvania—studied nearly 10,000 male individuals who lived in the city between the ages of 10 and 18. Incidence and prevalence of crime and delinquency were measured, as well as associated characteristics of the individuals involved and the incidents discovered therein. The subsequent Philadelphia Birth Cohort study was constructed similarly, however with two paramount differences. First, the birth year from which the cohort was constructed was 1958. Most important was the inclusion of females into the cohort, which greatly expanded the size of the cohort to over 27,000 individuals. This endeavor was spearheaded by Paul E. Tracy, in addition to the continued support and expertise of Marvin Wolfgang and Robert M. Figlio (1990).

The individuals involved in each cohort were studied retrospectively—the years of interest had already passed, and the data only needed to be collected. In order to gather the data, records from various school systems (public, private, and parochial) were used. These also helped to determine who lived in the city during the desired age range, e.g., the age during which delinquency can occur. Once the cohort was created and individuals selected, the researchers obtained crime data from the Juvenile Aid Division of the Philadelphia Police Department. In the second cohort, additional records were sought and used, specifically those from interviews and questionnaires administered to participants of the study. Later, Wolfgang would be involved in similar studies in Puerto Rico (a 1970 birth cohort) and China (a 1973 birth cohort).

> **Box 1.7: WHAT WE'VE LEARNED: Philadelphia Cohort Studies**
>
> Both Philadelphia Birth Cohort studies offered a wealth of information concerning the onset of juvenile delinquency, the perpetuation of criminal activity, and the cessation of crime. The studies continue to be influential and form the foundation of the study of criminal careers. Results showed that socioeconomic factors, such as family income, were more predictive of criminality than race. Age at onset (when the individual first commits a crime) helps predict the number of crimes later in one's life, and chronic offenders could be predicted based upon intelligence and success in school (as well as previous criminal behavior). While some findings were seen in both the original and the replication study, there were also differences between the 1945 and 1958 cohorts. For example, the prevalence of police contacts was lower in the replication study, the result of fewer arrests for minor offenses. One of the significant findings of the studies was the finding of the chronic six percent. Just over half of delinquent acts, and in increasing percentages in crimes of high severity, were committed by just six percent of the youth. The pattern emerged in each study, though the percentage of offenders that were considered chronic increased in the replication study (Tracy & Kempf-Leonard, 1996).

RACINE COHORT STUDIES

Philadelphia is not the only location in which multiple birth cohorts were studied. In Racine, Wisconsin, under the direction of Lyle Shannon, three different birth cohorts were studied. Much like the Wolfgang-involved studies, those from Racine were focused on the examination of crime onset, duration, and cessation, e.g., criminal careers. The Racine cohorts involved a total of more than 6,000 individuals born in the city in the years 1942, 1949, and 1955. Data collection procedures were quite similar: police records and court data were used as the primary form of criminal measurement. Personal interviews with members of the first two cohorts were conducted subsequently. Results from the Racine cohorts differ from those found in either Philadelphia study. Unlike the Philadelphia studies, in which offending rates were fairly similar across cohorts, the rate of serious crime doubled from the first to the third cohort in Racine. Although juvenile offenders were more likely to become adult offenders, there was little to no predictive ability from the data gathered in Racine: researchers could not predict which juvenile offender would continue to commit crime into adulthood (Shannon, 1982).

CAMBRIDGE STUDY

A third prominent cohort study in the fields of criminal justice and criminology has been taking place in Great Britain since 1961. The Cambridge Study in Delinquent Development began collecting data on 411 males, nearly all of which were born in 1953, when the boys were about eight years old. Originally directed by Donald West, the study's direction was transferred to David Farrington in 1981. The majority of the boys that were recruited into the study (399) were found on the registers of six primary schools in South London. These schools were within a one-mile radius of the research office West had established (Farrington, 2003). The remaining boys (12) were taken from a local school for the "the educationally subnormal" in order to make it more accurately represent the population of boys from the area (Farrington & West, 1990). The research team collected data from officially recorded convictions and self-reported offending, a result of several interviews during childhood and adolescence and into early adulthood. Results from the Cambridge study are fairly similar to other cohort studies when examining onset of delinquency and chronicity of offending within the sample studied. The more prolific offenders (the chronic offenders) begin to offend earlier and continue committing crime for longer periods of time. Several characteristics measured in the Cambridge study have helped explain what factors are associated with different criminal trajectories: family members with criminal pasts and behaviors, lower educational success, socioeconomic disadvantage, and individual cognitive and behavioral deficits (Farrington, Coid, Harnett, Jolliffe, Soteriou, Turner, & West, 2006).

ADMINISTRATIVE SOURCES

In addition to official statistics, surveys, and longitudinal research in the form of cohort studies, researchers use non-experimental sources of data from criminal justice agencies. Administrative data are that which are collected by an agency, department, organization, or other institutional body for the purposes of that body's operation. No specific research purpose is intended. However, these data have still been shown to be useful in criminal justice and criminological research. In criminal justice and criminology, there are some instances in which administrative data that are typically only found at the local level are collected and aggregated on a national level by agencies like the BJS.

CENSUS OF STATE AND LOCAL LAW ENFORCEMENT AGENCIES (CSLLEA)

The Census of State and Local Law Enforcement Agencies (CSLLEA) is a survey of all law enforcement agencies in the United States. Each reporting agency provides information specific to its jurisdiction, structure, and operation. Information ranges from characteristics of its personnel (e.g., number of officers) to types of specialty units and their functions. The Census, originally called the Directory Survey, is conducted every four years (though publication of data lags behind other data sources).

While the CSLLEA encompasses law enforcement in the United States in its entirety, alternative collection efforts are made on a smaller scale to obtain administrative data from these agencies. Using the CSLLEA as the sampling frame, the Law Enforcement Management and Administrative Statistics (LEMAS) survey has been conducted periodically since 1987. LEMAS collects information similar to that of the larger CSLLEA; however, there is greater detail in terms of what data items are collected. The survey expands the collection of variables with respect to agency personnel by including information on personnel demographics, agency policies and responsibilities, the use of various specialty units, and fiscal data, such as operating budgets and officer salaries.

ADMINISTRATIVE DATA:
This type of data collection involves the collection of information for purposes other than research, such as record keeping and agency management.

AGGREGATE:
In data analysis, the practice of collecting and grouping data into larger-level units, e.g., people into groups or students into classes.

Box 1.8: WHAT WE'VE LEARNED: Law Enforcement Management and Administrative Statistics

The use of LEMAS data has allowed researchers to have a more complete description of how the nation's law enforcement agencies are structured, their operation, and accountability measures, such as personnel and expenditure measures. Researchers have also used agency information in theory testing and conducting experimental research. For example, research has shown that agency practices vary significantly across departments. Agency characteristics such as size, workload, budget, and personnel demographics can affect the likelihood a crime results in arrest and the conditions of that arrest (e.g., type and length of time leading to it), and these characteristics have also been shown to be associated with local crime rates. In Roberts and Roberts' (2016) recent study, the authors found that agency workload is associated with a decrease in the likelihood an incident will be cleared. This association becomes stronger as the severity of a criminal incident decreases. This suggests that, while an increased workload is associated with a decreased chance of crime clearance, the decrease will be significantly less for more serious crimes. For example, within a single agency, incidents of increasing severity are more likely to be cleared. When comparing multiple agencies observing a similar incident, the greatest chance of crime clearance would be found in the agency with the lowest workload.

CENSUS OF JAILS

A second source of administrative data, among many others, related to criminal justice and criminology in the United States is the Census of Jails. Beginning in 1970, the Census of Jails has periodically collected data from jail facilities on several variables of interest. These include the number of inmates (gender, race, and age distribution), status of the inmates, offense for which the inmate is confined, program participation of inmates, and facility expenditures—to name just a few. The Census of Jails collects data on all jail detention facilities in the United States. Using this collection of data from over 3,000 facilities, smaller-scale collections are undertaken.

Operating in a similar fashion to the CSLLEA, the Census of Jails serves as the sampling frame for the Annual Survey of Jails (ASJ), as well as the Survey of Inmates in Local Jails. The ASJ, previously known as the National Survey of Jails, began in 1982 and is conducted on a periodic basis. Data provided differ from that found in the Census of Jails. Data concerning the jail population are obtained, as well as those which relate to admissions and releases, staff characteristics, inmate misconduct, supervision status, and facility capacity and occupancy.

Box 1.9: WHAT WE'VE LEARNED: Census of Jails

Data from the Census of Jails, as well as the Annual Survey of Jails, provide descriptive information concerning the nature of our nation's correctional facilities: who is in them, why they are in them (e.g., supervision status and offense type), the flow of inmates in and out of jail, and accountability measures, such as expenditures and capacity levels. Researchers have also used these administrative data sources to examine a variety of research questions concerning criminal justice outcomes, such as arrest, sentencing, and behaviors within the confines of the facility. For example, research has examined how the demographic makeup of an institution can impact inmate behavior. A recent study shows that jails in which there exists an imbalance in terms of racial composition have higher rates of inmate-on-staff assaults (Williams & Porter, 2016). Interestingly, the strength and significance of this relationship may depend on the relative level of imbalance. Williams and Porter (2016) found that the relationship between imbalanced racial composition and inmate-on-staff assaults exists at both extremes. Jails in which there are under-represented groups as a proportion of the population have higher rates of inmate-on-staff assault. Similarly, jails in which there are over-represented groups as a proportion of the population have higher rates of inmate-on-staff-assault.

SECONDARY DATA ANALYSIS:
The practice of using existing data that have been collected for another purpose.

PRIMARY SOURCES

The majority of research conducted in the fields of criminal justice and criminology is the result of secondary data analysis. This form of analysis involves the use of data that have already been collected, collated, and/or aggregated. The data, however, have been collected for the purposes of other research endeavors or, like administrative data sources, without research intentions. Thus, despite the relative ease in obtaining data in terms of time and financial costs, researchers are constrained in their research questions and analytical techniques employable as a result of *borrowing* data, so to speak. Rarely do data already gathered contain all the variables of interest, and rarely are they measured in the desired form and obtained from the desired population to meet the needs of the secondary analyst. As a result, disclaimers and caveats are often found within the limitations section of journal articles, texts, and research reports.

When original data are collected, it is often done on a small scale, unlike the data found in the aforementioned cohort studies. What is usually lacking in quantity is often made up for in quality. Conducting original data collection allows the researcher to employ methods (and subsequent analytical techniques) tailor-made for his/her specific research purposes. As a result, the data collected can be done so from cases of the highest interest, in the most appropriate and desired form(s), and in a way to meet all anticipated goals of the study.

Box 1.10: WHAT WE'VE LEARNED: Primary Sources

Primary data sources allow researchers to form very specific research questions. From these questions, researchers can access cases and collect data in the most appropriate way(s) to answer their questions. At times, the data collection and analysis can be large-scale, but this is often not the case. For example, using data from a small set of face-to-face interviews, considerations of parole board members were evaluated to determine the most important factors in deciding upon an inmate's release from prison: misconduct, participation, and completion of programming and one's reentry narrative (Connor, 2016). Dr. Connor analyzed interviews from a total of 17 former or active parole board members in his study. Nearly all (16 of 17) indicated that misconduct during the time of incarceration was a critical factor in determining whether an individual was ready for early release. Similarly, most (15 of 17) valued the successful completion of a prison program as influential in their decision-making process. Many of the respondents also stated that no inmate would be granted early release without a clearly formulated reentry plan. Some (5 of 17) discussed the need for inmates to accept responsibility for their behavior. Finally, some (6 of 17) mentioned taking into consideration the group with which they serve and their input in making a determination of parole.

SUMMARY

As preeminent criminologist Edwin Sutherland stated approximately 70 years ago, "The statistics of crime are known as the most unreliable and difficult of all statistics (1947)." This unreliability is strongly associated with the difficulty in obtaining accurate measurements of crime. Various repositories of criminal justice and criminological data, such as the Sourcebook of Criminal Justice Statistics at the University of Albany, offer a variety of resources for students and scholars alike. The Inter-University Consortium for Political and Social Research (ICPSR) also offers an abundant amount of data from which to study. Each dataset was compiled and is composed of specific information to address a social concern and answer important criminal justice and criminological research questions. No one dataset will answer all questions, nor will any two datasets answer the same research question similarly. Knowing the strengths and limitations of a study allows a researcher of any background or skillset to appropriately analyze data to answer questions, articulate findings, and offer suggestions for the fields of criminal justice and criminology. With the base knowledge of the origins of data, one can proceed to understanding its elements that allow for its analysis.

Sources of criminal justice and criminological data have three important differences. Besides the methodology by and the location and time from which the data are gathered, the various data sources vary based on their *by, from,* and *for* qualities. There are several agencies, institutions, and offices—in addition to groups and individuals—that collect and use data in the criminal justice and criminological contexts. At a local level, there are law enforcement agencies, court systems, and jail and prison facilities that collect various types of data. These data are collected at the state and federal levels, as well. Small-scale data collection is often employed by small agencies, groups, and even individuals. The origin of the data that provides it also differs. Data can be collected from the same varied sources: agencies, institutions, offices, groups, and individuals. Finally, the purposes of each form of data collection varies. Some data are collected for description, to provide measures of crime-related phenomena and characteristics of those that are offenders, victims, and criminal justice professionals. Some data are collected for explanation and prediction, to answer research questions, test theories and hypotheses, and influence policy. And, some data are collected for administrative purposes, to provide accountability and inform management of the group or institutional body it describes.

CHAPTER REVIEW QUESTIONS

1. Explain why the number of crimes in the United States is different according to the UCR and the NIBRS.

2. Explain why the number of crimes in the United States is different according to the UCR and the NCVS.

3. How did the second Philadelphia Birth Cohort Study improve upon the data collection efforts found in the first? If a similar study was conducted today, what other improvements could be added?

4. Discuss any disadvantages associated with relying upon omnibus surveys in criminal justice and criminological research.

5. Discuss one way in which a previously discussed data source has been used in criminal justice and/or criminological research or practice. Discuss another way that it could be used in the future.

CHAPTER REVIEW EXERCISES

1. Visit the UCR website: http://www.ucrdatatool.gov
Click the *Go to the table-building tool* tab. Next, select the *Agencies* tab, and then the *Single agency reported crime* tab. Use the drop-down menu to find and select your home state. Select *Next*. Find your hometown's law enforcement

agency, if possible. If it is unavailable, find the agency closest to your hometown. Use the drop-down menu to select *Violent crime rates* and *Property crime rates*. Finally, select *Get Table*. What patterns do you see? Have violent and property crime increased, decreased, or remained steady over time?

2. Visit the JRSA website: http://www.jrsa.org/ibrrc/background-status/nibrs-states.html
Find your home state, and select it. If possible, find and select your hometown. Does your state and/or hometown report incident-based data to NIBRS? If your state and/or hometown submits data to NIBRS, what was the date of certification? Why might some states (and towns) participate and others do not?

3. Visit the UCR website: https://www.ucr.fbi.gov/ucr-publications
Select the most recent year from *Crime in the United States*. Select *Violent Crime* and *Property Crime*. How many violent and property crime offenses were recorded?
Visit the NCVS website: https://bjs.gov
Select *Victims*. Under *Data Collection & Surveys,* select *National Crime Victimization Survey (NCVS)*. Select the most recent publication titled *Criminal Victimization*. View the *PDF* of the report. How many violent and property victimizations occurred? Explain the discrepancy you observed between the two measurements.

4. Visit the Bureau of Justice Statistics' website: https://bjs.gov
Using the search bar, search for two additional administrative data sources using the search terms "Census" and "Survey," separately. Explain when each instrument began, the most recent year data are available, and what information is provided.

5. Using your institution's library resources, find a peer-reviewed journal article that uses one of the data sources discussed in this chapter in its research. Discuss the article, the research question(s), how the data source was used, and what the researchers found.

REFERENCES

Act to Establish the Department of Justice. (1870). ch. 150, 16 Stat. (pp. 162–165).

Addington, L.A. (2008). Assessing the extent of nonresponse bias on NIBRS estimates of violent crime. *Journal of Contemporary Criminal Justice, 24*(1), 32–49.

Beattie, R.H. (1955). Problems of criminal statistics in the United States. *Journal of Criminal Law, Criminology, and Police Science, (46)*2, 178–186.

Bulwer, H.L. (1836). *France, social, literary, political*, Vol. 1, Book 1, *Crime*. London, UK: Richard Bentley.

Bureau of Justice Statistics. (n.d.). *The National Crime Statistics Exchange (NCS-X)*. Washington, D.C.: U.S. Department of Justice.

Carolina Population Center. (2016a). *Publications Database*. Retrieved from http://www.cpc.unc.edu/projects/addhealth/publications/database.

Carolina Population Center. (2016b). *About*. Retrieved from http://www.cpc.unc.edu/projects/addhealth/about.

Centers for Disease Control and Prevention. (2016). *Intimate partner violence: Data sources*. Retrieved from http://www.cdc.gov/violenceprevention/intimatepartnerviolence/datasources.html.

Chilton, R., & Regoeczi, W.C. (2007). Impact of employment, family structure, and income on NIBRS offense, victim, offender, and arrest rates. *Justice Research and Policy, 9*(2), 9–29.

Christie, Nils. (1960). *Unge norske lovovertredere*. Oslo, Norway: Universitetsforlaget.

Connor, D.P. (2016). How to Get Out of Prison: Views from Parole Board Members. *Corrections, (1)*2, 107–126.

Currie, J. & Tekin, E. (2012). Understanding the cycle: Childhood maltreatment and future crime. *Journal of Human Resources, 47*(2), 509–549.

Department of Justice Appropriation Authorization Act. (1978). Fiscal Year 1979, Pub. L. No. 95-624, §14, 92 Stat. 3459.

Farrington, D.P. (2003). Key Results from the first forty years of the Cambridge Study in Delinquent Development. In Thornberry and Krohn (Eds.) *Taking Stock of Delinquency: An Overview of Findings from Contemporary Longitudinal Studies*. New York, NY: Kluwer.

Farrington, D.P. & West, D.J. (1990). The Cambridge Study in Delinquent Development: A long-term follow-up of 411 London males. In Kerner and Kaiser (Eds.) *Kriminalitat*. Berlin, Germany: Springer Berlin Heidelberg.

Farrington, D.P., Coid, J.W., Harnett, L., Jolliffe, D., Soteriou, N., Turner, R. & West, D.J. (2006). *Criminal Careers and life success: New findings from the Cambridge Study in Delinquent Development*. Research Study No. 281. London: Home Office.

Federal Bureau of Investigation. (2010). *Variables affecting crime*. Retrieved from https://www2.fbi.gov/ucr/hc2009/variables.html.

Federal Bureau of Investigation. (2013). *National incident-based reporting system (NIBRS) user manual*. Washington, D.C.: U.S. Department of Justice.

Federal Bureau of Investigation. (2015a). *Crime in the United States*. Washington, D.C.: U.S. Department of Justice.

Federal Bureau of Investigation. (2015b). *Data declaration: Number of agencies and population covered by population group, 2014.* Washington, D.C.: U.S Department of Justice.

Federal Bureau of Investigation. (2015c). *Effects of NIBRS on crime statistics.* Washington, D.C.: U.S. Department of Justice.

Federal Bureau of Investigation. (2016). *Uniform crime reporting program data: Offenses known and clearance by arrest, 2014.* ICPSR36391-v1. Ann Arbor, MI: Inter-University Consortium for Political and Social Research [distributor], 2016-03-02.

Hirschel, D. & Buzawa, E. (2008). *An examination of the factors that impact the likelihood of arrest in intimate partner violence cases.* Annual Meeting of the Justice Research Statistical Association. Retrieved from http://www.jrsa.org/events/conference/presentations-09/David_Hirschel.pdf.

International Association of Chiefs of Police. (n.d.). *History.* Retrieved from http://www.iacp.org/History.

Inter-University Consortium for Political and Social Research. (2016). *National Longitudinal Study of Adolescent to Adult Health (Add Health), 1994–2008 [Public Use] (ICPSR 21600).* Retrieved from http://www.icpsr.umich.edu/icpsrweb/DSDR/studies/21600.

McCormack, P.D., Pattavina, A., & Tracy, P.E. (2017). Assessing the coverage and representativeness of the National Incident-Based Reporting System. *Crime & Delinquency, 63*(4), 493–516.

Morrison, W.D. (1897). The interpretation of criminal statistics. *Journal of the Royal Statistical Society,* LX, I, 1–24.

National Opinion Research Center. (n.d.). *An introduction to the general social survey.* Retrieved from http://gss.norc.org/About-The-GSS.

National Opinion Research Center (2015). *Crime and law enforcement in America: Racial and ethnic difference in attitudes toward the criminal justice system.* Retrieved from http://www.apnorc.org/PDFs/Crime/Crime%20Trends_FINAL.pdf.

National Opinion Research Center. (2016). *General social surveys, 1972–2014: Cumulative Codebook.* Chicago, IL: University of Chicago.

Poggio, E.C., Kennedy, S.D., Chaiken, J.M., & Carlson, K.E. (1985). *Blueprint for the future of the Uniform Crime Reporting Program.* Washington, D.C.: U.S. Department of Justice.

Rand, M.R. (2006). The National Crime Victimization Survey; 34 years of measuring crime in the United States. *Statistical Journal of the United Nations ECE, 23,* 289–301.

Rantala, R.R., & Edwards, T.J. (2000). *Effects of NIBRS on crime statistics.* Washington, D.C.: Bureau of Justice Statistics.

Reaves, B.A. (1993). *Using NIBRS data to analyze violent crime.* Washington, D.C.: Bureau of Justice Statistics.

Roberts, A. (2009). Contributions of the National Incident-Based Reporting System. *Sociology Compass, 3*(3), 433–458.

Roberts, A. & Roberts, J.M. (2016). Crime clearance and temporal variation in police investigative workload: Evidence from National Incident-Based Reporting System (NIBRS) data. *Journal of Quantitative Criminology, 32* (4), 651–674.

Roberts, D.J. (1997). *Implementing the National Incident-Based Reporting System: A project status report.* Washington, D.C.: U.S. Department of Justice.

Sellin, T., & Wolfgang, M. (1964). *The measurement of delinquency.* Oxford, UK: Wiley.

Shannon, L. (1982). *Assessing the relationship of adult criminal careers to juvenile careers.* Washington, D.C.: U.S. Department of Justice.

Sutherland, E. (1947). *Principles of criminology* (4th ed.). Chicago, IL: J.P. Lippincott.

Tjaden, P., & Thoennes, N. (2000). *Full report of the prevalence, incidence, and consequences of violence against women: Findings from the National Violence Against Women Survey.* Washington, D.C.: National Institute of Justice.

Tracy, P.E., & Kempf-Leonard, K. (1996). *Continuity and discontinuity in criminal careers.* New York, NY: Plenum.

Tracy, P.E., Wolfgang, M.E., & Figlio, R.M. (1990). *Delinquency careers in two birth cohorts.* New York, NY: Plenum.

Truman, J.L., & Morgan, R.E. (2016). *Criminal victimization, 2015.* Washington, D.C.: Bureau of Justice Statistics.

Williams, C. & Porter, J.R. (2016). An examination of inmate physical assaults on jail correctional staff: Exploring inmate-level and jail-level conditions in the United States. *Deviant Behavior, 37*(11), 1239–1251.

Wolfgang, M.E. (1958). *Patterns in criminal homicide.* Philadelphia, PA: University of Pennsylvania Press.

Wolfgang, M.E. (1963). Uniform crime reports: A critical appraisal. *University of Pennsylvania Law Review, 111,* 708–738.

Wolfgang, M.E., Figlio, R.M., & Sellin, T. (1972). *Delinquency in a birth cohort.* Chicago, IL: University of Chicago Press.

IMAGE CREDITS

PURPOSES OF ANALYSIS AND ELEMENTS OF DATA

INTRODUCTION: WHAT WE SHOULD KNOW BEFORE WE ANALYZE

Like the police, the behavioral scientist is oriented toward behavior in organizational systems. In designing behavioral research that has relevance … he confronts problems of operationalizing.
(Reiss and Black, 1967)

For as long as the fields of criminal justice and criminology have sought to measure and analyze, the initial issues have persisted of defining what will be measured and how those individuals, groups, places, etc. will be measured. As famed sociologist Robert J. Sampson noted in his 2012 Presidential Address to the American Society of Criminology, "… hundreds of operational definitions have been proposed, but the perceived problem continues" (2013). While Sampson is discussing his particular area of expertise—neighborhoods—in this address, this "perceived problem" is ubiquitous across all concepts. The problem he describes is that of defining concepts and measuring them appropriately and, perhaps, consistently. The implications of such measurement differences are far reaching. How a concept is defined and subsequently measured affects later analyses and, usually, the resultant findings. While all disciplines and fields of inquiry can define and measure concepts differently, social sciences such as criminal justice and criminology rely on this practice in the formation and development of theory and the practical applications that are informed by research.

Consider the following questions:

1. How can Hirschi's (1969) concepts of belief, attachment, commitment, and involvement be measured?

2. Can data only be obtained from and used to describe individual people?

3. Why are criminal justice and criminology related data collected and analyzed?

All disciplines within the field of social science encounter the same problem when conducting research. Many concepts and objects of theory can be interpreted subjectively. When the meanings of concepts are interpreted differently, the methods by which they are measured can differ as well. This would, of course, impact the results and conclusions of a study. The impact of a condition on an outcome may differ based on the way(s) in which the concept was measured. Hirschi's (1969) monumental text spawned such inconsistencies. For example, attachment can be measured several ways, e.g., to what or whom an individual is attached. The same applies to the other three concepts of his social bond theory. Other research questions may lend themselves to consistent measurement of concepts. Regardless of *how* data are collected and analyzed, the intent of research often lies within one of two frameworks: description and inference. This chapter examines the purposes of analysis and the elements of data.

LEARNING OBJECTIVES

By the end of this chapter, students will be able to:
1: Identify the various components of the research cycle
2: Discuss the components of the research cycle in relation to the analysis of data
3: Explain the qualities of each level of measurement
4: Evaluate the strengths and limitations of each level of measurement
5: Assess the advantages and limitations of different units of analysis

KEY TERMS

CONCEPTUALIZATION
EXHAUSTIVE
INTERVAL
LEVEL OF MEASUREMENT
MUTUALLY EXCLUSIVE
NOMINAL
OPERATIONALIZATION
ORDINAL
QUALITATIVE RESEARCH
QUANTITATIVE RESEARCH
RATIO

THE RESEARCH CYCLE

A common misconception is that there is a "beginning" and an "end" to all research. In the social sciences, this is generally untrue. In criminal justice and criminology research, many questions are answerable with high degrees of certainty, but not with complete certainty (this will be examined further when learning about and conducting various forms of analysis). Instead, research is cyclical and many research questions are asked and answered only to be repeated later by others with different, and presumably improved, data and measurement. More detailed or complete data, more representative samples, more comprehensive data collection instruments and procedures, alternative forms of measurement, and higher levels of data analysis can continually be incorporated into research to study the same issue(s) and answer the same research question(s). This highlights the cyclical nature of research in criminal justice and criminology.

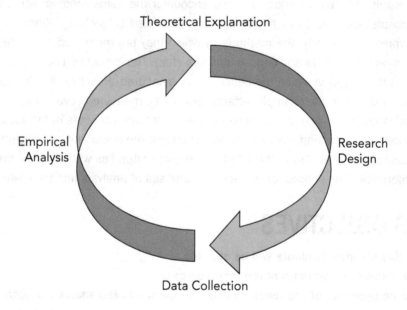

Figure 2.1 Research Cycle

The specific steps of conducting a research study vary based on the individual intricacies and complexities of the study. However, regardless of the research question(s), the data to be collected, the analyses to be conducted, and the consequences of the findings, most studies follow a very similar process. This process can be described generally using the research cycle. Research can be used both to inform and develop theory, or theory may inform the basis of a study. For example, some theories have been developed to explain observed conditions or respond to findings of research (e.g., Blalock, 1967). Alternately, prior research has been the basis or impetus for many studies, informing the ways in which concepts are measured, data are collected, and hypotheses are constructed (see Pratt, 2016, for a discussion of theory testing). The hypothesis creation stage of the research process is done with consideration paid to the data that are to be collected and analyzed. It would not be fruitful if the researcher(s) generated hypotheses based upon data that would ultimately be unavailable or inappropriate for the study at hand. Once hypotheses are made, the research design stage of a study provides the blueprint by which cases will be selected and data will be gathered. More generally, "research design" may refer to all processes involved in the planning and implementation of a research study. However, in viewing the research cycle through its individual stages, it may be more beneficial to view "research design" as being specific to the planning and implementation involved in the collection of data needed to test the hypotheses that have been generated. Once those procedures have been defined, only data collection and analysis are left—the latter of which is the focus of this text.

> **Box 2.1: WHAT WE'VE LEARNED: Research Cycle**
>
> A renowned scholar in his own right, Travis C. Pratt (2016) provides 11 guidelines for testing criminology theories, those of which are directly related to the research cycle. For example, he explicitly states that no single study is perfect. Thus, researchers, authors, and data analysts should "expect to make revisions" (2016, p. 45) along the way. He also notes that, in criminology, the research process is one of iteration, where repetition and improvement are expected. Some of these improvements may be incremental, and others may be significant—often the result of major departures from previous work. Furthermore, he contends that the future of criminology and theory testing lies in the improvement of the way constructs are measured and data are collected. Although individual studies may stand alone on the basis of their specific research question(s), they are, especially when testing theory, situated within a larger body of research that has seen development and refinement over time—embodying the research cycle. In order for new knowledge to be produced, "how theory and methods are fundamentally intertwined" (p. 46) must be recognized. The reciprocal nature of theory testing is evidence of just that. To develop theory, advancements in methodology are required. Yet, to develop methodology, guidance from theory is needed. Clearly, each element of the research cycle extends from and to another—proving that there is no end to the study of crime.

The process of conducting criminal justice and criminology research is cyclical. When findings from one study impact the understanding or development of theory, inductive research is being conducted. Inductive research is focused on generating or refining theory following data acquisition and analysis. Many exploratory studies are considered inductive, as they may not be initiated, in terms of their construction and implementation, to test hypotheses. Often, many of the "firsts"—original studies that are the first to examine a topic—are exploratory and seek only to acquire foundational information on a topic. From these data, theory may be developed using the inductive process.

An alternate process is deductive research. Deductive research, in a sense, "begins" the research process by formulating questions or problem statements from theory. This formulation forms the basis of identifying and selecting the best, most appropriate research methods to address and answer the research question(s). This is perhaps the more traditional and most frequently used or explained type of research and reasoning. In deductive research, one generally begins with an informed hypothesis or group of hypotheses. The subsequent steps in the research process, such as conceptualization, operationalization, data collection, and analysis, are conducted in such a way to specifically test that hypothesis, or those hypotheses, as generated from current theory.

CONCEPTUALIZATION

All stages of research, from hypothesis construction and data collection to analysis and discussion, require specific attention paid to the data that have been collected in terms of what they represent. All forms of research, be they inductive or deductive, are centered on the acquisition of knowledge via the assignment of attributes. The type of research being conducted is very closely related to the type of attributes studied. For example, quantitative research concerns attributes that can be assigned a numerical value and treated as having numerical characteristics in the context of statistical measurement. Qualitative research may contain some of these elements, but this type of research is generally associated with attributes that may not have assigned numerical values—particularly when the research is focused on understanding or learning more about, not measuring, concepts and ideas. Some attributes are inherently qualitative—they cannot be assigned a numerical value in the traditional sense.

QUANTITATIVE RESEARCH:
This type of research involves the collection of data that can be expressed in numbers, often to be used in statistical analysis.

QUALITATIVE RESEARCH:
This type of research involves the collection of data that describe qualities or characteristics, often expressed in narrative form.

CONCEPTUALIZATION:
The process of assigning labels and meaning to attributes or characteristics, e.g., defining a concept.

OPERATIONALIZATION:
The process of defining measurable qualities of concepts, e.g., determining how a concept will be measured.

For research questions to be answered, attributes or characteristics of interest must be identified and defined. The discussion of attributes or characteristics is focused on conceptualization, which is the assignment of abstract labels and the specification of meaning to concepts. Essentially, conceptualization is labeling and defining what is meant by certain constructs or terms. This assignment of labels and provision of definitions is done for all elements of research under study. These attributes or characteristics become variables through conceptualization and, subsequently, operationalization.

OPERATIONALIZATION

Once attributes are clearly defined and variables are created, the next consideration in the research process is operationalization. Operationalization involves the creation of criteria to serve as the basis by which the variables are measured. The operationalization of variables can have a profound impact on the subsequent steps in research. If a variable is to be measured a specific way, then specific data must be gathered and only specific forms of analysis may be utilized later in the study. For example, if the outcome of "crime" is to be measured by the number of crimes reported in a jurisdiction, then only the frequency of criminal incidents is required for data, and the count data will require specific

---

Box 2.2: WHAT WE'VE LEARNED: Operationalization

Examining the impact of operationalization, i.e., how something is measured, Ostermann, Salerno, and Hyatt (2015) compared the recidivism outcomes of over 12,000 prisoners in New Jersey to see if the ways in which recidivism was measured impacted research findings. Specifically, they analyzed data from prisoners who were released in 2008 to either parole or unconditional release. They then identified 10 different operationalizations of recidivism and found that the way in which that outcome was defined and measured impacted the findings of parole supervision effectiveness. These operationalizations included rearrest, a combined indicator of rearrest or parole revocation, four different forms of reconvictions, and four different forms of reincarceration. There are several distinct characteristics that were identified across the various forms of reconviction and reincarceration. Across the four types of reconviction measures, either the arrest date or disposition date was used to assess the length of time it took one to recidivate. In addition to these different indicators of time, some reconviction measures also included parole revocation in their outcome measure. Similar patterns were observed across the various reincarceration measures. Some researchers have used the arrest date, while others have used the booking date. Like the reconviction measures, some reincarceration measures also included parole revocations. Thus, of equal importance to *what* you measure is *how* you measure it.

forms of analysis later. Alternately, if the outcome of "crime" is to be measured by the crime rate, then the frequency of criminal incidents and the frequency of individuals (the population) is required, and the forms of analysis available to the researcher will differ on account of the outcome being continuous. Thus, slight changes in the definition and measurement of variables can have an appreciable effect on the study and resultant findings, as has been found in criminal justice and criminology research (see Chamlin & Cochran, 2004).

LEVELS OF MEASUREMENT

Concepts can be operationalized differently by different people, at different times, and in different places. Not all concepts and their resultant variable measurements mean the same thing to everybody. This is a consideration, and sometimes a concern, in social sciences—particularly criminal justice and criminology. Concepts may be understood and interpreted differently, which in turn, affect how they will be measured. Take, for example, the idea of "wealth." It is a concept that alludes to one's economic attainment and position in society, and it is a concept often used in research. But there are an innumerable number of ways to measure that concept, as research has shown. The fields of criminal justice and criminology routinely encounter concepts defined differently and variables measured differently. These differences can be explained via a variable's level of measurement. Levels of measurement describe the characteristics of variables' measurement, specifically how they are measured and their underlying assumptions. For statistical and analytical purposes, as we'll see more so in subsequent chapters, certain levels of measurement are more appropriate for certain data displays, descriptions, and analyses. It is imperative, when analyzing data, to use the appropriate *type* or *form* of a variable.

CATEGORICAL VARIABLES

Categorical variables are those in which "groups" are made to distinguish between different values of a variable. These may also be referred to as qualitative variables, or discrete variables. There are two forms of categorical variables: nominal and ordinal. Each of these forms of categorical variables has its own corresponding properties, uses, and advantages. Some choose to identify ordinal variables separately from categorical variables, but for the purposes of initial comprehension, it is beneficial to recognize the similarities between nominal and ordinal level measurement. We will account for the differences between the two subsequently, particularly during the analysis stage(s) of the text. These variables include values that are named or labeled. There is no quantitative, e.g., numerical, connotation to these levels of measurement. When variables are identified or, more specifically, created in these forms, they must be done so in a way that is both mutually exclusive and exhaustive. To be mutually exclusive, there can be no overlap between categories of the variable. Each category must

LEVEL OF MEASUREMENT: The nature of information assigned to and provided by variables; there are four different classifications.

NOMINAL: The lowest level of measurement in which variable values are categorical with no sequential, chronological, or hierarchical order.

ORDINAL: The second lowest level of measurement in which variable values are categorical with a sequential, chronological, or hierarchical order.

represent a distinct value of that variable. To be exhaustive, every possible case must have a category available or made in which to be represented.

NOMINAL

Nominal variables are those in which multiple categories are identified and/or created to represent a quality or characteristic. The fundamental assumption with a variable that is measured at the nominal level is that there is no ordering or hierarchy of its values. No one value is "higher" or "lower," or "greater" or "lesser," etc. than another. These measures are considered the lowest level of measurement due to their simplicity and limited use in terms of display, description, and analysis. Perhaps the most frequently used nominal variables in criminal justice and criminology research are demographic variables: *sex* and *race*, for example. The variable of *sex* is measured with two distinct categories: male and female. There is no implication as to an ordering or hierarchy of the two categories. The same can be said for *race* or any other nominal level measurement.

Box 2.3: WHAT WE'VE LEARNED: Nominal

The Bureau of Justice Statistics publishes annual bulletins based on the data received from the National Crime Victimization Survey (NCVS). National estimates of rates of victimization are presented, as well as the incidence of crime, e.g., the frequency totals. These figures are delineated by nominal measures, such as victim characteristics and crime type. In the year 2015, according to the NCVS, it is estimated that there were more male victims than female victims; more white victims than all other races combined; and most victims were single and never married. Violent crime is measured and presented in six categories, with three additional subcategories therein. For example, the total number of assaults is provided, as well as the number of aggravated and simple assaults that make up the total. The incidence of domestic violence is also displayed, with intimate partner violence accounting for a portion of those incidents. From these delineations, we can see that there are approximately three times as many simple assaults as aggravated assaults and about half of all domestic violence victimizations is the result of intimate partner violence. A similar breakdown of nominal categories can be seen in the presentation of property crime figures (Truman & Morgan, 2016).

ORDINAL

Ordinal variables are those in which multiple categories are identified and/or created to represent a quality or characteristic; however, there is an underlying

MUTUALLY EXCLUSIVE:
The characteristic of variables in which multiple values do not overlap; two values cannot occur simultaneously.

EXHAUSTIVE:
The characteristic of variables in which all possible values are accounted for and at least one value is available for each case.

assumption that, across the various values of the variable, there is an ordering or hierarchy. Values can be, and are, "higher" or "lower," or "greater" or "lesser," etc. than another. These measures are considered the second lowest level of measurement also due to their simplicity and limited range of uses. However, as we'll see in subsequent chapters, the ordered nature of these variables provides more possibilities for display, description, and analysis. These variables are commonly used by all students, perhaps even unbeknownst to them. The *year* or *grade* of schooling can be measured in an ordinal way: freshman, sophomore, junior, senior, graduate, etc. Each value represents a distinct group or category, but there is an agreed upon ordering to them. The same can be used in the professional landscape of criminal justice and criminology. For example, with police rank, a student may graduate and become a police officer, then a detective, then a sergeant, etc. Each value of the variable *police rank* is categorical, represented distinctly in a commonly understood and agreed upon order. There is no requirement concerning the direction of an ordinal variable's values: the order can be ascending or descending. However, like the nominal level of measurement, the values of ordinal measures must also be mutually exclusive and exhaustive.

INTERVAL:
The second highest level of measurement in which continuous variables have a known and meaningful distance between values, a known hierarchy, and an arbitrary zero; values can be negative.

RATIO:
The highest level of measurement in which continuous variables have a known and meaningful distance between values, a known hierarchy, and a meaningful zero; values cannot be negative.

Box 2.4: WHAT WE'VE LEARNED: Ordinal

Professors Carkin and Tracy (2015) incorporated the use of ordinal measures in a very novel way when examining trajectories of criminal offending. Instead of using ordinal measurement in their predictor variables, i.e., independent variables, they measured their dependent variable at the ordinal level. In doing so, they were able to examine the progression and escalation of criminal offending, based on records of juvenile offending, and found that the ordered "path" of a juvenile significantly predicted their subsequent adult path. The four categorical paths used were non-offenders, limited, frequent, and chronic. Non-offenders were those who were never arrested for a delinquent act or adult crime; limited offenders had limited experience in delinquency or one to two adult crimes; frequent offenders were those that have committed three to four offenses and; chronic offenders, since data from the 1958 Philadelphia Birth Cohort were used, were those that committed five or more crimes. Results showed that across the four ordered paths, age-at-onset increased, age-at-last offense increased, the severity of offense increased, the amount of serious offenses increased, and the amount of minor offenses decreased. The study also uncovered some interesting findings, such as 37% of the male chronic delinquents were non-offenders as adults and 71.4% of the female chronic delinquents were non-offenders as adults.

CONTINUOUS VARIABLES

Continuous variables are those in which values are measured numerically. There are two forms of continuous variables, interval and ratio, each with corresponding properties, uses, and advantages. There are some very important distinctions to be made between the two levels of continuous measurement that are important to note for conceptual reasons. Luckily, however, for the purposes of analysis, such distinctions are not of particular concern as we treat both interval and ratio level data similarly. There are also some important distinctions to make between numerically presented variables that are continuous and those that may, instead, be classified as discrete. Recall that discrete variables, being in some ways analogous to categorical variables, indicate that values are mutually exclusive and exhaustive. That is, each possible value must be represented distinctly from others and these representations, e.g., groups or categories, must be present and available for all possible values. There are some variables that have a numerical connotation but are considered discrete. This is an important distinction in advanced data analysis, as many statistical tests and functions can still be conducted without distinction between discrete numerical data and continuous numerical data. The most appropriate example of discrete, though numerical, data in criminal justice and criminology is count data. When variables are measured based on counts, or frequencies, they are considered discrete. What differentiates these types of variables from continuously measured numerical variables is the (in)ability to have values between the counts. For example, an offender can be arrested 2 times, 4 times, even 22 times! However, with count data, there can be no value between those counts. An offender cannot be arrested 2.5 times, 4.5 times, or 22.5 times. Thus, this form of numerical data, in relying on the count or frequency of a value, is considered discrete and may be analytically treated differently than other numerical data.

Box 2.5: WHAT WE'VE LEARNED: Count Data

Many of the factors and outcomes associated with criminal justice and criminology are measured using count data. Some suggest the number of crimes, one of most common outcomes analyzed, may be most appropriate when analyzing crime data because of the inherent nature of the event. Although the Uniform Crime Reports (UCR) state there were nearly 1.2 million violent and approximately 8 million property crimes in 2015, and the NCVS estimates there were 5 million violent and nearly 14.6 million property victimizations in the same year, crime is a relatively rare phenomenon. At the individual level, most individuals are neither victims nor perpetrators of crimes in any given year. Similarly, there are many jurisdictions—whether measured by agency, town, or even county—that may report no crimes in a given year. To account for any substantive and statistical issues that may arise when inappropriately treating count data as a continuous variable, Osgood (2000) advocated for, and demonstrated, alternative analytical techniques for analyzing crime rates. Instead of utilizing a traditional set of techniques that examined crime rates in a continuous fashion, he suggested, with good reason, to use the number of crimes (a discrete variable) and analyze it accordingly. His research suggested that this may prove advantageous both substantively and statistically.

INTERVAL AND RATIO

In variable construction, i.e., conceptualization and operationalization, as one ascends to the higher levels of measurement, additional properties are exhibited. Interval and ratio level variables, in addition to having the ability to be categorized and ordered, also exhibit a meaningful and measurable distance between values. What differentiates interval from ratio measures is the meaningfulness of zero. Ratio level measures have an absolute zero, meaning zero acts as the lower bound for these variables: there is no conceptual or numerical possibility of having a negative value. This is not true for interval measures. Interval measures have the conceptual and numerical possibility of having negative values.

As one ascends to a higher level of measurement, e.g., nominal to ordinal to interval/ratio, the fundamental properties of those lower-level variables remain as properties of the higher-level variables. Higher-level variables tend to be measured more precisely, allowing for greater, but also, if desired, more crude measurement possibilities. For example, a variable measured at the interval/ratio level, such as income, can remain at this high, continuous level or can be collapsed or aggregated and grouped in a categorical fashion. The reverse is not true. A lower-level variable, as a function of its measurement and properties, cannot be described at a higher level.

Levels of Measurement	Attribute
Nominal	Race, Sex, Political Affiliation
Ordinal	Level of Agreement
Interval	Net Wealth, IQ
Ratio	Age, Income

Figure 2.2 Levels of Measurement Examples

UNITS OF ANALYSIS

When concepts are defined and measured, there must be careful attention paid to what those variables describe and represent. As a result, one must be cognizant of the unit of analysis that is being examined. The unit of analysis refers to the individual case, or unit, under study. What is being measured, analyzed, and subsequently discussed is the unit of analysis. These are "what" or "who" a researcher is trying to study and describe. In criminal justice and criminology research, there are several forms this unit can take, i.e., what or who a researcher can study. Perhaps the most traditional units of analysis are individuals and groups. Researchers also examine other forms of aggregates, such as organizations or geographical units, such as when one is attempting to study crime rates. Units of analysis, in the context of geography, may be measured using census tracts, cities, states, or even countries. Social artifacts may also be studied. Social artifacts are often tangible objects that might be analyzed such as news reports, books, songs, court cases, traffic accidents, or even events such as riots. These non-traditional sources of data are typically used when the content or information provided is unavailable in a traditional sense, e.g., there is no "dataset" available.

Units of analysis and operationalization are inexorably linked elements of criminal justice and criminology research. The ways in which concepts are defined and measured must be done with respect to the unit of analysis they are meant to describe. For example, if a researcher intends to study an individual and includes *race* as an important measure, it is most appropriate to use the race of the individual. However, if a researcher intends to study cities, it would likely be most appropriate to use measurements of race that describe the city, such as proportions, percentages, or counts. Regardless of what or whom is under study, careful consideration to defining concepts and appropriately measuring them to represent the intended unit of analysis must be made.

Units of Analysis	Criminal Justice and Criminology Examples
Individuals	Victims, Offenders, Officers
Groups	Neighborhoods, Cities, Countries
Organizations	Agencies/Departments
Social Artifacts	Newspapers, Social Media Content

Figure 2.3 Units of Analysis Examples

Box 2.6: WHAT WE'VE LEARNED: Units of Analysis

Researchers Klein and Cooper (2016) sought to answer two questions concerning the case of Jerry Sandusky, the former assistant coach of Penn State University's football team. The researchers examined over 200 news articles, as their unit of analysis, to see how Sandusky and his trial were portrayed in the print media. To select cases for analysis, the authors examined only media coverage during the trial. They examined national, regional, and local news sources. Five themes were measured when analyzing the content of the articles: jury selection, representation of sexual abuse, testimony from victims, Sandusky's defense, and jury deliberation. Through their analysis of the content of the news articles, they found that there were many instances of incomplete or incorrect information concerning the trial. For example, from the 4.6% of the articles that mentioned how long the jury deliberated, five different lengths of time were reported. Only one article correctly reported the length of time the jury deliberated: two days. The researchers reported that no noticeable efforts were made to correct or retract incorrect reporting. Finally, they found that Sandusky was portrayed less negatively than the offenses he was tried for. This contrasted the pretrial coverage in which both Sandusky and his alleged crimes were portrayed equally negatively.

PURPOSE OF DATA ANALYSIS

As we have learned, studying the phenomenon of crime involves a significant amount of time and attention paid to a variety of elements of data and stages in the planning process by which that data will be obtained. Following the identification of a research problem or question, concepts are defined, and strict guidelines are created by which they will be measured. Data are collected and analyzed, resulting in several possible outcomes—none of which are mutually exclusive, such as: the research question is answered, the results inform practitioners, the results refine and develop theory, extant literature is either confirmed or contradicted, and the study serves as the foundation for future research. To achieve these outcomes, researchers utilize two linked, but fundamentally different, forms of statistics: descriptive and inferential.

DESCRIPTIVE STATISTICS AND DATA ANALYSIS

Data analysis that involves the collection and analysis of information to better understand the cases included in the study utilizes descriptive statistics. This form of data analysis is focused solely at examining, identifying trends or patterns in, and explaining phenomena of the cases under study. There is no allusion or extrapolation to a larger group. This results in the calculation of statistics—values that describe the sample. In this sense, descriptive data analysis is focused on statistically describing only the sample. Samples are almost always used in data analysis, as it would be nearly impossible to account for every person, group, city, etc. in the population. The time, energy, and financial resources needed to collect data from a population would be outrageously, if not impossibly, high. When this form of analysis is conducted, the cases are often described using various graphical displays of data (Chapter 3) and descriptive statistics, such as measures of central tendency (Chapter 4) and measures of variability and dispersion (Chapter 5). Description is appropriate when the purpose of the research is to statistically summarize characteristics of the group under study, not the larger group from which the sample was derived.

Box 2.7: WHAT WE'VE LEARNED: Descriptive Statistics

Recently, a group of researchers—all of whom are from the Drexel University College of Medicine or the University's School of Public Health—studied victims of interpersonal violence that were participating in a hospital-based violence intervention program. Corbin, Purtle, Rich, Adams, Yee, and Bloom (2013) sought out to assess the prevalence of negative outcomes, such as post-traumatic stress disorder (PTSD) and adverse childhood experiences (ACEs). The researchers collected data during a one-year period from 35 individuals who were violently injured. Using screening instruments and administrative data, the group can be described as follows: nearly all were male (91.4%), were African American (80%), and were victims of gunshot wounds (71.4%), and approximately half (48.5%) had previously had a violent injury (p. 1024). The PTSD screening instrument found that most (75%) had met full PTSD criteria for diagnosis, nearly all met criteria for re-experiencing the event (90.6%), as well as arousal (87.5%) and avoidance (81.3%) criteria. Finally, in terms of the ACE screening instrument, all respondents reported at least one adverse childhood experience and half had experienced at least four. The most prevalent experience of abuse was recurrent emotional abuse (34.4%), of neglect was emotional neglect (37.5%), and of household dysfunction was parental separation/divorce (90.6%). More than half of the respondents also noted a member of the household was incarcerated (53.1%), and half noted there was substance abuse in the household. Because of this small sample, and the research design utilized, the authors stressed that these descriptive statistics should not be generalized to other programs at other times.

INFERENTIAL STATISTICS AND DATA ANALYSIS

The larger group from which a sample is derived is known as the population. Data analysis that involves the collection and analysis of information to better understand the population utilizes inferential statistics. This form of data analysis is focused on utilizing data obtained from a sample, one that is representative of the population from which it is drawn, to generalize findings to the larger group. Examination of the sample data, using analytical techniques, allows for characteristics to be estimated and conclusions to be made about the population. These estimations are known as parameters or values of a population. Just like with descriptive statistics, inferential statistics involves the use of graphical displays of data, measures of central tendency, and measures of variability and dispersion. However, to make inferences about the population, analytical techniques such as those used to test equality (Chapter 6) and test associations (Chapter 7) are required. Thus, it is possible to use the same sample data for description and inference. Inference is appropriate when the purpose of the research is to statistically summarize, via estimation, characteristics of the population by using a smaller subset of data.

Box 2.8: WHAT WE'VE LEARNED: Inferential Statistics and Data Analysis

In a recent study, Dr. Scott Walfield (2016) sought to examine several elements of exceptional clearances, e.g., when a case was "closed" but did not result in an arrest. He wanted to know the prevalence of exceptional clearances, if it was consistent across departments, what factors and circumstances of a crime are related to cases being exceptionally cleared, and what characteristics of the responding law enforcement agency are related to how cases are cleared. To study this, he examined incident-level data from the National Incident-Based Reporting System (NIBRS) and organizational data from the Law Enforcement Management and Administrative Statistics (LEMAS) survey. Since not all incidents that are in NIBRS have organizational information in LEMAS, and not all organizations represented in LEMAS are found in NIBRS, he had to compare the cases which were to be included in his analysis and which were not. This comparison would help determine how generalizable his inferential analyses would be, e.g., how well his sample data can describe the uncaptured population. His comparisons yielded mostly minor differences. The major difference found between the cases analyzed and those that were not was the region in which the incident occurred. The percentage of cases in the South and Northeast were similar; however, there was an 11.5% and 8.9% difference of cases in the Midwest and West, respectively (p. 1780). As a result, the data used may over-represent the Western region and under-represent the Midwestern region of the United States.

To make inferences about the population, the data analyzed should be generalizable. The characteristics of the sample should, as closely as possible, be statistically similar to the characteristics of the population from which it was drawn. Chapters 6 and 7 will discuss statistical tests that can be conducted to examine this similarity. As you read in Box 2.8: WHAT WE'VE LEARNED: Inferential Statistics and Data Analysis, Walfield (2016) compared the cases that were included in his analysis and those that were not. If the cases in each group were statistically similar, based on the characteristics of interest, the findings would be more generalizable. Since the cases in each group were not statistically similar across all characteristics, the findings are less generalizable. To increase the generalizability of research, we can think of the characteristics of the various data sources discussed in Chapter 1. For example, with surveys like the NCVS and NVAWS that are nationally representative, a sample was drawn to represent the population utilizing random sampling procedures. In random sampling, each case has an equal chance of being selected from the population. If data are collected using a random sampling procedure, there is a very high likelihood that the characteristics of the sample resemble those of the population, which will result in the findings of the study being generalizable. If an alternative procedure is used, tests such as those employed by Walfield are advisable to determine generalizability. This will increase the validity of any inferences made at the conclusion of the study.

SUMMARY

The analysis of data, despite previous practice and perhaps conventional wisdom, may be a final stage in a single research study, but it represents, perhaps, the start of future studies. From one set of findings, another researcher may find him/herself filled with ideas and questions from which they will design and conduct a new study. Further, the analysis of data may answer one research question, or address one set of hypotheses, while illuminating the need to ask more research questions and generate more hypotheses. Hindelang (1978) famously asked, is minority overrepresentation in the criminal justice system a function of differential involvement, differential treatment, or a combination thereof? His findings suggested that overrepresentation in the criminal justice system was largely the result of differential involvement. While this individual study did answer the question posed, it spawned future studies that attempted to answer *why* Hindelang found what he found, e.g., why some racial groups commit crimes at higher rates than others (see Unnever & Gabbidon, 2011, for a recent theoretical explanation). This cycle continued, and it continues this day—all the while altering and improving upon the various research designs employed. From data construction and collection, i.e., conceptualization and operationalization, to analysis—which must be directly related to the research question—to the hypotheses generated and the variables' levels of measurement, studying a phenomenon like crime is a continual and seemingly never-ending process.

This process, as Pratt (2016) notes, is needed in criminal justice and, specifically, criminological research. In order to improve and develop theory, these fields require advances in research methodology. Concepts and data must be improved and developed, too. These improvements take time and are often the result of asking a research question differently, collecting data from a different unit of analysis, or measuring a concept in a way that has not been done before. In this sense, the research cycle reflects, and may even perpetuate, the advancement of the criminal justice and criminology fields. This advancement can improve how phenomena such as crime are described, resulting in a greater understanding of such elements of crime as its prevalence, the characteristics of those that are victims of and perpetrate crime, and the characteristics of and processes used by those that respond to crime. As new criminal justice and criminology-related issues arise, the fields are more prepared theoretically, methodologically, and analytically to answer questions and test hypotheses posed by researchers.

CHAPTER REVIEW QUESTIONS

1. Explain how the inductive and deductive research processes are different in their relation to criminal justice and criminology theory.

2. Explain how one researcher, studying one topic, can conduct several studies—characterizing the research cycle.

3. Discuss the difference between an attribute and a variable. What processes must be undertaken for an attribute to become a variable?

4. Explain the differences across the four levels of measurement.

5. What is a unit of analysis? Cite an attribute, and explain how it can be examined, e.g. measured, using different units of analysis.

CHAPTER REVIEW EXERCISES

1. Review the UCR by visiting the offense definitions website:
https://www.ucrdatatool.goe/offenses.cfm
Examine the definitions provided for the Part I (Index) crimes. How can one classify these nominally? How can one classify these ordinally? Which do you think is the most appropriate level of measurement to use? Explain.

2. Identify an attribute used in criminal justice and criminology research. Provide a definition for the concept. Attempt to operationalize it using all four levels of measurement. Discuss the attribute and what levels of measurement could characterize it.

3. Visit the NCVS website: http://www.bjs.gov
Select *Victims*. Under *Data Collection & Surveys*, select *National Crime Victimization Survey (NCVS)*. Select the most recent publication titled *Criminal Victimization*. View the *PDF* of the report. Identify a variable that is measured at each level of measurement (nominal, ordinal, and interval/ratio).

4. Review the discussion of the UCR, NIBRS, and the NCVS. What are the respective units of analysis when each is gathering and reporting data? Explain.

5. Using your institution's library resources, find a peer-reviewed journal article that uses crime rates as a variable in the analysis. Find another that uses crime totals (e.g., counts) as a variable in the analysis. Discuss the articles, the research questions, the variables' levels of measurement, the reasoning for using the crime rate or total, and what the researchers found.

REFERENCES

Balbi, A., & Guerry, A.M. (1829). *Statistique compare de l'état de l'instruction et du nombre des crimes dans les divers arrondissements des academies et des cours royales de France.* Paris, France: Jules Renouard.

Carkin, D. M. & Tracy, P.E. (2015). Moffitt revisited: Delinquent and criminal career paths in the 1958 Philadelphia birth cohort. *Journal of Law and Criminal Justice, 3*(1), 14–39.

Chamlin, M. B. & Cochran, J.K. (2004). An excursus on the population size-crime relationship. *Western Criminology Review, 5*(2), 119–130.

Corbin, T.J., Purtle, J., Rich, L.J., Adams, E.J., Yee, G., & Bloom, S.L. (2013). The prevalence of trauma and childhood adversity in an urban, hospital-based violence intervention program. *Journal of Health Care for the Poor and Underserved, 24,* 1021–1030.

Hindelang, M. (1978). Race and involvement in common law personal crimes. *American Sociological Review, 43,* 93–109.

Hirschi, T. (1969). *Causes of Delinquency.* Berkeley, CA: University of California Press.

Klein, J.L., & Cooper, D.T. (2016). Trial by error: A content analysis of media coverage surrounding the Jerry Sandusky trial. *Justice Policy Journal, 13*(1), 1–29.

Osgood, D.W. (2000). Poisson-based regression analysis of aggregate crime rates. *Journal of Quantitative Criminology, 16*(1), 21–43.

Ostermann, M., Salerno, L.M., & Hyatt, J.M. (2015). How different operationalizations of recidivism impact conclusions of effectiveness of parole supervision. *Journal of Research in Crime and Delinquency 52*(6), 771–796.

Pratt, T.C. (2016). Theory testing in criminology. In Alex R. Piquero (Ed.) *The Handbook of Criminological Theory* (pp. 37–49). Malden, MA: Wiley-Blackwell.

Reiss, A.J. & Black, D.J. (1967). Interrogation and the criminal process. *The Annals of the American Academy of Political and Social Science, 374,* 47–57.

Sampson, R.J. (2013). The place of context: A theory and strategy for criminology's hard problems. *Criminology, 51*(1), 1–31.

Truman, J.L. & Morgan, R.E. (2016). *Criminal victimization, 2015.* NCJ 250180. Washington, D.C.: Bureau of Justice Statistics, U.S. Department of Justice.

Unnever, J.D., & Gabbidon, S.L. (2011). *A theory of African American offending: Race, racism, and crime.* New York, NY: Routledge.

Walfield, S. (2016). When a cleared rape is not cleared: A multilevel study of arrest and exceptional clearance. *Journal of Intimate Partner Violence, 31*(9), 1767–1792.

CHAPTER 3

GRAPHICAL DISPLAYS OF DATA

INTRODUCTION: VISUALIZING DATA IN CHARTS AND GRAPHS

Graphs are used for many different purposes. They can be used to store quantitative data, to communicate conclusions, or to discover new information. Some types of plots are better for one purpose, and some are better for another. ... Most of the displays may never be seen in a published report, but they are not designed for publication. ... Graphical techniques can be important in the discovery phase of analysis. (Church, 1979)

While highly complex forms of analysis are utilized in criminal justice and criminology research, they are by no means required, and they are often unnecessary. Sometimes, simply looking at the data, or "exploring" it, in various ways can be preferable to conducting complex and sophisticated statistical tests (Tukey, 1977). At minimum, visualizing data with displays, such as tables and graphs, provides a basis for organizing, presenting, and understanding data. For some, creating tables and graphs are the "first steps" to answering a research question. They are created for the purpose of examining the data to discover patterns before more sophisticated analysis. For others, creating tables and graphs from data can provide the answers to the research question(s) posed. Not all research questions require advanced analysis. Simplicity and parsimony is nearly always preferable to complexity and sophistication, especially when it is unnecessary. Regardless of their use, all forms of tables and graphs have specific assumptions, requirements, purposes, and accompanying advantages and disadvantages.

Consider the following questions:

1. What is the racial/ethnic distribution of inmates that are incarcerated in the United States?

2. How have violent and property crime rates in the United States changed over time?

3. Are crimes concentrated in certain areas of a city, or are they evenly dispersed?

Data collected for criminal justice and criminology-related research do not necessarily require advanced statistical calculations or complex and sophisticated analyses. In fact, some questions, like the three posed above, can be answered without much computation. Instead, they can be answered with the creation of various visual depictions, or graphical displays, of data. Many of the same types of tables, graphs, charts, plots, and other visual depictions of data are used across the social sciences. It is likely that most seem familiar, having been taught or referenced perhaps since the latter years of primary school. By using simple charts and graphs, one can clearly display descriptive information of data. For example, demographic information of those involved at various stages of the criminal justice system can be shown in a non-numerical way. Temporal patterns can be depicted, displaying how values have, or have not, changed over time. Crime data can also be linked with geographical data, often to inform criminal justice agency responses. Uses are not limited to these examples. This chapter examines the histories, requirements, and uses of the various forms of graphical displays of data.

LEARNING OBJECTIVES

By the end of this chapter, students will be able to:

1: Identify the various forms of graphical displays of data

2: Discuss the requirements of each form of graphical display of data

3: Explain the purpose of each form of graphical display of data

4: Evaluate the strengths of each form of graphical display of data

5: Assess the advantages and limitations of each form of graphical display of data

KEY TERMS

BAR CHART

BOX PLOT

CLASS INTERVALS

CROSS-TABULATION

FREQUENCY DISTRIBUTION

HISTOGRAM

LINE CHART

PAIRED OCCURRENCES

PIE CHART

SCATTERPLOT

TABLE

DISPLAYING CATEGORICAL VARIABLES

Data can be measured in a variety of ways. Each level of measurement has advantages and disadvantages associated with its respective use. Related, each level of measurement can be graphically

TABLE:
A graphical display of data that displays information in rows and/or columns to show values, frequencies, or other important characteristics of a variable.

FREQUENCY DISTRIBUTION:
A tabular representation of data that shows the occurrence or frequencies of a variable's values.

displayed in a variety of ways—with each display having advantages and disadvantages associated with its respective use. The purpose of each graphical display of data is important to consider, e.g., what its creator is attempting to convey to the reader. This is of paramount importance, as the intersection of the data used, how the data are measured, and the type of graphical display chosen impacts what the reader "takes away" from the display. Thus, each is created with a specific purpose in mind: to display data in the most appropriate, effective, and simple way possible.

FREQUENCY DISTRIBUTIONS

The first, and most simple, type of data display is the frequency distribution. A frequency distribution is a chart or table that shows the relative distribution of values across a single variable. A frequency distribution provides numerical data, in the form of counts, for one variable that is measured across multiple units. In essence, what is being measured is *how many* cases there are of the measured values or categories of a variable of interest. Since this type of chart provides frequencies, specific values of a variable are not examined and analyzed. The frequency distribution shows how many cases of the variable, and its various values, are found in the data. Often, these charts contain information in addition to the frequencies to contextualize the information being presented, such as proportions or percentages. These values are provided as a result of group differences in frequency totals, which is a common feature of data. Proportions compare the number of cases in a category to the total number of cases in the distribution. The proportion value indicates the relative frequency of a variable value. Percentages show the frequency of occurrence for each variable value per 100 cases. Proportions and percentages can be calculated for both nominal and ordinal variables in a frequency distribution.

Proportion

$$\frac{frequencies\ of\ a\ value}{total\ frequency}$$

Percentage

$$\frac{frequencies\ of\ a\ value}{total\ frequency} \times 100$$

Figure 3.1 Equations for Proportions and Percentages

For some datasets, especially larger ones, frequencies may be presented in a cumulative fashion. The cumulative frequency is the total number of cases having any given score and a score that is lower. Thus, in order to create and provide the cumulative frequencies of a distribution, the data must be measured at least at the ordinal level. The same cumulative value can be calculated and provided for proportions and percentages. Regardless of the type of frequency distribution—simple or cumulative—there are requirements that each must meet. First, all possible values of a variable must be accounted for and provided in the chart. Second, all cases must be accounted for and provided in the chart. This results in the cumulative proportion and cumulative percentage equaling 1.0 and 100, respectively.

Class Standing	f
Freshman	0
Sophomore	3
Junior	12
Senior	4
	Total = 19

Figure 3.2 Frequency Distribution

Box 3.1: WHAT WE'VE LEARNED: Frequency Distributions with Categorical Data

The Death Penalty Information Center (DPIC) is a national non-profit organization that collects, examines, and disseminates information to the public on issues related to capital punishment in the United States. Founded in 1990, the DPIC's website continually updates a *Fact Sheet* about the death penalty in the United States. While utilizing a variety of graphical displays, one of the most telling displays is the frequency distribution depicting *Executions by State Since 1976*—the year in which the United States Supreme Court reinstated the death penalty following the *Gregg v. Georgia* (1976) ruling. The frequency distribution shows that, overwhelmingly, Texas leads the nation in total executions since reinstatement (over 540). The next closest states, Oklahoma and Virginia, have had slightly over 110 in that same time period. Another very telling frequency distribution shows the number of death row inmates by state, as of October 2016. This tabular display of data shows the distribution of 2,902 death row inmates across 33 states, federal jurisdictions, and military jurisdictions. Perhaps surprisingly, Texas is third on the list with 254 inmates currently awaiting execution. Florida is second with 395, and California houses the most death row inmates with 745. When examining both of these frequencies together, interesting patterns emerge. For example, as of October 2016 there were 62 death row inmates under federal jurisdiction, yet there have been only 3 executions by the government since 1976. Many of the 35 jurisdictions are housing more death row inmates at one point in time than they executed in the previous 40 years. Notable exceptions include several southern states. Interestingly, New Hampshire houses one death row inmate, yet the state hasn't executed a prisoner since 1939 (DPIC, 2017).

CROSS-TABULATIONS (CONTINGENCY TABLES)

Frequency distributions are the simplest way of viewing, in chart form, the distribution of values of a variable in a dataset. However, analysis may require further inquiry. In order to further expand upon the examination of the distribution of values of a variable in a dataset, a cross-tabulation (cross-tab) may be created. Also known as contingency tables, cross-tabs are tabular displays of data that show frequencies of two or more variables. Often, they are created to show the relative frequencies and percentages of one variable, such as an independent variable, across an additional variable, such as a dependent variable. A cross-tab builds upon a frequency distribution by adding a second variable to show how cases are distributed across

CROSS-TABULATION: Also known as a cross-tab, a tabular representation of data that shows the paired occurrences or frequencies of two variables.

PAIRED OCCURRENCES: Also known as joint frequencies, when multiple variable values are simultaneously represented in a case; cases having specific values of two variables.

both variables. The joint frequencies represent what are referred to as paired occurrences, which indicate the number of times (the frequency) in a dataset the cases have the respective values of both variables. By rule of thumb, if the variables being examined are an independent variable and a dependent variable, the independent variable is located on the column, and the dependent variable is located on the row. Associated percentages for the paired occurrences can be provided, in addition to the frequencies, to show the relative frequency compared to the total number of cases. This number of cases, and its related percentage, can be relative to the row total, column total, or overall total. The percentage that is used is selected and presented based on which is more appropriate according to the analyst's research question and line of inquiry.

Column Percent

$$\frac{\textit{frequency}}{\textit{column total}} \times 100$$

Row Percent

$$\frac{\textit{frequency}}{\textit{row total}} \times 100$$

Total Percent

$$\frac{\textit{frequency}}{\textit{total}} \times 100$$

Figure 3.3 Equations for Cross-Tab Percentages

Box 3.2: WHAT WE'VE LEARNED: Cross-Tabulations with Categorical Data

In collaboration with the Thorn organization, the Crimes Against Children Research Center at the University of New Hampshire conducted a survey of persons who had been a target of threats to expose sexual images. The survey collected data on this practice, colloquially known as "sextortion," from more than 1,600 individuals age 18 to 25. The ultimate goal was to "inform strategies to reduce these incidents" (Wolnak & Finkelhor, 2016, p. 5). The first step was obtaining demographic information of the respondents and data concerning their relationship status. Using both of these variables, the researchers constructed a cross-tab to show the paired occurrences of gender and relationship status. Of the survey respondents, an overwhelming majority of them were female. However, when examining online relationships compared to face-to-face relationships, a greater proportion of males were found to be in online relationships than face-to-face relationships. In all, over 40 cross-tabs were examined, comparing demographics, behaviors, and outcomes with relationship status. One such cross-tab examined how perpetrators obtained the image. This cross-tab showed a significant difference between online and face-to-face relationships in the proportion of respondents that knowingly provided an image to the perpetrator. Approximately 60% of those in an online relationship did, while nearly 80% in a face-to-face relationship did.

Class Standing	Male	Female	Total
Freshman	0	0	0
Sophomore	2	1	3
Junior	6	6	12
Senior	4	0	4
	12	7	19

Figure 3.4 Cross-Tabulation (Cross-Tab)

BAR CHARTS:
A graphical representation of data in which parallel rectangular bars are plotted to show the relative frequency or percentage of a discrete variable's value.

BAR CHARTS

The history of bar charts can be traced back, approximately, to the year 1350 when either Nicole Oresme or Jacobus de Sancto Martino presented perhaps the first bar charts to examine acceleration. The authorship has been debated for some time. Regardless, across various scientific disciplines, the charts were focused on the visualization of measurable quantities as they relate to one another. While this contribution was not specific to criminal justice and criminology, the practice of creating bar charts to show quantities, specifically of values of a variable relative to one another, is still seen today.

Figure 3.5 Nicole Oresme's Bar Charts

Bar charts (or graphs—the terms are interchangeable) are used to graphically display frequencies of variable values relative to one another. Frequencies, or the associated percentages of a variable's values, can be displayed in a bar chart. The length or height, depending on construction, of the bars is proportional to the frequency or percentage of the variable value. Values with more cases, e.g., higher frequencies, will have longer or taller bars. Typically, these graphical displays show categorical variables. Being able to accommodate a higher number of categories than pie charts, bar charts are widely used in criminal justice and criminology research. Bar charts have relatively few requirements for display: the bars are proportional in length or height to the frequency or percentage of the respective values; the bars have equal width; the bars are equally spaced; the bars do not touch; the variable is discrete and; the variable values are mutually exclusive and exhaustive.

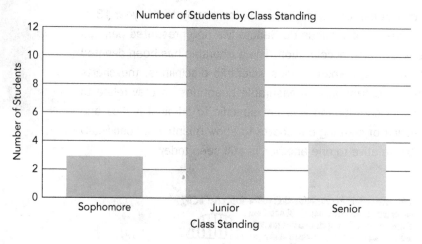

Figure 3.6 Bar Chart

Box 3.3: WHAT WE'VE LEARNED: Bar Charts with Categorical Data

Recently, the Bureau of Justice Statistics released a special report that discusses an analysis of police vehicle pursuits. Utilizing data from the years 2012 and 2013, it is estimated that approximately 68,000 vehicle pursuits were conducted by general state and local law enforcement agencies. The first bar chart in the report delineates this total by agency type. Local police departments conducted approximately 40,000 vehicle pursuits, sheriffs' offices nearly 18,000, and state police and highway patrol agencies the remaining 10,000. The report provides several additional graphical displays of data, including frequency distributions, cross-tabulations, line charts, and bar charts. One such bar chart displays data collected several years prior. The bar chart shows that among 115 law enforcement agencies, between 2009 and 2013, the most frequent "primary reason for termination" of police vehicle pursuits was the stopping of the driver. This accounted for 29% of the data. The discontinuation of pursuit by police followed at 25%; the violator eluding police at approximately 17%; a collision occurred at 15%; the violator exited the jurisdiction at 10%; alternative police intervention occurred at approximately 9%; and approximately 2% had a vehicle disabled. Perhaps unsurprisingly the penultimate bar chart shows the three most frequent "primary reasons" for the stop preceding the pursuit were driving related: other traffic offense, speeding, and reckless driving (Reaves, 2017).

PIE CHARTS

PIE CHART:
A graphical representation of data in which a circle is divided into sections to show the relative frequency or percentage of a variable's value.

The history of pie charts is curiously related to that of the bar chart. Some credit William Playfair (1786) with the invention of the bar chart, some three hundred years after Oresme (or de Sancto Martino). Playfair's use of the bar chart followed the assumptions and requirements that are familiar to analysts today, such as the equality in width and spacing and the lack of "touch" between the bars. His work used bars to signify distinct groups. Although those technicalities and the resultant credit may be up for debate, there is no debate about Playfair's other contributions. In his later work, Playfair (1801) became the first to use a pie chart to show frequencies or percentages, not only relative to each value of a variable but also relative to the entire distribution.

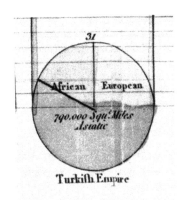

Figure 3.7 William Playfair's Pie Chart

Pie charts—or circle charts as Playfair (1801) described them—are used to graphically display frequencies of variable values relative to one another and relative to the entire distribution. Frequencies or the associated percentages of a variable's values can be displayed in a pie chart. Since the variable's values are displayed relative to one another as part of the entire distribution, the presentation of frequencies versus percentages is often only a matter of personal preference. The size of the "slice" is proportional to the frequency or percentage of the variable value, so they are identical except for their labels. Values with more cases, e.g., higher frequencies, will have larger "slices." Pie charts may be inappropriate to examine the distribution of variables with many values, particularly those that have a small number of cases. Pie charts are often used in criminal justice and criminology research to display variable distributions that have only a few values. Pie charts have few requirements for display: the "slices" are proportional in size to the frequency or percentage of the respective values; the variable is discrete; and the variable values are mutually exclusive and exhaustive.

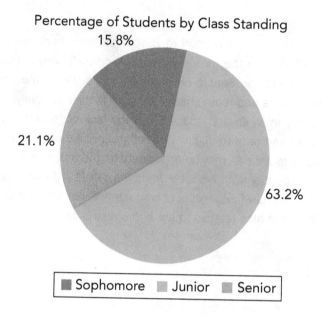

Figure 3.8 Pie Chart

CRIME MAPS

Like with the aforementioned graphical displays of crime, it may come as a surprise to know that the examination of spatial distributions of crime data has origins in Europe during the 1800s. Two contemporaries, André-Michel Guerry of France and Adolphe Quetelet of Belgium, studied the impact of geography on various social outcomes, including, but not limited to, crime. Guerry and geographer Adriano Balbi (1829) created the first maps of crime in their single-page sheet of maps titled "*Statistique Comparée de létat de l'Instruction et du Nombre des Crimes.*"

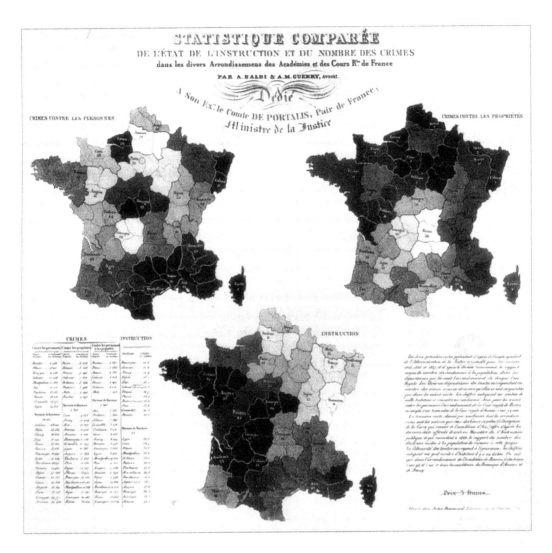

Figure 3.9 Guerry and Balbi's Maps

At approximately the same time that Guerry and Balbi were completing their work, Adolphe Quetelet was providing groundbreaking statistical and methodological advances in the social sciences (Beirne, 1987). Quetelet worked for Belgium, France, and later Great Britain, teaching, training, and developing new methods of statistical analysis for social science disciplines. He contributed significantly to various disciplines, not just statistics and criminology. In fact, criminology was not yet a recognized discipline until several decades later. Quetelet (1832) published similar maps to Guerry and Balbi; however, he examined larger areas. His research on crime, time, and space helped provide the theoretical and empirical foundations for environmental criminology and routine activities theory. Most of these early maps used continuous data, so they will be discussed in greater detail later in the chapter.

Crime mapping in the United States, particularly in the areas of sociology and criminology, lagged behind their use by European counterparts. At the time of Guerry and Quetelet, the United States, as a nation, was only about 60 years old, a far cry from an established sovereignty. In fact, at the time of Guerry and Balbi's (1829) publication, the United States was a country of just 24 states. The 25th state (Arkansas) was not admitted to the Union until one year after Quetelet's (1835) subsequent work. As a result, it would not be until several decades later that crime and demographic information were collected on a regular basis, let alone used for geographic visualization. When created, those early maps were called spot maps, which were described in a U.S. Federal Bureau of Investigation bulletin:

> Spot maps have been used for a number of years by traffic bureaus in police departments throughout the country for the purpose of furnishing a clear, quick, and comprehensive picture of the accident situation and to indicate at a glance the points in the city which present the greatest hazard. Spot maps have also been used in a similar fashion to show the crime hazards of the city. For example, some departments show on a spot map one type of pin indicating the location of the theft of each automobile and a pin of a different shape or color to indicate the location of its recovery. The advantage of a spot map lies in its maintenance and interpretation. (1944, p. 34)

These spot maps are fairly common, even today—for a variety of applications unrelated to criminal justice and criminology. Have you ever used the internet to search "restaurants near me" or searched for driving directions on a laptop or smartphone? The results will likely have a "pin" indicating the location of your search term(s) and perhaps even many clustered together.

The use of mapping in the field of American criminology did not gain traction until the 1920s. Researchers from the Chicago School of sociologists developed very sophisticated maps of neighborhoods in Chicago—quite impressive for the lack of technology available to them at the time. Several urban sociologists affiliated with the University of Chicago (a school with a very prominent sociological tradition) examined characteristics of the urban environment to explain outcomes, such as crime in American cities. These sociologists included, among others, Robert Park, Ernest Burgess, Frederic Thrasher, Clifford Shaw, and Earl Myers—all of which influenced urban sociologists and criminologists directly and indirectly for decades to come.

These researchers studied Chicago by mapping out levels of crime and other social characteristics, just as their European predecessors had done. However, the geographic specificity and application of sociological theory they incorporated into their research set them apart from the likes of Guerry and Quetelet. Their focus was one called the concentric zone model. Thrasher (1927) examined the gangs within Chicago by layering their location and distribution on a concentric neighborhood map. He discovered that gangs were typically found in areas of the city where social control is weakened and social disorganization is heightened. Similar concentric maps were used by Park, Burgess, and McKenzie (1925) and Shaw and Myers (1929). Naturally, similar conclusions were made—areas with poverty, social disorganization, and physical disrepair (e.g., elements of "Broken Windows") are clustered with incidents of crime and delinquency.

In order to create the crime map, Shaw and Myers painstakingly analyzed the addresses of approximately 9,000 juvenile delinquents in Chicago. By hand, they marked the location of the addresses on the city map (see Figure 3.10). Simple spot maps like this use data that are categorical in nature. The variable in this case, delinquency, has two values: occurrence and no occurrence. When there is the presence of a predetermined variable value, the location, or spot, is plotted on the map. The absence of the variable results in the absence of "spots" on the map. In the case of Shaw and Myers (1929), when there was recorded delinquency (the presence of that value: occurrence), the location was plotted on the Chicago map.

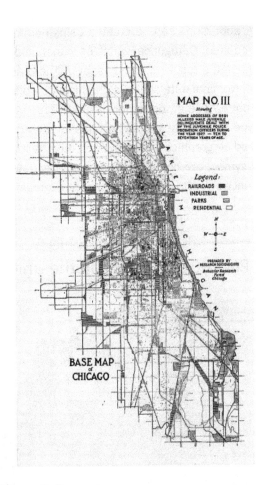

Figure 3.10 Shaw's Map of Chicago Delinquents

Box 3.5: WHAT WE'VE LEARNED: Crime Maps with Categorical Data

The National Institute of Justice (NIJ) provides various technological tools for law enforcement, one of which is the *CrimeStat* program. Available for download, along with documentation, workbook, and a sample dataset, the *CrimeStat* program allows for, among other things, the input of locations or spots of criminal incidents. These locations are plotted on a map for visual inspection and more detailed and complex analyses. Levine (2006) provided an overview of the program's most recent additions. He also illustrated the various plotting capabilities of the program with several examples. The first example plotted burglaries that occurred in Precinct 12 of Baltimore County. Using the date of the incident, he was able to depict the burglaries in different shades based on when they occurred: June of 1997 or July of 1997. Another crime map depicts the area of Central Houston. Data from 1999–2001 were combined and plotted on one map, indicating the location of driving while intoxicated (DWI) crashes. Finally, based on an example of West Baltimore County, he provided a spot map of robbery locations. Using this visual information, and knowledge of the areas in which the robberies occurred most frequently, he concluded that most are concentrated at commercial strips along various highways in the county, specifically State Highway 26.

As a form of crime mapping, spot maps can be created using nominal or ordinal data, as only the presence of a variable value is required. Categorical variables with multiple values that could be plotted on a map may have different shapes, sizes, or colored "spots." There are several other ways in which categorical data may be mapped. Nominal data could be graphically displayed on a crime map with areas of different colors, symbols, or patterns, e.g., dotted or dashed sections, to indicate the presence of a particular variable value. This type of data could also have labels affixed to "spots" to differentiate the values present. Ordinal data could be graphically displayed on a crime map in a variety of ways, as well. Differences in size, shape, and symbol are common ways to differentiate ranked categories. The most common practice is using differences in color. Typically, data are aggregated to larger geographical units with ordinal data.

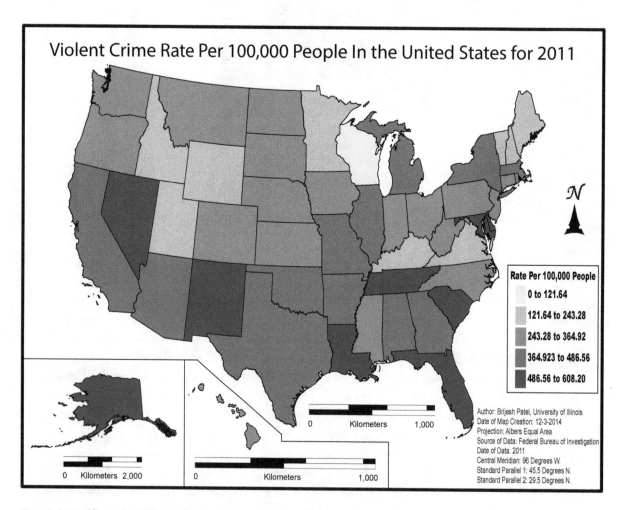

Figure 3.11 Choropleth Map of Crime Rates

DISPLAYING CONTINUOUS VARIABLES

There are many advantages to measuring data at a higher level, i.e., at the interval/ratio level, compared to measuring data at the nominal or ordinal levels. All forms of description, analysis, and presentation that are available to categorical variables are also available to continuous variables, even if some data work is required. For example, some variables may need to be aggregated into groups.

In addition to what is available to lower levels of measurement, interval/ratio data also have graphical displays available to them that cannot be used to describe nominal and ordinal measures. With more options available to these types of data, special attention should be paid to what is most appropriate to use. Each form of graphical display of data has its own set of strengths and weaknesses. Some are better suited than others to describe a particular phenomenon, answer a specific question, or display a distinct type of data. Thus, like the aforementioned graphical displays, each is created with a specific purpose in mind: to display data in the most appropriate, effective, and simple way possible.

FREQUENCY DISTRIBUTIONS

Frequency distributions are available, and sometimes used, to display data that are continuous or numerical. There is no level of measurement requirement for this type of graphical display of data. For continuous variables, the frequency distribution provides counts, or how many times a specific variable value is observed in a dataset. Compared to frequency distributions that examine the relative frequencies of variables measured at the nominal and ordinal levels, displaying continuous variables often results in an exorbitant number of values. When a frequency distribution is created that has an extensive number of variable values, the variable and its values are often aggregated into groups into class intervals. These groups, as a lower level of measurement (ordinal), must meet the requirements of that data: groups must be mutually exclusive and exhaustive.

CLASS INTERVALS:
In data analysis, when data are aggregated into groups to reflect a range of values.

Age	f
0-19	7
20-24	10
24-29	2
	Total = 19

Figure 3.12 Frequency Distribution with Class Intervals

If this was not done, the resultant frequency distribution would be very difficult to read or even be presented due to size. For example, if the age of an offender is measured, and the values are found to range from age 15 to 49, the accompanying frequency distribution would require 35 different frequencies—each to represent one of the ages between, and including, 15 and 49. Even with fewer values (see Figure 3.13), the table may be unnecessarily large for the information it is meant to convey.

Age	f
17	2
18	3
19	2
20	4
21	1
22	5
23	0
24	0
25	0
26	0
27	0
28	0
29	1
30	1
	Total = 19

Figure 3.13 Frequency Distribution with Many Values

CROSS-TABULATIONS (CONTINGENCY TABLES)

Like frequency distributions, cross-tabulations (cross-tabs) are available for the examination of data measured at all levels. If the variables being examined are an independent variable and a dependent variable, the independent variable is located on the column, and the dependent variable is located on the row. Associated percentages for the paired occurrences can be provided, in addition to the frequencies, to show the relative frequency compared to the total number of cases. This number of cases, and its

Age	Male	Female	Total
17	1	1	2
18	1	2	3
19	2	0	2
20	2	2	4
21	1	0	1
22	2	3	5
23	0	0	0
24	0	0	0
25	0	0	0
26	0	0	0
27	0	0	0
28	0	1	1
29	0	1	1
Total	9	10	19

Figure 3.14 Cross-Tab with Many Values

related percentage, can be relative to the row total, column total, or overall total. The percentage that is used is selected and presented based on which is more appropriate according to the analyst's research question and line of inquiry. However, also like frequency distributions, cross-tabs are generally inappropriate when there are a substantial number of variable values. In order to more effectively display data involving a variable that is measured continuously, the variable may be aggregated or grouped to create a categorical variable. This will allow for the examination of paired occurrences across two variables. This will also provide clarity and ease in visualization, interpretation, and subsequent analyses.

PIE CHARTS

Pie charts are also available, and sometimes used, to display data that are numerical—or continuous. Like frequency distributions, there is no level of measurement requirement for this type of graphical display of data. For continuous variables, pie charts are able to show relative frequencies or percentages of specific variable values observed in a dataset. The same disadvantage to using frequency distributions exists with using pie charts to show the relative frequencies and/or percentages of a continuous variable. It is possible that the variable may have an inordinate number of values to display.

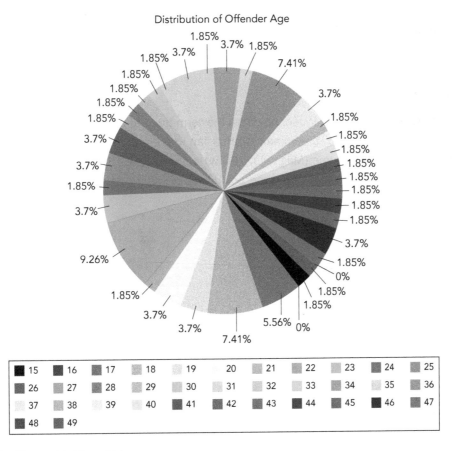

Figure 3.15 Pie Chart with Many Values

Consider the previous example. If the age of an offender is measured, and values are found to range from age 15 to 49, the accompanying pie chart would require as many "slices" as there are different values in the dataset. If all values from 15 through 49 are represented in the dataset, like in the frequency distribution, the pie chart will be required to display 35 different "slices"—each representing a single age. Sometimes, it may be of substantive and/or practical interest to make groups of different sizes. Groupings of different sizes are referred to as unequal class intervals. These groups, as a lower level of measurement (ordinal), must still meet the requirements of that data: groups must be mutually exclusive and exhaustive.

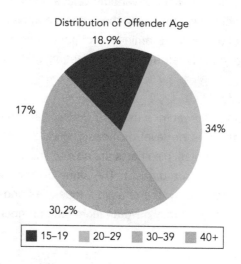

Distribution of Offender Age

18.9%

17%

34%

30.2%

■ 15–19   ■ 20–29   ■ 30–39   ■ 40+

Figure 3.16 Pie Chart with Unequal Class Intervals

HISTOGRAMS

The history of histograms, and their use, predates the term used to describe them. The word histogram was coined and first discussed by preeminent statistician Karl Pearson in 1895, having been used some years earlier in a series of lectures (Magnello, 2005; Pearson, 1895; Stigler, 1986). However, it was at least several decades earlier when their use could first be seen, particularly in criminal justice and criminology research (Dietz & Kalof, 2009).

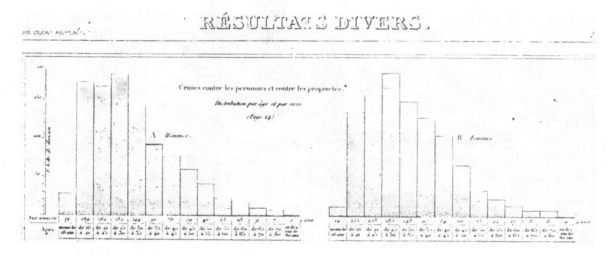

Figure 3.17 Guerry's Histogram

Histograms are quite similar to bar charts. In fact, many are unable to distinguish one from the other. Some software programs do so by creating and labeling them differently. For example, Microsoft Excel has bar charts with horizontal presentations and vertical presentations (denoted as column charts). Histograms are also presented vertically. Like bar charts, histograms represent data using "bars." However, there are very important differences that make the two distinct from one another. It is important to note the difference(s) between bar charts and histograms. Bar charts, generally, display the frequency or percentage of a discrete variable. This variable is most appropriately measured at the nominal level. Since there is no continuity between the values of a nominal variable, a bar chart has space between the bars. Histograms display variables measured at higher levels where there may be continuity, thus the bars are joined to show continuity along the scale: they connect or "touch" each other.

HISTOGRAM:
A graphical representation of data in which parallel rectangular bars are plotted to show the relative frequency or percentage of a continuous variable's value.

LINE CHART:
A graphical representation of data in which multiple data points connected by lines are plotted to show continuity or series data values over time.

Box 3.6: WHAT WE'VE LEARNED: Histograms

André-Michel Guerry, in his 1833 seminal work on the social statistics of France, was the first to use histograms to show patterns of criminal behavior. In the appendix to the volume, he provides several histograms that examine, among other things, crime rates by age, sex, month, and offense type. His first histograms, *Crimes contre les personnes et contre les proprieties: Distribution par age et par sexo*, provided one display for males (*hommes*) and one display for females (*femmes*). The histogram for males shows that the highest crime rates are found for those age 25 to 30, followed closely by those age 16 to 21. The histogram for females also shows the highest crime rates are found for those age 25 to 30, followed by those age 21 to 25. His second set of histograms depicts crime rates over time (rates for each month). The first, displaying personal crime data, shows June with the highest crime rate and January with the lowest. The histogram displaying property crime data shows contrasting results: July has the lowest crime rates, and December has the highest. His final pair of histograms compares the rate of suicide, by age and type, for males. He finds the highest rate of suicide by firearm is found for those age 20 to 30, while the highest rate of suicide by hanging is found for those age 50 to 60 (Friendly, 2008; Guerry, 1833).

LINE CHARTS

William Playfair (1786), inventor of the bar chart—to some—and the pie chart, was also the first to produce and publish a line chart. A line chart is a graphical display of data that can be used to display changes in a continuous variable, or variables, over time. Line charts can also be used to show changes in variables across groups over a specified time period. The line is produced by plotting values of a variable across another variable that is measured continuously, such as in months or years. In criminal justice and criminology research, rates of crime, such as offending rates and victimization rates, are commonly displayed in this manner. Variables that are measured and displayed over time allow for the discovery and examination of trends or patterns in a dataset.

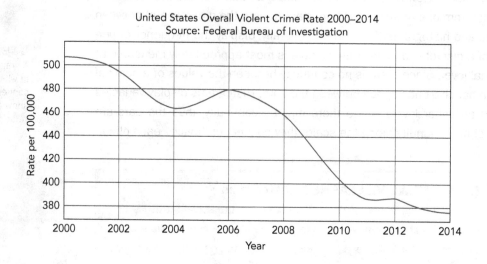

Figure 3.18 Line Chart with Crime Rates

Some data can be graphically displayed in either a histogram or a line chart. Although the data requirements are similar, e.g., the variable must be continuous, how the data are plotted may differ. Data that may be displayed in the form of a line chart are continuous data that are displayed longitudinally, or over time, such as rates. Data that may be displayed in the form of a histogram or a line chart are typically shown by reporting and displaying the variable values' frequencies or percentages.

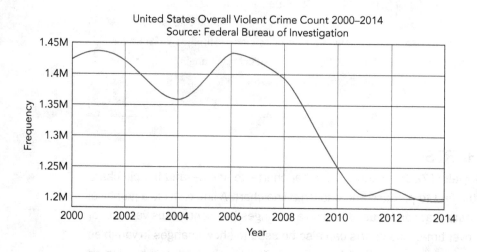

Figure 3.19 Line Charts with Frequencies

Box 3.7: WHAT WE'VE LEARNED: Line Charts

The U.S. Department of Justice and the Bureau of Justice Statistics publishes reports concerning many areas of criminal justice and criminology on an annual basis. A recent bulletin, *Correctional Populations in the United States, 2015,* examines the total population under the supervision of United States corrections systems in a 15-year time period. Using a combined histogram and line chart, the bulletin shows not only the frequencies, or the population on an annual basis, via the histogram, but also the yearly percent change of that population. The line chart indicates that from 2008 until the most recently available data in 2015, the total population under correctional supervision in the United States has declined. Not only was there an overall decline for the seven-year period, but for each year, a reduction was observed. While the year 2007 represented the height of correctional supervision, 2008 was not far behind. In 2007, the total correctional population was 7,339,600. In 2008, it was 7,312,600—a decrease of three-tenths of a percent. Beginning in 2008, however, steady decreases were observed during most years. As a result, from the peak year of 2007 to the most recent data of 2015, the number of persons supervised by United States adult correctional systems declined by approximately 600,000, or 8% (Kaeble & Glaze, 2016).

BOX PLOTS

The history of the box plot, or the box-and-whisker plot as some first learn it, is a bit less storied, or at least more recent, than some of the other graphical displays of data discussed thus far. In his widely influential text, *Exploratory Data Analysis* (1977), John W. Tukey advocated for the use of many graphical displays in the exploration of a dataset. Tukey was particularly interested in taking information that was traditionally displayed numerically and exploring the ways in which it could be displayed graphically. One of the displays that he developed to explore variables was the box plot.

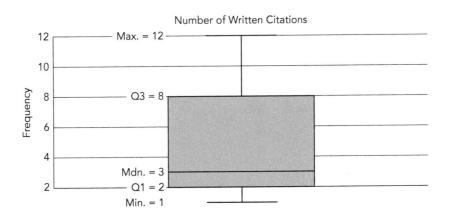

Figure 3.20 Box Plot

A box plot is a graphical display of data that is created with five variable values. The values needed to create a box plot are the minimum, maximum, first quartile, median, and the third quartile. Chapters 4 and 5 will explain and examine those values in greater detail. The box plot, created from those five values, provides a standardized summary of a variable. This allows for the comparison of distributions,

BOX PLOT:
A graphical representation of data in which the distribution of data is depicted using a number line, rectangle, and various descriptive statistics, including the minimum value, the first quartile, the median, the third quartile, and the maximum value.

either of multiple variables or multiple groups of a single variable. The "box" is created using the values of the first quartile and the third quartile. The median is identified within the "box." The minimum and maximum values produce the "whiskers," which extend from the "box" in opposite directions based on the respective values. There are several variations and additions one can make to a box plot, depending on the analyst's preference and the data available.

Box 3.8: WHAT WE'VE LEARNED: Box Plots

In a comparison of groups, specifically two different time periods, several prominent scholars teamed up to take Tukey's suggestion and put it into practice. Applying *exploratory* data analysis, Messner, Anselin, Baller, Hawkins, Deane, and Tolnay (1999) examined spatial patterns of county homicide rates. The researchers examined diffusion of homicides for two different time periods in St. Louis (1984–1988 and 1988–1993). The first time period represented a period of relative stability, in which homicide rates fluctuated very little. The second time period represented a period of marked increase. Homicide rates increased each year to their peak in 1993. From their analysis, they found there may be some diffusion of homicide from one county to another, and areas that are considered rural and agricultural may serve as a barrier to such diffusion. Examination of box plots shows that there were differences of homicide rates between the two different time periods, largely a result of outliers that emerged in the later time period. These outliers may have been the result of diffusion. From the first time period to the second time period, areas with higher rates of homicide could be found throughout city. However, as the authors note, "the 'south-west vs. northeast' division deteriorates over time" (p. 437). The south and west areas no longer evidenced higher levels of homicide; those areas could now almost exclusively be found in the northeast area.

SCATTERPLOTS

The history of the scatterplot is far less precise and definitive than the other graphical displays of data (see Friendly and Denis, 2005, for a discussion). The use of "plots," by placing data points to represent the coinciding values of two variables on a plane, has been in practice for several hundred years. Early cartographers created maps using "plotting" methods, mathematicians plotted values from equations in planar form, and astronomers examined weather patterns using early forms of this graphical display. J.F.W. Herschel (1833) was the first to describe how to create a scatterplot and to advocate for its use; thus, he is often credited with the formation of the scatterplot as we know and use it today.

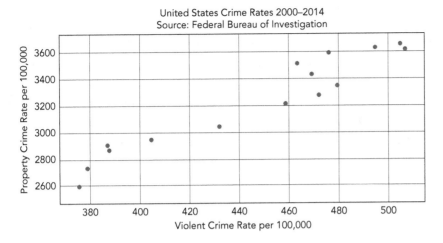

Figure 3.21 Scatterplot

SCATTERPLOT:
A graphical representation of data in which individual data points are plotted using values of two variables, one presenting on the Y-axis and one presenting on the X-axis.

A scatterplot is a graphical display of data that is created using paired data, which are continuous and representative of two variables. Each pair pertains to an individual case within the dataset. Scatterplots tend to be used with large datasets to examine patterns or relationships between the two included

Box 3.9: WHAT WE'VE LEARNED: Scatterplots

Researchers Fajnzylber, Lederman, and Loayza (2002) were interested in studying whether economic characteristics of a country had similar effects on crime for different crime types. In their study, they investigated the link between income inequality and violent crime at the national level. Using multiple scatterplots, a measure of income inequality (the Gini coefficient) was paired with rates of robbery and homicide. The data used were from 37 countries during the period of 1970–1994 (for robbery) and 39 countries during the period of 1965–1995 (for homicide). The authors displayed this relationship across groups by differentiating the "points" by geographic region: Sub-Saharan Africa was represented by a dark triangle, East and South Asia by a circle, Eastern Europe by a light triangle, Latin America by a square, and Organisation for Economic Cooperation and Development (OECD) countries by a diamond. Latin American countries were shown to have the highest levels of income inequality and crime rates. Eastern European and OECD countries were shown to have the lowest levels of income inequality and crime rates. Despite the delineation of regions by the authors, similar patterns were observed. An increase in the income inequality of a nation had a significant and positive effect on crime rates—at least for robbery and homicide.

variables. Each variable is represented on a different axis of the chart. If a dependent variable is included in the scatterplot, it is placed on the Y-axis (or the vertical axis) while the independent variable is placed on the X-axis (or the horizontal axis). The paired data are plotted so that each data point on the chart, or "dot," represents one case. Scatterplots allow for the examination of patterns or relationships between two continuous variables within groups, across groups, and even across variables. Scatterplots also allow for the detection and examination of outliers. Despite those possibilities, the strength of having large amounts of data may become a weakness if there are patterns or relationships that are indiscernible as a result of having "too much" in the plot. Like the other graphical displays discussed, the simplest option is often preferable.

CRIME MAPS

As discussed earlier, the maps created by the likes of Guerry, Balbi, and Quetelet were the first to graphically display crime data using maps. The data used by Guerry and Balbi were a combination of crime data obtained from the *Compte Général*, as well as data from France's census spanning the years of 1825–1827. Using the combination of these data, Guerry and Balbi were able to calculate various crime rates, including population per crime and inhabitants per student. The maps they developed examined crimes against property, crimes against persons, and levels of education. Guerry and Balbi were able to uncover some interesting relationships. First, the northeastern portion of France was better educated. Second, areas with high levels of property crime have relatively low levels of violent crime ("attacks on people"). Finally, areas with higher levels of property crime were inhabited with individuals of higher levels of education. The second and third discoveries were in direct contrast to popular beliefs at the time.

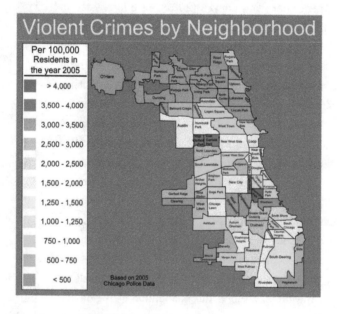

Figure 3.22 Hot Spot Map

In each of Guerry and Balbi's maps, regions were shaded darker with increasing crime or decreasing education. The regions used to form geographical boundaries were education districts. Shading locations is often incorporated into crime maps, by using a gradient of color, such as various grey hues, ranging from white to black. However, only in recent years have technologies evolved to become accessible for nearly all data analysts to more accurately depict the continuous data required for a crime map. Today, not only is shading available, but so are gradients of different colors. Perhaps the most well-known type of crime map using continuous data is a heat, or "hot spot," map. These types of maps are often used to show differences in crime frequencies or rates, the latter which constitutes continuous data. These maps typically use a range of colors: from dark blue to bright red, a cold and a warm color. The colder colors, such as different shades of blue and green, represent relatively low values of the variable in a particular area. The hotter colors, such as different shades of orange and red, represent relatively high values of the variable in a particular area. More neutral colors, such as different shades of yellow, represent the middle values of the variable in a particular area. It is important to note when viewing a hot spot map that a "cold" area does not necessarily mean that there is a low value of a variable. It means that these areas represent the lowest values in the dataset. The same can be said for "hot" areas not necessarily meaning that there is a high value of a variable. It means that these areas represent the highest values in the dataset.

Box 3.10: WHAT WE'VE LEARNED: Crime Maps with Continuous Data

The emergence of social media platforms, such as Facebook, LinkedIn, and Instagram, have allowed individuals to connect with one another remotely and in real time using only a smart phone or similar device with an Internet connection. The applications have also provided invaluable information for criminal justice professionals and researchers. In recent years, several scholars have studied the use of social media and its relationship to crime. At the University of Freidburg in Germany, three researchers have done just that. Researchers Johannes Bendler, Antal Ratku, and Dirk Neumann (2014) incorporated social media data with traditional environmental measures that are theoretically and statistically related to crime. The researchers included more than 600,000 geo-tagged Twitter status messages into their crime prediction models to see if it increased its accuracy. These messages provided a precise geographical location and a specific time, so researchers were able to know exactly where and when a tweet was posted. Results suggested that social media can improve crime prediction with respect to where these events occur. In this study, Twitter statuses helped statistically explain burglary, motor vehicle theft, robbery, and theft/larceny. They did not help explain other violent crimes. As a result, it was suggested that although property crime increases as the population increases, the traditional measure of population does not reflect mobility. Thus, social presence in an area may be a better predictor of crime.

Graphical Display	Data Best Suited For	Best To Show
Frequency Distribution	Categorical	Distribution of one variable
Cross-Tab	Categorical	Distribution across two variables
Bar Chart	Categorical	Frequencies, percentages
Pie Chart	Categorical	Frequencies, percentages
Histogram	Continuous	Frequencies, percentages
Line Chart	Continuous	Trends over time
Box Plot	Continuous	Descriptive statistics
Scatterplot	Continuous	Relationships
Map	Continuous	Geographic differences

Figure 3.23 Graphical Displays of Data Summary

SUMMARY

Perhaps Edward R. Tufte put it best when he said, "Excellence in statistical graphics consists of complex ideas communicated with clarity, precision, and efficiency. … Graphics *reveal* data" (2001, p. 1). The purpose of graphical displays of data is to show data in the simplest and comprehendible manner, based on the intent of the specific display and the data available. Creating graphical displays of data can be the start of analysis or statistical inquiry, or, as Tukey (1977) may suggest, the initial steps of exploration, or graphical displays of data can represent the end or outcome of analysis. Tables may organize available data needed to answer a relatively simple research question, such as that found in a frequency distribution. Charts can examine distributions and provide visual representations of group differences, such as those in a bar chart. Plots might present variables from a dataset that are easier to comprehend than if the numerical values were simply displayed in a table. The box plot or scatter plot offer this advantage. There are countless variants of the aforementioned graphical displays, and even more types of tables, charts, and graphs that were not discussed. What is consistent across all graphical displays of data is their utility and the general requirement of specific data. Each graphical display is available and appropriate for particular types of data, determined by either *how* something is measured (e.g., at the nominal level) or *what* is being measured (e.g., values over time).

When these characteristics of data are decided upon, so too are the methods by which the data can be graphically displayed. Employing specific data collection instruments and measurement techniques may allow for a greater number of graphical displays of data to be created. When data are measured at the interval/ratio level, most, if not all, forms of data visualization are available to the researcher(s). Interval/ratio data can be displayed with the same tables, charts, and graphs that nominal and ordinal data can be displayed with. This can be done by keeping the interval/ratio data intact, as measured, or this can be done via aggregation. Interval/ratio data can be grouped into categories. Whether or not this occurs depends on what the researcher wishes to convey, and how s/he wishes to graphically convey it. Regardless of what level of data is used and what type of graphical display is created, the goal of achieving simplicity and parsimony remains. "Analysis" of data does not require statistical computation. Sometimes, data visualization is the most effective way to answer a research question.

CHAPTER REVIEW QUESTIONS

1. Explain how frequency distributions and cross-tabs can be created with continuous data.

2. Explain how bar charts and pie charts can be used to display the same data.

3. Discuss the differences between a bar chart and a histogram. What type of data is used for each? How do they differ, substantively and visually?

4. Which graphical display of data is most appropriate, and most often used, to show changes of a continuous variable over time?

5. What is a box plot? List the level of measurement the variable must be and the values needed to create one.

CHAPTER REVIEW EXERCISES

1. Visit the Death Penalty Information Center website:

https://deathpenaltyinfo.org

Select *Fact Sheet.* Identify one graphical display of data that you would alter. Explain what changes you would make to improve it. Specifically, if applicable, discuss issues of operationalization, inappropriate use of display, and/or inappropriate (or ineffective) use of data.

2. Identify one of the graphical displays of data discussed. Provide an example of how it could be used to display data in criminal justice and criminology research. What level of measurement(s) would be required?

3. Visit the NCVS website: http://www.bjs.gov

Select *Victims.* Under *Data Collection & Surveys,* select *National Crime Victimization Survey (NCVS).* Select the most recent publication entitled *Criminal Victimization.* View the *PDF* of the report. Identify a frequency distribution, a cross-tab, and a line chart. Explain what each of the graphical displays of data is showing.

4. Are there are any attributes that, as a result of different operationalizations, could be graphically displayed using all of the forms discussed? Identify or create a variable that can be graphically displayed in multiple formats. Explain the variable and its construction and what displays are available to it.

5. Using your institution's library resources, find two peer-reviewed journal articles that are of interest to you that examine data graphically. What form(s) of graphical displays of data are used? Compare the articles, the displays, and the data used. Discuss the appropriateness of displays, based on its data and purpose, and what you learned from them as a viewer.

REFERENCES

Balbi, A., & Guerry, A.M. (1829). *Statistique comparée de l'état de l'instruction et du nombre des crimes dans les divers arrondissements des Académies et des Cours Royales de France.* Paris, France: Jules Renouard.

Bendler, J., Ratku, A., & Neumann, D. (2014). Crime mapping through geospatial social media activity. Paper presented at the *Thirty Fifth Conference on Information Systems, Auckland 2014.*

Beime, P. (1993). *Inventing criminology.* Albany, NY: State University of New York Press

Church, R.M. (1979). How to look at data: A review of John W. Tukey's exploratory data analysis. *Journal of the Experimental Analysis of Behavior, 31*(3), 433–440.

De Sancto Martino, J. (1482). *Tractatus de latitudinibus formarum.* Padua, Italy: Matheaus Cerdonis.

Dietz, T. & Kalof, L. (2009). *Introduction to social statistics: The logic of statistical reasoning.* Malden, MA: Wiley-Blackwell.

Fajnzylber, P., Lederman, D., & Loayza, N. (2002). Inequality and violent crime. *Journal of Law and Economics, 45*(1), 1–39.

Friendly, M., & Denis, D. (2005). The early origins and developments of the scatterplot. *Journal of the History of the Behavioral Science, 41*(2), 103–130.

Friendly, M. (2008). La vie et l'oeuvre d' André-Michel Guerry (1802–1866). *Mémoires de l'Académie de Touraine, 20.*

Gregg v. Georgia. (1976). 428 U.S. 153.

Guerry, A.M. (1833). *Essai sur la statistique morale de la France.* Paris, France: Crochard.

Herschel, J.F.W. (1833). On the investigation of the orbits of revolving double stars. *Memoirs of the Royal Astronomical Society, 5,* 171–222.

Kaeble, D. & Glaze, L. (2016). *Correctional populations in the United States, 2015.* U.S. Department of Justice. Retrieved from https://www.bjs.gov/content/pub/pdf/cpus15.pdf.

Levine, N. (2006). Crime mapping and the Crimestat Program. *Geographical Analysis, 38*(1), 41–56.

Mangello, M. E. (2005). Karl Pearson and the origins of modern statistics: An elastician becomes a statistician. *The Rutherford Journal: The New Zealand Journal for the History and Philosophy of Science and Technology, 1.* Retrieved from http://www.rutherfordjournal.org/article010107.html.

Messner, S.F., Anselin, L., Baller, R.D., Hawkins, D.F., Deane, G., & Tolnay, S.E. (1999). The spatial patterning of county homicide rates: An application of exploratory spatial data analysis. *Journal of Quantitative Criminology, 15*(4), 423–450.

Mitchell, K.J., Jones, L.M., Turner, H.A., Shattuck, A., & Wolak, J. (2016). The role of technology in peer harassment: Does it amplify harm for youth? *Psychology of Violence, 6*(2), 193–204.

Mitchell, K.J., Jones, L.M., Turner, H., Blachman-Demner, D., & Kracke, K. (2016). The role of technology in youth harassment victimization. Washington, D.C.: U.S. Department of Justice.

Park, R.E., Burgess, E.W., & McKenzie, R.D. (1925). *The city*. Chicago, IL: University of Chicago Press.

Pearson, K. (1895). Contributions to the Mathematical Theory of Evolution- II: Skew variation in homogenous material. *Philosophical Transactions of the Royal Society of London. A, 186,* 343–414.

Pearson, K. (1904). *On the Theory of Contingency and its relation to association and normal correlation.* New York, NY: Drapers' Co. Memoirs.

Playfair, W. (1786). *The commercial and political atlas: Representing, by means of stained copper-plate charts, the progress of the commerce, revenues, expenditure and debts of England during the whole of the eighteenth century.* London, UK: Debrett, Robinson, and Sewell.

Playfair, W. (1801). *Statistical breviary; Shewing, on the principle entirely new, the resources of every state and kingdom in Europe.* London, UK: Wallis.

Quetelet A. (1832). Nouveaux memoire de l'Academie Royale des Sciences et Belles-Lettres de Bruxelles. *Recherches sur le poids de l'homme aux different ages,* p. VII.

Quetelet, A. (1835). *Sur l'homme et le développement de ses facultés, ou Essai de physique sociale.* Paris, France: Bachelier.

Reaves, B.A. (2017). *Police vehicle pursuits, 2012–13.* Washington, D.C.: Bureau of Justice Statistics.

Shaw, C.R., & E.D. Myers (1929). The juvenile delinquent. In *Illinois Crime Survey.* Chicago, IL: Illinois Association for Criminal Justice.

Stigler, S.M. (1986). *The history of statistics: The measurement of uncertainty before 1900.* Cambridge, MA: Harvard University Press, Belknap Press.

Stigler, S.M. (2002). The missing early history of contingency tables. *Annales de la Faculte des Sciences de Toulouse, 11,* 563–573.

The Death Penalty Center. (2017). *Facts about the Death Penalty* (Updated: April 7, 2017). Retrieved from https://deathpenaltyinfo.org/documents/FactSheet.pdf.

Thrasher, F.M. (1927). *The gang.* Chicago, IL: University of Chicago Press.

Tufte, E.R. (2001). *The visual display of quantitative information* (2nd Edition). Cheshire, CT: Graphics Press.

Tukey, J.W. (1977). *Exploratory data analysis.* Reading, MA: Addison-Wesley.

U.S. Federal Bureau of Investigation. (1944). *Spot maps in crime prevention.* FBI Law Enforcement Bulletin. Washington, D.C.: U.S. Department of Justice.

Wolak, J. & Finkelhor, D. (2016). *Sextortion: Findings from a survey of 1631 victims.* Durham, N.H.: University of New Hampshire: Crimes Against Children Research Center.

IMAGE CREDITS

SECTION II

DESCRIPTIVE STATISTICS

This section provides a general discussion of samples (versus populations), as well as distributions (such as the assumption of the normal curve) and, briefly, the central limit theorem as it relates to data analysis. This section will provide you with the fundamental knowledge and skills needed to understand statistical concepts and perform rudimentary statistical calculations. Each chapter herein explains, with the use of examples and practical application, the components, uses, and most appropriate times to use particular descriptive statistics.

4

MEASURES OF CENTRAL TENDENCY

INTRODUCTION: WHAT DO YOU MEAN, AVERAGE?

The typical criminal slayer is a young man in his twenties who kills another man only slightly older. Both are of the same race. ... Men kill and are killed between four and five times more frequently than women. ... A woman killing a woman is extremely rare. (Wolfgang, 1961, p. 48)

Although the patterns observed in Dr. Wolfgang's study may slightly differ from national level data obtained today, the methods used by which the *typical* criminal can be described are still in use today. To describe the "typical criminal slayer," Dr. Wolfgang needed only to utilize the most basic statistical calculations. In Chapter 3, we learned how to describe data using frequency distributions and graphical displays in order to appropriately and effectively visualize the data. While this practice of data analysis is important, it is but one available practice of data analysis, one that should be used in conjunction with summary statistics like those used in Wolfgang's (1958) original study. Combined, these analyses can help one better describe a variable's distribution. Researchers in the fields of criminal justice and criminology are often interested in summary statistics, such as averages, because these values tell us about the center or middle of a distribution. An average can indicate where data points tend to cluster, where the middle value of a distribution is located, or it can provide a single value to represent all values in a distribution.

Consider the following questions:

1. What is the most common race among police officers in the United States?

2. What is the *median* household income for people living in Oak Park, compared to Chicago, Illinois?

3. What is the average violent crime rate across all cities and towns of Massachusetts?

Each of these questions refers to an *average* or, more specifically, a measure of central tendency. In Chapter 3, we learned to describe data using frequency distributions and graphical displays—to appropriately and effectively show all of the data with one visual representation. While this practice is important, it is only one available tool of data analysis, one that should be used in conjunction with summary statistics to help us better describe our data. Measures of central tendency, like visual representations of data, can take information from all cases in a dataset and create a single, representative value. As a result, this additional type of data analysis, by using more complex statistical calculations, can provide additional information by which data and the variables therein can be described. Summary statistics, in the form of the mode, median, and mean, are central to subsequent analyses, specifically in the area of inferential statistics and data analysis. This chapter examines the histories, calculations, and uses of the various measures of central tendency.

LEARNING OBJECTIVES

By the end of this chapter, students will be able to:

1: Identify the various measures of central tendency

2: Discuss the level of measurement requirements of each measure of central tendency

3: Explain how one variable can have different values of each measure of central tendency

4: Evaluate the strengths of each measure of central tendency

5: Assess the advantages and limitations of each measure of central tendency

KEY TERMS

BIMODAL

DISTRIBUTION

MEAN

MEDIAN

MODE

MULTIMODAL

NORMAL DISTRIBUTION

OUTLIER

CENTRAL TENDENCY AND NORMAL DISTRIBUTIONS

To understand the characteristics of each measure of central tendency, one must first examine and understand distributions. Recall the discussion of a frequency distribution in Chapter 3. The shape of a distribution can be seen when data, such as that found in a frequency distribution, is tabulated in the form

DISTRIBUTION:
In data analysis, the pattern or arrangement of data.

NORMAL DISTRIBUTION:
A pattern or arrangement of data that is bell shaped and often occurs naturally across many phenomena, having distinct characteristics, such as symmetry and central tendency coincidence.

of a bar chart or, sometimes more appropriately, a histogram. This allows for the understanding of how each measure of central tendency is related and when it is most appropriate to use each one. The characteristics or shape of a distribution is a very important factor that can influence a researcher's decision when reporting measures of central tendency. Distributions that are shaped differently may have a different central tendency measure that is most appropriate to use to describe it. In a perfectly normal distribution, which, at times, is called a normal curve or bell curve, there are several prominent characteristics:

1. All central tendency measures coincide and are equal

2. The distribution is symmetrical

3. The distribution is unimodal

4. The distribution is asymptotic

5. The proportion of data under the curve is equal to 1.0

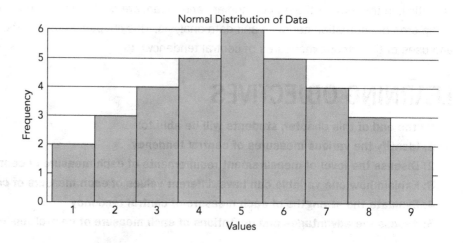

Figure 4.1 A Normal Distribution

In a perfectly normal distribution, the three central tendency measures (mode, median, and mean) are all identical and equal to one another. They have the same value. The values that are lower than the central tendency measures are equidistant from them and found with the same frequency as the values that are higher than the central tendency measures. For example, any value that is lower than the central tendency measures would have a corresponding value that is greater than the central tendency measures of equal magnitude. For example, suppose the central tendency measures are equal to 6. If there is a value of 3, there would also be a value of 9. In addition, their frequencies, or how many times those values occur, would be equal to one another—and less than the frequency of the central tendency measures. The distribution would have one single mode that depicts, along with the other central tendency measures, the peak of the distribution. This value represents the value that is found with the highest frequency in the dataset: it appears the most. The final two characteristics can be explained together. All data points lie between the baseline (visually, the x-axis) and the curve, and the tails of the curve extend indefinitely in both directions. Theoretically, this allows for the possibility of any extreme value. If the curve "touched" or crossed the x-axis, this would create and require a minimum and maximum value. While some extreme values in criminal justice and criminology research are not possible, such as an extreme (or any) negative value of the number of criminal offenses, the normal distribution approximates the distributions of a substantial number of phenomena and is the basis for much of the statistical work in criminal justice and criminology. In addition, it is representative of a probability distribution, that which does not necessarily conform to values of actual phenomena. Additional distribution shapes will be discussed in Chapter 5.

Box 4.1 WHAT WE'VE LEARNED: Normal Distributions

While the unfortunate events of the Columbine and Jonesboro shootings occurred two decades ago, attention paid to crime and violence at school has only recently become a focus of research and policy. Little is known about juvenile crime committed while on school property. Using 2010 National Incident-Based Reporting System data, the Texas School Safety Center (TSSC) examined the rates of offending throughout the school day to determine when crime occurred most and if there were differences in offending rates by time period. To do so, the TSSC isolated cases that occurred on school property in the state of Texas. Based on the nearly 4,000 cases analyzed, the TSSC found that the percentage of crimes committed for each hour between 7:00 a.m. and 4:00 p.m. approximated a normal distribution. The time periods with the lowest rate of offending were the initial and final hours, 7:00 a.m. and 4:00 p.m., respectively. During the 7:00 a.m. time period, only 2.5% of the offenses occurred, while 6.3% of the offenses occurred during the 4:00 p.m. time period. The time periods with the highest rates of offending were in the middle of the day, 11:00 a.m. and 12:00 p.m. During the 11:00 a.m. time period, 12.6% of the offenses occurred, while 13% of the offenses occurred during the 12:00 p.m. time period (TSSC, n.d.).

CATEGORICAL VARIABLES

Recall the previous discussion of levels of measurement in Chapter 2. All variables are measured, or operationalized, in different ways. With each level of measurement comes distinct characteristics and possible applications that impact what subsequent statistical and analytical techniques can be used. Lower levels of measurement are those in which variables are measured at the nominal or ordinal level. Both of these levels of measurement (nominal and ordinal) are categorical in nature: groups are made to distinguish between different values of a variable. Ordinal measures, remember, have an ordering or hierarchy. Thus, the various values of an ordinal variable, e.g., the groups, can be sequenced in either an ascending or descending order. When examining categorical variables, there are two possible measures of central tendency available: the mode and the median.

MODE

The first measure of central tendency is the mode. The mode was used as an indicator long before a term was coined for it (Walker, 1929). In fact, the term "mode" was not used to describe the statistical

MODE:
The most frequently occurring value of a variable.

BIMODAL:
The characteristic of having two values of a variable in a distribution with the same highest frequency.

MULTIMODAL:
The characteristic of having more than two values of a variable in a distribution with the same highest frequency.

concept until 1895 by Karl Pearson (David, 1995). Abbreviated as *Mo*, the mode is the most common or frequently occurring value in a distribution. More specifically, it is the value or category of a variable in a dataset that occurs more than any other category or score, i.e., it has the greatest probability of occurring. The mode is the only measure of central tendency available for nominal level variables. It can, however, be used to describe the most common value in any distribution, regardless of the level of measurement. The mode describes nothing about the ordering of variables or variation within variables, it simply refers to the value or category of a variable that appears most often in the distribution.

Determining the mode of a variable is quite simple. To find the mode, locate the value or category that occurs most often in a distribution. The mode can be easily found by inspection, rather than by computation. Keep in mind that the mode is not the frequency of the most common value or category but the value or the most common category itself.

Box 4.2: Example of the Mode (Mo) for Categorical Variables

Suppose you survey your Data Analysis class and find you have 12 male students and 7 female students. What is the mode of this nominal variable, *sex*? The mode is *male*, because that is the value or category of the variable that occurs most often. The mode is not 12. The mode is the actual value or category occurring most frequently, NOT the frequency. Suppose you further inquire about the class standing of each of the students in the class and find 3 sophomore students, 12 junior students, and 4 senior students. What is the mode of this ordinal variable, *class standing*? The mode is *junior*, because that is the value or category of the variable that occurs most often. The mode is not 12. Like before, the mode is the actual value or category occurring most frequently, NOT the frequency. In this example, the mode was obtained for a nominal and an ordinal variable, *sex* and *class standing*. The mode can also be obtained for a variable measured at the interval/ratio level, such as *age* or *GPA*.

Not all distributions are unimodal, in which there is only a single value or category of greatest frequency. Some frequency distributions contain two or more modes. When viewed graphically, distributions that have two points of maximum frequency are characterized by two peaks. These distributions are referred to as being bimodal. A distribution with more than two modes is defined as a multimodal distribution. When this type of distribution is viewed graphically, there are more than two peaks, indicating several values or categories of greatest frequency.

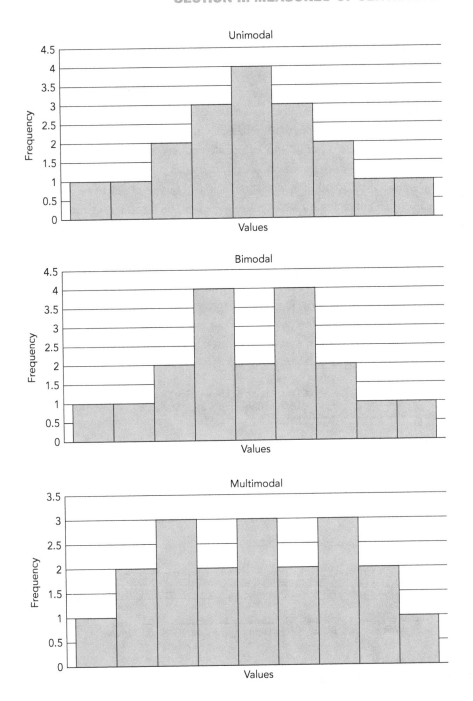

Figure 4.2 Unimodal, Bimodal, Multimodal Distributions

Box 4.3: WHAT WE'VE LEARNED: Mode (Mo) for Categorical Variables

In the introduction of this chapter, you were asked to think about the most common race of police officers in the United States. Today, there are more than 18,000 law enforcement agencies of various types and sizes that report data to the FBI on an annual basis. Some law enforcement agencies have: local jurisdiction, such as a municipal department; regional jurisdiction, such as state police; national jurisdiction, such as federal agencies; and special jurisdiction, such as campus police departments and transit police. Some agencies have as few as one officer, while others, like the New York City Police Department, have more than 30,000 officers. The racial distribution of officers varies by agency size, type, and location. When national data were first collected in 1987, racial minorities made up 14.6% of all officers. Today, that number has nearly doubled. According to the Bureau of Justice Statistics (2015:2016), among local police departments: 72.8% of personnel is White; 12.2% Black/African-American; 11.6% Latino; 2.4% Asian/Native Hawaiian/Other Pacific Islander; .6% American Indian/Alaska Native and; .5% Two or More Races. Generally, similar patterns, though slightly different figures, are found among sheriffs' departments. In sheriffs' departments, Latinos make up the second largest racial category (10.7%), while Black/African-Americans make up the third largest (9.2%). Overall, there is more racial minority representation in local police departments than sheriffs' departments: 27.2% and 22.1%, respectively. As a result, the mode category for police officer race is *White*.

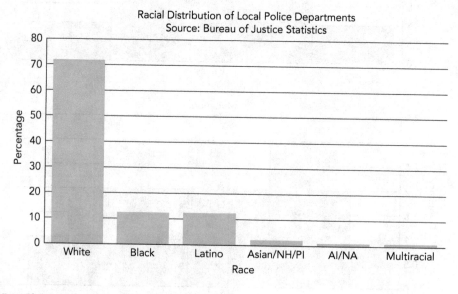

Figure 4.3 Bar Chart with a Categorical Variable

As a measure of central tendency, the mode has several advantages:

1. Provides one measure to represent the entire dataset

2. Utilizes every case in the dataset

3. Is not heavily influenced by extreme values, or outliers

4. Does not require mathematical calculation

5. Is available for every level of measurement

The primary strength of the mode is that it gives the most common, or most frequently observed, value of a variable in a distribution by taking into account every case and value in the dataset—even outliers. It is one of the only statistical measures that does not involve arithmetic. Mathematical calculation is not involved in the determination of the mode, so it is very easy for researchers to determine and for readers to understand. Additionally, it is the only measure of central tendency that can be employed with data measured at every level of measurement.

The mode also has several disadvantages, or weaknesses, that limit its use as the primary statistic for central tendency description:

1.   May not represent the middle-most or typical value

2.   Only accounts for the frequency of values, not the values themselves

3.   Is strongly influenced by sampling techniques

Despite, or perhaps as a function of, the mode's simplicity, it may not accurately represent the *central tendency*, or where values cluster for all variables. One of the most significant disadvantages of using the mode for description is that it only takes into consideration the frequency of the observed values in a dataset, not the values themselves. This is particularly important for variables measured at a higher level. Remember, it is possible for the mode to occur anywhere in a distribution, not necessarily near the center of it. Modes that are found at the low or high ends of a distribution are an unstable measure and cannot always be relied upon to give an accurate description of a variable's central tendency. As a result, alternative measures of central tendency are often utilized.

MEDIAN

The second measure of central tendency is the median. Abbreviated as *Md* or *Mdn*, the median is the middle-most point in a distribution. Often referred to as the 50th percentile point, this simply means that 50% of the data falls below the median and 50% falls above it. Thus, it represents the literal center of the distribution. It can be calculated with ordinal level and continuous data, but not nominal level data, since a requirement for the median is ordering. The median requires variables to have the ability to be rank ordered (i.e., placed in order from highest to lowest, lowest to highest, greatest to least, etc.). Keep in mind, the median does not imply or require the knowledge of the distance between each value, just the direction (above or below) of each value relative to the others.

The median and the mode have long been in use, though as measures of central tendency, their applications in statistics, relatively speaking, "... have been developed recently" (Zizek, 1913). The concept of the median, however, can be traced much further back to the writings of astronomers and

MEDIAN:
The middle-most value of a variable in a distribution, representing the 50th percentile point.

mathematicians in the 16th century (Eisenhart, 1974). The mathematician Edward Wright (1599) may very well be the first to specifically advocate for its use:

> ... but as when many arrows are shot at a marke, and the marke after-wards taken away, hee may been thought to worke according to reasons, who to find out the place where the marke stood, shall seeke out the middle place amongst all the arrows: *so amongst many different observations, the middlemost is likest to come nearest the truth* (emphasis added).

The median is a positional measure, which means that it is located instead of calculated. To begin the process of locating the median, the categories within the distribution need to be ranked in either ascending or descending order. Next, the *position of the median* for categorical (i.e., grouped) data must be calculated using the following formula:

$$\frac{n+1}{2}$$

Figure 4.4 Position of the Median Equation

where n = the number of cases.

For ordinal data, the total sample size (n) is the sum of all the frequencies. This formula is to help calculate the *position of the median*; it does not give you the median value or category. The final step is to identify the median. The value obtained from the formula refers to the position or location of the median category when all cases are ordered sequentially.

> **Box 4.4: Example of the Median (*Md* or *Mdn*) for Categorical Variables**
>
> Recall the previous example in Box 4.3: Example of the Mode (*Mo*) for Categorical Variables. Suppose you survey your Data Analysis class and find you have 3 sophomore students, 12 junior students, and 4 senior students. What is the median of this categorical, yet ordinal variable, *class standing*? The median variable value is *junior*. Using the median formula, where the number of cases (*n*) is 19, the location of the median is the 10th case. The number of cases is added to one, then divided by two. This results in the location of the median, the 10th case, sequentially. Thus, when the cases are sequentially ordered based on class standing, the median, or middle-most case, would have the value of *junior* for *class standing*. Suppose you surveyed a second section of the course and found 6 sophomore students, 4 junior students, and 10 senior students. What is the median, then?

The concluding question in Box 4.4: Example of the Median (*Md* or *Mdn*) for Categorical Variables highlights a very important concern when attempting to locate the median of an ordinal variable. In that example, the location of the median would be between the *junior* and *senior* class standing. Adding the number of cases to one, then dividing by two would result in a value that is not a whole number. Since the variable is ordinal, it is impossible to find the "middle" of those two values. Thus, utilizing the median as a measure of central tendency for ordinal variables is limited, at best, to data that contain an odd number of cases.

Box 4.5: WHAT WE'VE LEARNED: Median (*Md* or *Mdn*) for Categorical Variables

Researchers Hiller, Salvatore, and Taniguchi (2014) evaluated the internship program of the Department of Criminal Justice at Temple University. The evaluation sought to determine whether participation in the program increased career preparedness. To determine its efficacy, the researchers surveyed students before and after participation in the internship program. The researchers utilized a Likert scale to operationalize student answers in the survey (1 = "not at all important" through 7 = "very important"). Results showed that the modal and median responses to many of the questions concerning how important various reasons for doing the internship program were "very important," including the reasons: "I want to apply what I have learned in my criminal justice courses," "I believe the internship will look good on my resume," "I think it will help me get ready for a career in criminal justice," "I think it will help me to decide what I want to do for my career," and "I hope to learn career relevant skills" (Hiller et al., 2014, p. 6). There were five items in which the modal and median responses were different. The survey items that showed the largest difference were "I need it to fill 12 credit hours in my schedule" and "I think classes taught by professors in the CJ department do not teach me about the 'real' world." Each of these items resulted in higher levels of importance represented by the median and lower levels of importance represented by the mode.

As a measure of central tendency, the median has several advantages:

1. Can only be represented by one value

2. Is not influenced by outliers

3. It is easy to locate and understand

Unlike the mode, there will always be only one median. Compared to the mode, the median is also a more stable measure of central tendency. Stability in this sense refers to the fact that extreme scores at either end of a distribution (i.e., outliers) may exist but have little to no effect on the median. As a result, when the data do not reflect a normal distribution, the median is the most suitable measure of central tendency for description. The median always yields a value that divides a distribution of scores into two equal parts, which is what makes it such a desirable measure of central tendency.

The median also has several disadvantages, or weaknesses, that limit its use as the primary statistic for central tendency description:

1. Is representative of just one value of a variable

2. Is a stand-alone statistic

3. Is unavailable for nominal data and limited for ordinal data

Just like the mode, however, the median does not provide information about all of the values within a distribution. While all of the cases are used for its location, ultimately, the median value does not provide information about the rest of the dataset—just its center point. It is also limited in further application. It is generally not used beyond descriptive purposes or incorporated into more sophisticated analyses. Finally, as we saw in Box 4.4: Example of the Median (*Md* or *Mdn*) for Categorical Variables, the median can only be used with ordinal variables on limited occasions.

CONTINUOUS VARIABLES

Continue your review of the Chapter 2 discussion of levels of measurement. Variables that are not operationalized categorically are done so continuously. It is often helpful to think of continuous variables as "numerical" variables. Although that is not a perfect analogy, for most of the purposes of this text, it will suffice. Continuous variables are those that are measured at a higher level. The two levels are interval and ratio. What differentiates these levels from ordinal data are two characteristics. First, the values of the variables are not groups or categories. Instead, they represent some quantitative value. Second, the distance between each value is known and measurable. That is not the case with lower levels of measurement. Further differentiation is possible. Interval level data have an arbitrary zero point, meaning that "0" does not represent an absence of the variable. Alternately, ratio level data have a meaningful zero point; thus, the "0" does represent an absence of the variable. It may be helpful to remember that interval level data can have negative values, while ratio level data cannot.

MODE

The mode can also be used with continuous variables. Instead of representing the most frequently occurring category (as with nominal or ordinal data), the mode represents the most common value or score. If the data are in numerical or in tabular form, such as in a frequency distribution, the mode can be found by locating the value that has the greatest frequency, proportion, or percentage. Remember from Chapter 3 that simple frequency distributions consist of two columns. The left column, headed *X* or by the variable name, indicates what characteristic is being presented and contains the categories of analysis. The right column, headed frequency or *f*, indicates the number of cases in each category. More detailed frequency distributions will provide a proportion or percentage to accompany the frequency total for each value. See Box 4.6: Example of the Mode (*Mo*) for Continuous Variables for an example.

Box 4.6: Example of the Mode (*Mo*) for Continuous Variables

Suppose you were examining the frequency of officer complaints for a local police department. You obtained the number of citizen complaints against officers during their careers. The totals were:

1, 1, 2, 2, 2, 2, 2, 2, 2, 3, 3, 3, 4, 4, 5, 5, 5, 5, 6, 6, 6, 6, 7

What is the mode *number of officer complaints*? After carefully reviewing the number of complaints found in the distribution, you should see that *two* complaints is the most frequently occurring value. If the data are in tabular form, the determination is made very quickly.

Number of Citizen Complaints	f
1	2
2	7
3	3
4	2
5	4
6	4
7	1
	Total = 23

Figure 4.5 Frequency Distribution of Citizen Complaints

Like when displayed with a frequency distribution, if the data are in other graphical displays, the mode can be found by locating the value in the chart that has the tallest bar (bar chart and histogram) or the largest slice (pie chart).

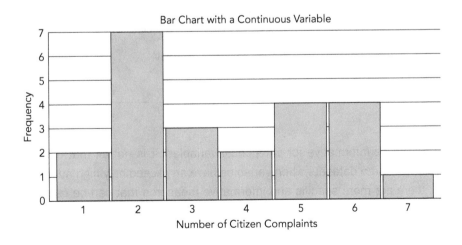

Figure 4.6 Bar Chart with a Continuous Variable

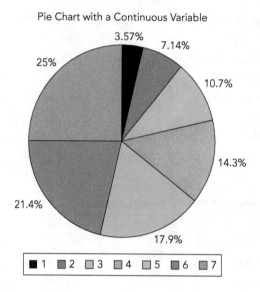

Figure 4.7 Pie Chart with a Continuous Variable

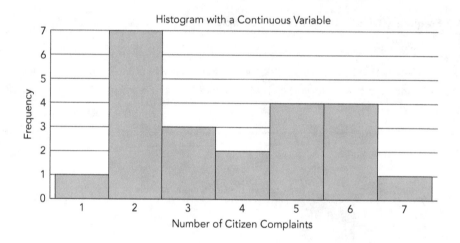

Figure 4.8 Histogram with a Continuous Variable

While the mode can be informative for categorical variables, it is not all that useful for continuous variables, particularly in large datasets when variables have an exceedingly high number of values. With continuous data, there are more specific and informative measures that can be calculated to enhance variable description.

MEDIAN

To begin the process of locating the median, the scores within the distribution need to be rank ordered. Next, the *position of the median* for continuous data must be calculated using the following formula—the same that was used for categorical data:

$$\frac{n+1}{2}$$

Figure 4.9 Position of the Median Equation

where n = the number of cases.

For continuous data, the total sample size (n) is the sum of all the frequencies. In distributions where n is an odd number, the median will be one of the values observed in the distribution. If n is an even number, the average (or mean) of the two middle scores is used to find the median. As a result, it is possible that the median could be a value that is not represented in the distribution.

Box 4.7: WHAT WE'VE LEARNED: Mode (*Mo*) for Continuous Variables

Recently, researchers Porter, Bushway, Tsao, & Smith (2016) examined the demographic composition of prisons within the United States. The researchers obtained these data to see how the prison boom of the latter decades of the 20th century may have changed the age distribution within prisons over that time period. By examining incarceration data spanning 40 years, the authors were, among other things, able to provide descriptive data concerning the measures of central tendency for the age of those incarcerated. Their inquiry suggests that the most frequently observed ages of inmates within carceral facilities were generally in the low-to-mid 20s from 1974–2004, except for the late 1990s, specifically 1997. The data showed that the modal age of prisoners was 23 years in 1974. By the next time period examined, 1979, there was no change in the modal age of prisoners. By the next time period, 1986, there was a slight increase—to 24 years. By 1991, the modal age of prisoners began to increase more steadily. At this point in time, the modal age was 27. The upward trend continued through the next time period, 1997, when the modal age of prisoners reached 33, which was the only year provided by the authors in which the modal age equaled the median age. Finally, in the last year under study, 2004, the modal age showed a decrease—down to 25 years.

Box 4.8: Example of the Median (*Md* or *Mdn*) for Continuous Variables

Suppose you were to continue your examination of the rate of officer complaints for a local police department. You previously obtained the number of citizen complaints against officers during their careers. The totals were:

1, 1, 2, 2, 2, 2, 2, 2, 2, 3, 3, 3, 4, 4, 5, 5, 5, 5, 6, 6, 6, 6, 7

What is the median number of officer complaints? Using the median formula, you should have come up with the value of "12." This is NOT the median, but the location of the median. Since the data are already ordered sequentially, the median will be the 12th value. For this dataset, the 12th and median value is 3 complaints.

MEAN:
The arithmetic average of a variable in a dataset, or the value that all cases would share if the sum of a variable was equally distributed across all cases in a dataset.

For example, while studying citizen complaints against officers as seen in Box 4.8: Example of the Median (*Md* or *Mdn*) for Continuous Variables, the data are all measured in whole numbers. Depending on the value of an additional case, it is possible that the median will be represented with a decimal. Let's say a new hire had received seven citizen complaints at a previous employer and you decided to add this to the dataset. The data would now look like this:

1, 1, 2, 2, 2, 2, 2, 2, 2, 3, 3, 3, 4, 4, 5, 5, 5, 5, 6, 6, 6, 6, 7, 7

What is the median? Using the median formula, you should have come up with a value of "12.5." This is NOT the median, but the location of the median. Now, the median will be the value between the 12th and 13th values, so to speak. The 12th and 13th values must be averaged together to obtain the median. In this case, by averaging three and four, the median becomes 3.5 citizen complaints.

The median for a continuous variable is more precise than that of an ordinal variable. This is a byproduct of the levels of measurement. Continuous data are measured at higher levels and have greater specificity than the lower level categorical data of an ordinal measure. As a result, we can only say the median is contained or found within a certain category when discussing ordinal data. When discussing continuous data, we can identify a specific, numerical value. Regardless of the level of measurement being described with the median, the same advantages and disadvantages apply.

MEAN

The final measure of central tendency is the mean, sometimes abbreviated as *Mn*. The mean can also be described as the arithmetic average or the average score or value among a group of scores in a distribution. The mean, unlike the other measures of central tendency, has two different representative symbols. The first, $\bar{x}$ (pronounced "x-bar"), is used to describe the mean of a sample. The mean of a population is symbolized with the Greek letter mu, μ (pronounced "myoo"). This also represents the mean of a normal distribution. Exclusively used with continuous variables, the mean is the arithmetic average of a numerical variable.

The first mention of the arithmetic average can be traced back nearly 3,000 years. For example, there were several different mean values defined in Greece, even before the time of Aristotle or Pythagoras, who made note of the standard arithmetic average (Bakker, 2003). The use of the mean in mathematics has a long and storied history, as well (Eisenhart, 1974; Plackett, 1958). Over the course of history, mathematics, specifically statistics, has seen many different *means*. Early astronomers and mathematicians, for example, would calculate a mean but only use values that "… they felt were of equal intrinsic accuracy" (Stigler, 1986, p. 16). At the time, there existed the requirement that all of the values were to be measured by the same individual, at the same time, in the same place, and with the same measuring instrument in order to be considered valid. This was problematic, and nearly impossible, at the time, due to the nature of the practice of measurement. Many early astronomers and mathematicians worked independently, but corresponded often with one another. Since these scholarly partnerships included measurements by different people, at different times, in different places, and with different measurement instruments, it was rare to see the mean calculated using each measured value before 1750, with rare exceptions such as that of Tycho Brahe in the late 16th century (Plackett, 1958) and Roger Cotes (1722), who suggested that all observations should be accounted for in order to calculate an accurate, representative measurement (Stigler, 1986).

The mean is calculated by summing all raw scores in a distribution and dividing by the total number of scores or cases. Just like the symbols used to denote the mean, there are two symbols to denote the number of cases. If the number of cases describes a sample, n is used. If the number of cases describes a population, N is used. There is no difference between the two in terms of calculation. The difference is largely symbolic. The following formula is used in calculating the mean for a distribution of scores for a sample:

$$\frac{\sum x}{n}$$

Figure 4.10 Mean Equation

where $\sum$ = "the sum of" (Greek letter sigma)
and x = each score or value in the distribution
          n = the total sample size.

Box 4.9: Example of the Mean (Mn) for Continuous Variables

Suppose you were to continue your examination of the frequency of officer complaints for a local police department. Thus far, you have determined the mode and located the median. The final central tendency measure of this continuous variable is the mean. You previously obtained the number of citizen complaints against officers during their careers. The totals were:

1, 1, 2, 2, 2, 2, 2, 2, 2, 3, 3, 3, 4, 4, 5, 5, 5, 5, 6, 6, 6, 6, 7

What is the mean *number of officer complaints*? Using the mean formula, you should have come up with the value of approximately "3.65." This is obtained by using the values provided and the mean formula. The equation should be identical to Figure 4.11. For this police department, the mean value of citizen complaints is approximately 3.65.

$$\frac{(1+1+2+2+2+2+2+2+2+3+3+3+4+4+5+5+5+5+6+6+6+6+7)}{23} = \frac{84}{23} = 3.65$$

Figure 4.11 Mean Example

If the data are in tabular form, such as in a frequency distribution, the mean can be calculated using a separate formula. Revisit the frequency distribution in Figure 4.5. The data from this frequency distribution, as currently displayed, can be used to calculate the mean number of citizen complaints by utilizing this formula:

$$\frac{\Sigma(fx)}{n}$$

Figure 4.12 Mean Equation for a Frequency Distribution

where Σ = "the sum of" (Greek letter sigma)
and fx = the product of the scores or values and their respective frequencies
             n = the number of cases.

To obtain the numerator, the individual scores or values (in this case, number of complaints) are multiplied by their respective frequencies. After these products are calculated, they are summed together to get one value. This value is the numerator. Like we saw in Box 4.8: Example of the Mean for Continuous Variables, this value is divided by the number of cases to obtain the mean.

Box 4.10: WHAT WE'VE LEARNED: Mean (Mn) for Continuous Variables

The National Registry of Exonerations (NRE) is a joint project of the University of California, Irvine, the University of Michigan, and Michigan State University. The registry compiles information about all known exonerations of innocent defendants in the United States since 1989. Consistently updated, the registry provides case and individual-specific information for each known exoneration. As of July 26, 2018, the registry documented 2,252 exonerations (n), accounting for 19,790 total years wrongly spent incarcerated (Σx). The mean number of years wrongly spent incarcerated, or "lost," for these known exonerations is 8.8 (NRE, n.d.). The state with the lowest mean number of years wrongly spent incarcerated is Maine. There have been three exonerations in the state, resulting in about 3 years lost for a mean value of approximately 1.14 years lost. The state with the highest mean number of years wrongly spent incarcerated is Louisiana. There have been 58 exonerations in the state, resulting in 800 years lost for a mean value of approximately 13.79 years. The NRE also delineates the data by crime type, including murder, sexual assault, child sex abuse, drugs, robbery, and other. Perhaps unsurprisingly, convictions of murder represent the highest mean value of years wrongly spent incarcerated.

As a measure of central tendency, the mean has several advantages:

1. Is simple to interpret

2. Utilizes data from all cases

3. Is less prone to fluctuation due to sampling

4. Is versatile in its application

The mean has several strengths that make it the most frequently used measure of central tendency in statistics. The term *average* is ubiquitous, and it is likely you have calculated the arithmetic average (mean) long before you took a formal statistics or data analysis course. The mean is the only measure of central tendency that uses information from every case in the dataset, which, in turn, promotes the consistency of its value across datasets. As the only measure of central tendency calculated exclusively for continuous variables, it is also used in more sophisticated analysis.

The mean also has several disadvantages, or weaknesses, that limit its use as the primary statistic for central tendency description:

1. Is sensitive to outliers

2. Is most appropriate for normal distributions

3. Is often an unobserved value in the dataset

Despite the substantial advantages to using the mean, it is not without its weaknesses. Since the mean uses information from every case in the dataset, there is the potential that some of those cases can be quite impactful. When a dataset contains extreme values, those that are much lower or much higher than where data cluster, the mean will be affected accordingly. As a result, while informative, it may be best to describe normal distributions that do not contain an inordinate amount of (asymmetrical) outliers. Finally, as we saw in Box 4.8: Example of the Mean (Mn) for Continuous Variables, the mean might be a value that is not seen in the dataset—or is even possible in the dataset (e.g., You cannot have 3.65 complaints).

Measure of Central Tendency	Levels of Measurement
Mode	Nominal, Ordinal, Interval, Ratio
Median	Ordinal, Interval, Ratio
Mean	Interval, Ratio

Figure 4.13 Measures of Central Tendency Summary

SUMMARY

Each measure of central tendency describes something different: the *most*, the *middle*, or the *average*. With these differences come both advantages and disadvantages to their respective uses. Choosing the most appropriate measure for description involves several factors, including the level of measurement, whether the distribution is "normal" or not, and the research objective. The mode only requires a count to determine the highest frequency of occurrence. Since there is no calculation involved, it can be found for both categorical and continuous data, and each level of measurement therein. Most importantly, it is the only measure that can be used with nominal level data. The median requires the sequential ordering of its categories. Therefore, it can only be obtained from ordinal level or continuous data, though continuous data are most suitable. This is particularly the case for datasets with an even number of cases. The calculation of the mean is done exclusively with continuous data. This measure considers the actual values of all the data points in a dataset, not the frequency or location of the values.

The shape of a distribution is the second factor that can influence a researcher's decision to use a particular measure of central tendency. The arithmetic average is a very informative descriptor of individual scores when a distribution is normal. However, when a distribution is not normal, the arithmetic average is less useful and can oftentimes be misleading. The degree to which a distribution is not normal is an important consideration when determining which measure of central tendency is most appropriate to use for describing a variable. You will learn more about this in the next chapter. Finally, the research objective must be considered when reporting these measures of central tendency. In most situations encountered by criminal justice and criminology researchers, the mode is useful only as a basic indicator of central tendency. However, if the researcher is looking for a more informative measure to describe a variable, the median and/or the mean would be the most appropriate indicators to describe central tendency of a variable. If the data do not have a normal distribution, the median is the most appropriate measure of central tendency to use for description. Regardless of the intent of the measurement, and the aforementioned considerations, it is common practice to at least calculate and examine, if not report, all three measures of central tendency. This provides the most complete picture of the variable, its values, and its distribution.

CHAPTER REVIEW QUESTIONS

1. Explain the characteristics of the normal distribution as it relates to measures of central tendency.

2. Explain the characteristics of a dataset when the median can be obtained for ordinal data and when it cannot be.

3. Discuss the level of measurement requirements for each measure of central tendency.

4. Which measure of central tendency suffers from the most significant disadvantages? Explain your position.

5. Which measure of central tendency offers the most significant advantages? Explain your position.

CHAPTER REVIEW EXERCISES

1. Visit the Uniform Crime Report website: https://ucr.fbi.gov/
Select *Crime in the United States*, then select the year 2015. Finally, select *Violent Crime*, and then *Robbery*. Locate the average dollar value of property stolen by robbery and the average dollar loss reported by banks. Find similar data for preceding years. How do the most recent data compare?

2. Identify one of the measures of central tendency discussed. Suppose you were to develop a survey of your class as in Box 4.2 and Box 4.4. For each level of measurement, list two variables, in addition to *sex* and *class standing*, for which you could collect data.

3. Visit the NCVS website: http://www.bjs.gov

Select *Victims*. Under *Data Collection & Surveys*, select *National Crime Victimization Survey (NCVS)*. Select the most recent publication titled *Criminal Victimization*. View the *PDF* of the report. What measure of central tendency, though perhaps not described as such, can be determined from the report? Explain.

4. Are there any criminal justice or criminological research questions for which all the measures of central tendency would be desired? Develop a research question and explain the data needed, how the data would be collected, and why the mode, median, and mean of particular variables would be of interest.

5. Using your institution's library resources, find a peer-reviewed journal article that is of interest to you that reports the three measures of central tendency. Discuss the article, the measures of central tendency, the appropriateness of their use, and what variable(s) they describe.

REFERENCES

Bakker, A. (2003). The early history of average values and implications for education. *Journal of Statistics Education, 11*(1). Retrieved from http://ww2.amstat.org/publications/jse/v11n1/bakker.html

Cotes, R. (1722). Aestimatio errorum in mixta mathesi, per variationes partium trianguli plani et sphaerici. In Smith, R. (Ed) *Harmonia Mensurarum*. Cambridge, England.

David, H.A. (1995). First (?) occurrences of common terms in mathematical statistics. *The American Statistician, 49*(2), 121–133.

Eisenhart, C. (1974). The development of the concept of the best mean of a set of measurements from antiquity to the present day. *1971 American Statistical Association Presidential Address*. Retrieved from https://www.york.ac.uk/depts/maths/histstat/eisenhart.pdf

Hiller, M.L., Salvatore, C., & Taniguchi, T. (2014). Evaluation of a criminal justice internship program: Why do students take it and does it improve career preparedness? *Journal of Criminal Justice Education, 25*(1), 1–15.

Morrison, W.D. (1891). *Crime and its causes*. London, UK: Swan Sonnenschein & Co.

National Registry of Exonerations. (n.d.) *Resources: Infographics: Interactive Data Display*. Retrieved from https://www.law.umich.edu/special/exoneration/Pages/Exonerations-in-the-United-States-Map.aspx

Plackett, R.L. (1958). Studies in the history of probability and statistics VII: The principle of the arithmetic mean. *Biometrika, 45*(1/2), 130–135.

Porter, L.C., Bushway, S.D., Tsao, H., & Smith, H.L. (2016). How the U.S. prison boom has changed the age distribution of the prison population. *Criminology, 54*(1), 30–55.

Stigler, S.M. (1986). *The history of statistics: The measurement of uncertainty before 1900*. Cambridge, MA: Harvard University Press.

Texas School Safety Center (TSSC). N.d. *Temporal differences in crime committed during school hours*. Retrieved from https://txssc.txstate.edu/topics/school-violence/articles/temporal-differences-in-crime

U.S. Census Bureau. (2016). *2015 American community survey, 1-year public use microdata sample (PUMS)*. Accessed from https://www.census.gov/programs-surveys/acs/data/pums.html

Walker, H.M. (1929). *Studies in the history of statistical methods: With special reference to certain educational problems*. Baltimore, MD: Williams & Wilkins Co.

Wolfgang, M.E. (1958). *Patterns in criminal homicide*. New York, NY: Wiley.

Wolfgang, M.E. (1961). A sociological analysis of criminal homicide. *Federal Probation, 25*, 48–55.

Wright, E. (1599). *Certaine errors in navigation, arising either of the ordinarie erroneous making or vsing of the sea chart, compasse, cross staffe, and tables of declination of the sunne, and fixed starres detected and corrected*. London, UK: V. Sims.

Zizek, F. (1913). *Statistical average: A methodological study*. New York, NY: Henry Holt and Company.

MEASURES OF VARIABILITY AND DISPERSION

5

INTRODUCTION: WHY THE DISTRIBUTION MATTERS

One of the major difficulties always involved in a compilation of data received from a large number of individual sources (in the case of the Uniform Crime Reports, several thousand agencies) is that there is a great deal of unevenness and variability in the data. (Beattie, 1959, p. 585)

In Chapter 4, we discussed and practiced multiple ways to describe a variable in a dataset with a single value. The measures of central tendency describe the most frequently occurring value, the middle-most value, and the arithmetic average of all values in a dataset. While these values can be informative, they do not describe or provide a depiction of the entirety of cases. As Beattie (1959) discusses, when there are multiple data compiled, there is a "great deal of unevenness and variability." Not all values are the same. We saw this in the discussion of the mode, median, and mean and how they are determined. Additional information is often sought to describe the spread of the data or how unlike each case is from the others, the distance each is from the *average*, and the relative locations of the measures of central tendency. Thus, just like our measures of central tendency, which describe where data cluster, we can quantify and describe the distance from these values that the rest of the data are located. There are several ways to quantify these values. Consider the following questions:

1. What is the distance, or difference, between the two most extreme values of a variable?

2. What is the typical distance any single value of a variable is located from the mean?

3. Is the variable's distribution normal, or are cases clustered at the lower end or higher end of values?

Each of these questions can be answered with specific, and sometimes complementary, measures that describe how different or spread apart the values of a variable are. By calculating these various measures, a researcher can quantify exactly how different values of a variable are based on the criteria and assumptions of each respective measure. Some measures quantify how different two values are, some measures quantify how different all measures are, e.g., how different from the mean the values in a dataset are, and other measures can be used to describe a byproduct of the difference in variable values: the shape of the distribution. Each measure, like the measures of central tendency discussed in Chapter 4, has its own set of requirements. Each has a requirement for the variable's level of measurement, and each is more appropriate than others to answer particular research questions or to describe the data in a specific manner. This chapter examines the histories, calculations, and uses of the various measures of variability and dispersion.

LEARNING OBJECTIVES

By the end of this chapter, students will be able to:

1: Identify the various measures of variability and dispersion

2: Discuss the level of measurement requirements of each measure of variability and dispersion

3: Explain how measures of variability and dispersion can describe the relative location of the measures of central tendency

4: Evaluate the strengths of each measure of variability and dispersion

5: Assess the advantages and limitations of each measure of variability and dispersion

KEY TERMS

DEVIATION

DISPERSION

INDEX OF QUALITATIVE VARIATION (IQV)

INTER-QUARTILE RANGE

KURTOSIS

LEPTOKURTIC

MESOKURTIC

NEGATIVE SKEW

PLATYKURTIC

POSITIVE SKEW

QUARTILE

RANGE

SKEWNESS

STANDARD DEVIATION

VARIABILITY

VARIATION RATIO

CATEGORICAL VARIABLES

The concepts of variability and dispersion have been in use by statisticians and mathematicians for over 100 years. For example, the first known occurrences of the term "dispersion" were seen in Wilhelm

Lexis' (1877) study of mortality, where he described and classified ages of death; in the work of Francis Ysidro Edgeworth (1892), a political economist who was the first to systematically study the normal distribution; and in the writings of Sir Arthur Lyon Bowley (1897), a statistician who is credited with creating the first English-language textbook for the study of statistics (David, 1995; Gorroochurn, 2016).

Measuring variability and dispersion for categorical variables, however, is problematic. Revisit Box 4.2: Examples of the Mode (Mo) for Categorical Variables. That example provided a hypothetical example of the only measure of central tendency available for nominal data. In that example, a survey found your Data Analysis class to have 12 male students and 7 female students. From that information, can you quantify how different each case is from the next on the basis of sex? In other words, is it possible to measure "how much" one individual value is different from another? Probably not. It is unconventional to attribute a quantitative characteristic to categorical data.

VARIATION RATIO (VR)

The most basic measure of variability and dispersion for categorical data is the variation ratio (VR). This measure, despite its simplicity, is often attributed to Linton C. Freeman (1965), a sociologist perhaps known more for his work in the area of social networks. The variation ratio represents the proportion of cases that are not in the modal category. Thus, it is the complement to the proportion of cases that are in the modal category. The formula for the variation ratio is as follows:

$$1 - \frac{f_m}{N}$$

Figure 5.1 Variation Ratio Equation

where f_m = the number of cases in the modal category
and N = the number of cases.

The variation ratio is particularly suited for when data are measured at the nominal level, though it can and has been used for ordinal data. The ratio can range from a minimum value of 0 to a maximum value of 1. A variation ratio of 0 indicates that there is no variability or dispersion in the variable. This would occur if all cases in a dataset have the same value in a variable. For example, if we were to examine the species of the students in this class, since everyone is of the Homo sapiens species, the variation ratio would equal 0. There are no differences in the values of the variable *species*. Statistically, this would only be possible if the frequency of the mode was equal to the number of cases, e.g., there was only one value with cases. A variation ratio

VARIABILITY:
In data analysis, the degree or extent to which individual values differ from other values in a dataset.

DISPERSION:
In data analysis, the degree or extent to which a dataset is spread out across its values.

VARIATION RATIO:
A measure of variability for nominal variables, representing the relative proportion of cases that are different from the mode; expressed as a decimal between 0.0 and 1.0.

of 1 indicates that there is complete variability in the variable. This is only statistically possible if the frequency of the mode is 0, e.g. there are no values with cases. Thus, in practice, a variation ratio of 1 is impossible and a variation ratio (infinitely) approaching 1 is possible. This would indicate that every value represented in the variable has an equal frequency. As the number of cases in the modal category decreases and/or the number of cases overall increases, the variation ratio approaches, but never equals, 1.

Box 5.1: Example of the Variation Ratio (VR)

Revisit the data from Box 4.2: Example of the Mode (*Mo*) for Categorical Data. In that hypothetical example, you surveyed your data analysis class to obtain the frequencies of the variable *sex*. From the data gathered from your survey, you found that there were 12 male students and 7 female students. What is the VR for the sex of your class? Using the VR formula, you should have come up with a value of approximately 0.37. This indicates a moderate level of variability of sex in the class, based on this measure.

$$1 - \frac{f_m}{N} = 1 - \frac{12}{19} = 1 - .63 = .37$$

Figure 5.2 Variation Ratio Equation Example

Using the same formula, calculate the VR based on the data in Box 4.4: Example of the Median (*Md* or *Mdn*) for Categorical Variables. Using the VR formula, you should have come up with a value of approximately 0.37 in the first example and 0.47 for the second.

$$1 - \frac{f_m}{N} = 1 - \frac{12}{19} = 1 - .63 = .37$$

$$1 - \frac{f_m}{N} = 1 - \frac{10}{19} = 1 - .53 = .47$$

Figure 5.3 Variation Ratio Equation Example #2

The variation ratio is rather limited in its ability to describe a variable within a dataset. This is due in large part to the limited information that categorical data, specifically nominal data, can provide. One of the strengths of the VR is its simplicity. To calculate this value, only two values are needed: the frequency of the mode and the number of cases in the dataset. A second strength is its standardization. As a proportion, it is easily interpreted. Beyond the use of description, however, the VR is limited and cannot be informative beyond quantifying how representative the mode is of the data (Weisberg, 2004).

> ### Box 5.2: WHAT WE'VE LEARNED: Variation Ratio (VR)
>
> While the VR is not commonly provided in research reports, journal articles, or even textbooks, it is easy to determine due to its simplicity in calculation. In addition, since most of those sources often provide raw data, e.g., frequencies, the VR may be reported in a different form, such as a percentage or a proportion. For example, in the most recent National Crime Victimization Survey Bulletin published by the Bureau of Justice Statistics (BJS), the percentage of violent crime reported to police in 2015 was 46.5% (Truman & Morgan, 2016). As a variable with two options (*Yes, the crime was reported* or *No, the crime wasn't reported*), the 46.5 value represents the variation ratio expressed as a percentage instead of a proportion. Since the percentage is less than 50, the complement would be the mode: *No, the crime wasn't reported*. Any categorical variable described in the bulletin may have this value calculated. The BJS estimates there were approximately 5 million violent victimizations and 14.6 million property victimizations in 2015. Using simple arithmetic, we could determine the variation ratio for offense type: approximately 0.26. Variables with a greater number of categories, which are frequently found in the data, may evidence a larger VR value. For example, when examining victim age, we find the variation ratio to be 0.74.

INDEX OF QUALITATIVE VARIATION: A measure of variability for nominal and ordinal variables, representing the proportion of observed variable values relative to the maximum possible paired variable value differences in a dataset; expressed as a decimal between 0.0 and 1.0.

INDEX OF QUALITATIVE VARIATION (IQV)

As a result, measures of variability and dispersion have been mostly restricted to the examination of continuous variables. Since measures of variability and dispersion measure the magnitude of difference between values in a dataset, the inherent nature of categorical data has historically limited their statistical description (Kader & Perry, 2007). However, that is not because there are not measures available for categorical data. This may be due to how these measures are obtained for categorical data, what they describe, and the subsequent interpretation—all of which differ from the measures available for continuous data.

Traditionally, variability and dispersion is understood to describe "how *much* the observations differ from one another." With categorical data, the measurement and interpretation is different. With categorical data, variability and dispersion are understood to describe "how *often* the observations differ from one another" (Perry & Kader, 2005, p. 59). As a result, due to the characteristics of categorical data, any measure of variability and dispersion takes into account the frequency of specific values, while the focus of continuous data is typically the values themselves.

There are several different measurements of variability and dispersion for categorical data. In fact, Allen R. Wilcox (1973) developed six that were published in just one paper. Wilcox discussed his family of measures by their requirements. First, the measure of variability must not depend on the number of cases and the number of categories (though those values are used in its calculation). Second, the measurement must have a standard range of values. Like other measures we have discussed so far, e.g., proportions, and others to come, Wilcox's measure has a range of 0 to 1. The third condition describes the nature of the distribution when the measure is at the minimum value, 0, and at the maximum value, 1. Wilcox states that the measure is at the minimum value of 0 "... if all cases fall within one category" (p. 325–326). He goes on to state that the maximum value of 1 "... occurs if, and only if, an identical number of cases fall within each category" (p. 326).

These principles exist today in the form of perhaps the most commonly used and referred to measure of variability and dispersion for categorical data—the index of qualitative variation (IQV). By some accounts, this was first introduced by Mueller and Schuessler (1961). The measure has also been referred to as the coefficient of unlikeability (Kader & Perry, 2007). The index of qualitative variation was developed, and initially used, to measure variability of nominal variables with two values. However, over time, it has been applied to measure variability of ordinal variables and those with several possible values. Ranging from 0 to 1, the IQV is the proportion of different variable value pairings relative to the maximum possible differences. More commonly, the equation used to calculate the IQV provides a value ranging from 0 to 100, interpretable as a percentage. Thus, as the frequencies of each category become more similar, the IQV decreases. As the frequencies of each category become less similar, the IQV increases. The lower the value, the more similar the cases are across that variable. The higher the value, the less similar the cases are across that variable. To calculate the IQV, the following formula is used:

$$\frac{K\left(100^2 - \sum pct^2\right)}{100^2(K-1)}$$

Figure 5.4 Index of Qualitative Variation Equation

where   K = the number of categories

and $\sum Pct^2$ = "the sum of" (Greek letter sigma) the squared percentages.

Box 5.3: Example of the Index of Qualitative Variation (IQV)

Revisit the data from Box 4.2: Example of the Mode (*Mo*) for Categorical Data. In that hypothetical example, you surveyed your data analysis class to obtain the frequencies of the variable *sex*. From the data gathered from your survey, you found that there were 12 male students and 7 female students. What is the IQV for the sex of your class? Using the IQV formula, you should have come up with the value of approximately 0.93. This indicates a very high degree of variability of sex in the class, based on this measure.

$$\frac{K\left(100^2 - \sum Pct^2\right)}{100^2(K-1)} = \frac{2\left(100^2 - (63.16^2 + 36.85^2)\right)}{100^2(2-1)} = \frac{2\left(100^2 - (5346.26)\right)}{100^2(2-1)} = \frac{2(4653.74)}{10000} = .93$$

Figure 5.5 Index of Qualitative Variation Example

Using the same formula, calculate the IQV based on the data in Box 4.4: Example of the Median (*Md* or *Mdn*) for Categorical Variables. Using the IQV formula, you should have come up with a value of approximately 0.80 in the first example and 0.93 for the second.

$$\frac{K(100^2 - \sum pct^2)}{100^2(K-1)} = \frac{3(100^2 - (15.79^2 + 21.05^2 + 63.16^2))}{100^2(3-1)} = \frac{3(100^2 - (4681.44))}{100^2(3-1)} = \frac{3(5318.56)}{20000} = .80$$

Figure 5.6 Index of Qualitative Variation Example #2

The VR and IQV have several strengths and weaknesses, some of which may be considered one and the same:

1. Utilize data with lower levels of measurement

2. Are commonly used, as there are few measures available

3. Are not needed (or used) for other statistical procedures

Inherently, categorical data provide less information than data measured at higher levels. The available measurements of variability and dispersion for categorical data are few and far between. The characteristics of nominal and ordinal level data limit how they can be measured. Beyond the index of qualitative variation, which is infrequently used, only a handful of other variability and dispersion measures are available for categorical data. Having alternative measures of variability and dispersion for categorical data can prove problematic. The various measures are calculated differently, providing different results and interpretations. As a result, the operationalization of the index of qualitative variation remains very important. Finally, while providing some information, the index of qualitative variation is not very useful in statistical analysis beyond description.

Box 5.4: WHAT WE'VE LEARNED: Index of Qualitative Variation (IQV)

There have been several forms of the IQV developed and utilized over time. One of the more common uses for these indices in criminal justice and criminological research is to measure the variation of racial/ethnic heterogeneity. Using an index derived from Agresti and Agresti (1978), a team of researchers in the Netherlands sought to explain burglary rates in urban neighborhoods. Analyzing data from 89 neighborhoods, Bernasco and Luykx (2003) found that there was a relatively low level of variability of racial/ethnic composition in these areas. In this study, ethnicity was measured based on the country of birth of the residents and their parents. This allowed the researchers to identify natives and individuals with origins in common, neighboring countries. Across neighborhoods, the mean value of ethnic heterogeneity was 0.36. The researchers note that in their analysis, the value of 0.36 represents the probability that two randomly selected members of a neighborhood are of different racial or ethnic origin. This measure is traditionally associated with the lack of social cohesion and collective efficacy in a neighborhood. As a result, they hypothesize that "Higher levels of ethnic heterogeneity increase residential burglary rates" (p. 978). Confirming this, the results showed that ethnic heterogeneity did share a positive relationship with burglary rates. As the variability increased, e.g., there was more racial/ethnic heterogeneity, so too did the burglary rates.

RANGE:
A measure of variability representing the difference or distance between the minimum and maximum values of a variable in a dataset.

Measure of Variability	Range of Values	Levels of Measurement
Variation Ratio	0 to 1	Nominal
Index of Qualitative Variation	0 to 1	Nominal, Ordinal

Figure 5.7 Variation Ratio and Index of Qualitative Variation Comparison

CONTINUOUS VARIABLES

While there are few options when measuring variability and dispersion for categorical variables, there are several options available for continuous variables. The characteristics of continuous data allow for the increase in possible measurements. Recall from Chapter 4 that continuous variables are "numerical" in nature. As a result, these variables have an additional measure of central tendency available for calculation—the mean. Thus, interval and ratio data allow for the examination of the *spread* of data. Being measured at the highest level of measurement allows for the determination of variability and dispersion based on variable *values* instead of *categories*, e.g., the magnitude by which two values differ from one another and the typical magnitude by which all values differ from the measures of central tendency, specifically the mean.

RANGE

The most basic measure of variability and dispersion for continuous variables is the range. The range was first described as a statistical concept by Reverend Humphrey Lloyd, an Irish physicist (David, 1995). Lloyd's (1848) work included the study of magnetism and meteorology. The range can only be measured for variables measured at the interval or ratio level. These levels of measurement, unlike nominal and ordinal level data, represent variables that have some quantitative value. In addition, and equally important for calculating the range, these levels of measurement have a known and measurable distance between values. The range itself is a measurement of the distance between values—two specific values. To obtain the range of a continuous variable, use the following formula:

$$H - L$$

Figure 5.8 Range Equation

where H = the highest value of the variable
and L = the lowest value of the variable.

Box 5.5: Example of the Range

Revisit the data from Box 4.6: Example of the Mode (*Mo*) for Continuous Variables. In that hypothetical example, you collected data concerning the number of citizen complaints against officers during their careers. The totals were:

1, 1, 2, 2, 2, 2, 2, 2, 3, 3, 3, 4, 4, 5, 5, 5, 5, 6, 6, 6, 6, 7

What is the range of the number of citizen complaints against officers during their careers? Using the range formula, you should have come up with a value of six.

$$H - L = 7 - 1 = 6$$

Figure 5.9 Range Equation Example

If the data are in tabular form, such as in a grouped frequency distribution, the range can be calculated using a different formula. See Figure 5.9. The data from this frequency distribution, as currently displayed, can be used to calculate the range of citizens' complaints against officers during their career using the following formula (found in the final column):

Number of Citizen Complaints	Frequency	Midpoint of Interval	$m_H - m_L$
0–1	2	.5 (m_L)	
2–3	10	2.5	
4–5	6	4.5	
6–7	5	6.5 (m_H)	$6.5 - .5 = 6$

Figure 5.10 Range Example #2

where m_H = the midpoint of the highest class interval
and m_L = the midpoint of the lowest class interval.

As a measure of variability and dispersion, the range has several advantages:

1. Describes all data with one value

2. Can be calculated for multiple data forms

3. Is easy to calculate

4. Is easy to interpret

The range, like other descriptive measures—not just those of variability and dispersion—describes an entire dataset with a single value. As a result, it accounts for all variable values in its calculation. The range can be calculated when data are presented in several data forms and if the data are measured at the interval or ratio level. The range can be calculated for data in its raw form, as in Figure 5.9, and it can be calculated for grouped data, as in Figure 5.10. The equation used for its calculation requires

---

Box 5.6: WHAT WE'VE LEARNED: Range

Recently, a group of researchers sought to assess whether the location of alcohol establishments in a neighborhood impacted the amount of crime the area experienced. Toomey, Erickson, Carlin, Lenk, Quick, Jones, & Harwood (2012) examined the association of alcohol establishment density with the number of assaults, rapes, robberies, and total violent crime. To calculate alcohol establishment density, they collected data from the local municipality's regulatory agency (Minneapolis Department of Regulatory Services). In sum, they were able to identify 623 licensed alcohol establishments: 503 on-premises and 120 off-premises. Their measure represented the number of establishments per roadway mile. Three such measures were created: total establishment density, on-premise establishment density, and off-premise establishment density. In their analysis of 83 neighborhoods, they found stark differences in several of their variables. Within their one-city analysis, the neighborhoods differed drastically, showing several characteristics positively associated with crime. For example, the range for the population in the neighborhoods was 15,119, for the number of alcohol establishments 124, and for the number of total crime incidents 272, among other reported differences. Across all neighborhoods, the total establishment density was associated with increases in all offense categories measured: rape, robbery, assault, and total crime. This pattern was also observed for on-premises establishment density. Off-premises establishment density was only significantly related to robbery and assault.

---

knowing just the extreme values of the variable: the highest value and the lowest value. The result is an easily interpreted value that describes the difference between both "ends" of the distribution.

The range also has several disadvantages, or weaknesses, that limit its use as the primary statistic for variability and dispersion description:

1. Only uses the extreme values of the data

2. Is affected by outliers

3. Only describes spread, not shape

While the range encompasses all variable values in its calculation, its determination relies upon only the most extreme values: the highest and the lowest. Although all variable values fall between those extremes, their individual values are not incorporated into the calculation. As a result, if the highest and/or lowest values are outliers, the range may provide an inaccurate description of the *spread* of the distribution. In fact, the range *only* provides a measure of the *spread* of the distribution, not its shape. Thus, the variability that may exist between the two values is unknown and unaccounted for, which limits the ability to fully describe the data.

QUARTILES

Related to the concept of the range is the measurement of quartiles. The word quartile as a concept has been in use since at least the 16th century. Astronomers used the term to describe locations based on radians. As a descriptive measure of data, quartiles were first described by Francis Galton, an English statistician, in 1882 (sometimes credited as 1883). Galton was the chair of a committee that produced several reports on the physical characteristics of inhabitants of the British Isles, which included Scotland, Ireland, England, and Wales. The physical characteristics the committee was required to measure and report on included:

(1) Stature. (2) Weight. (3) Girth of chest. (4) Colour of eyes (complexion). (5) Hair (complexion). (6) Breathing capacity. (7). Strength of arm. (8). Sight. (9). Span of arms. To these might have been added others, especially—(10) Size and shape of head. (11) Length of lower limbs as shown by the difference between the sitting and standing positions. (12) Girth, length, and breadth of other parts of the body. (Galton, 1882)

Galton's committee collected and reported a significant amount of individual data. From this data, they sought to provide representative values by calculating various *averages*—including the traditional mean we are familiar with today. The report specifically identifies the methodological contributions of Galton, stating that "… he introduces his method of the calculation of … quartiles" (p. 255).

Quartiles represent values within a distribution that divide it in fourths, or quarters. The practice of using a value to represent the relative location of other values might be familiar. This is the same procedure when calculating percentiles and the ranking of values relative to other values in the distribution. If you have taken standardized tests, such as those for college admission, your scores may have been reported to you in the form of a percentile. Quartiles represent specific percentiles due to their location. Since quartiles divide a distribution in four, there are three quartile values. The quartiles represent the 25th, 50th, and 75th percentile locations within a distribution. The 25th percentile is equal to the first quartile (Q_1), the 50th percentile is equal to the second quartile (Q_2), and the 75th percentile is equal to the third quartile (Q_3).

The first quartile represents the value of which 25% of the data lie below (and 75% lie above); the second quartile the value of which 50% lie below (and 50% lie above) and; the third quartile represents the value of which 75% of the data lie below (and 25% lie above). Since the second quartile (50% percentile) divides the distribution in half, it is represented by the median. Thus, Q1 and Q3 are the medians of the lower and upper halves of the distributions, respectively. When determining quartile values, the minimum and maximum values are often presented, as we saw in Chapter 3 with the creation of box plots. There are multiple ways to find the quartiles of a distribution. See Box 5.7: Example of Quartiles for examples.

Do the results from Box 5.7: Example of Quartiles reflect the values between which each quarter of the distribution lies? For example, is 25% of the distribution less than 2; is 50% of the distribution less than 3, and; is 75% of the distribution less than 5? In this case, no. However, in large(r) datasets that are normally distributed, these patterns will be more evident.

QUARTILES:
In data analysis, three values representing an equal division of the distribution of a variable into four sequential groups: the 25th, 50th, and 75th percentile data points.

INTER-QUARTILE RANGE (IQR):
In data analysis, a measure of dispersion representing the difference or distance between the first and third quartiles; the middle-most 50% of the data.

Box 5.7: Example of Quartiles

Suppose you were to continue your examination of officer complaints for a local police department. In that hypothetical example, you collected data concerning the number of citizen complaints against officers during their careers. The totals were:

1, 1, 2, 2, 2, 2, 2, 2, 2, 3, 3, 3, 4, 4, 5, 5, 5, 5, 6, 6, 6, 6, 7

What are the three quartile values of the number of citizen complaints against officers during their careers? Your answer may depend on the procedures you used. The two simplest and commonly used will be discussed. The only difference is what happens with Q_2 (the median) after it has been found: is it included or excluded when finding the median of the lower and upper halves of the distribution? Find the three quartile values when including the median and excluding the median when finding Q_1 and Q_3.

Using your knowledge of median calculation, you should have come up with the following values when including the median: $Q_1 = 2$, $Q_2 = 3$, and $Q_3 = 5$. You should have come up with the following values when excluding the median: $Q_1 = 2$, $Q_2 = 3$, and $Q_3 = 5$. In this dataset, there is no difference, but that is not always the case.

Dispersion Measure	Values	Calculation and Representation
Range	Min., Max.	Distance between two (lowest and highest) values, encompassing all values
Quartile	Q1, Q2 (median), Q3	Location of three values, equally dividing all values into four groups

Figure 5.11 Range and Quartile Comparison

There is also a measure of variability and dispersion that combines characteristics of the range and the quartiles of a distribution. The inter-quartile range (IQR) operates in a similar manner to the range by utilizing two values that serve as an upper and lower boundary. These two values that serve as an upper and lower boundary are the first (Q_1) and third (Q_3) quartiles. By obtaining this value, one can determine where in a distribution the middle 50th of all values are concentrated. This is often used in addition to the range and quartile values to identify the *spread* of data that is clustered in the middle of the distribution. To obtain the IQR, the following formula is used:

$$Q_3 - Q_1$$

Figure 5.12 Interquartile Range Equation

where Q_1 = the value of the first quartile

and Q_3 = the value of the third quartile.

Box 5.8: WHAT WE'VE LEARNED: Quartiles

In their comparison of groups, specifically two different time periods, several prominent scholars examined spatial patterns of county homicide rates. Messner et al. (1999) collected data to see if there were differences in crime rates across counties and over time. From their data, the researchers sought to test if diffusion of homicides for two time periods in St. Louis (1984–1988 and 1988–1993) occurred. They found there may be some diffusion of homicide from one county to another, and areas that are considered rural and agricultural may serve as a barrier to such diffusion. They conducted several statistical tests and provided several graphical displays of data, such as maps, line charts, and box plots. Examination of the box plots show that there were differences in homicide rates between the two time periods, largely a result of outliers that emerged in the later time period. This was visually evident in the box plot. Viewing the plot showed the values represented by the quartiles varied across the two time periods. When outliers were excluded, the latter period (1988–1993) produced a "considerably smaller inter-quartile range" (Messner et al., 1999, p. 438). In this study, an outlier was a county with a homicide rate greater than the IQR and at least 1.5 times its value.

As a measure of variability and dispersion, the use of quartiles has several advantages:

1. Easy to determine

2. Easy to interpret

3. Not affected by outliers

The value of each quartile is very easy to determine. All that is needed is the set of data and knowledge of how to find the median. This was learned in Chapter 4. Once this is known, there is only one thing needed: a decision. As Box 5.7: Example of Quartiles showed, there is more than one way to determine where the quartiles lie in the distribution. This depends on the median: if it is included or excluded in the determination of the first quartile (Q_1) and the third quartile (Q_3). Once the quartiles are located, they are very easily interpreted. Each represents an equal division of the distribution. Finally, although included in the determination of the location of the quartiles, the extreme values of outliers do not impact the quartile values.

The use of quartiles has several disadvantages, or weaknesses, that limit their use as the primary statistic for variability and dispersion:

1. Are limited to quantitative data

2. Offer limited information about spread

3. Are prone to fluctuation due to sampling

DEVIATION:
In data analysis, a measure of dispersion that represents the difference or distance between two variable values.

Quartiles are restricted to quantitative data. Most appropriate are their use when they are calculated using continuous variables, which are measured at the interval or ratio levels. However, they can be, and have been, used to describe ordinal data, as well. The quartile values are not very informative about the variable's distribution. They provide locations of values that divide the distribution into four equal parts, which can be somewhat informative—especially if the IQR is considered. However, quartiles provide no information regarding dispersion between the values. Finally, since the determination of quartiles is based on location, not values, they are more prone to fluctuation due to sampling, especially when the number of cases is low. When data are not normally distributed, quartiles and the IQR will be limited in the information they provide (see the discussion of Box 5.7: Example of Quartiles).

DEVIATION

By this point, we have seen how to calculate several measures of variability and dispersion, all of which describe different types of data in different ways. Like we saw with measures of central tendency, as the level of measurement of data moves from categorical to continuous data, there are more measures that can be calculated. These are often more specific, providing information that may be complementary to the previous measures.

Disadvantages to some of the aforementioned measures of variability and dispersion include the inability to describe those characteristics between located values. When the range and quartiles are calculated and found, there is no description about the variability and dispersion of individual values, just the percentage of the distribution between the determined values. For example, when determining the range of a distribution a researcher has only knowledge about the spread. There is no information regarding the location of values within the range. Similarly, when determining the quartiles of a distribution, a researcher has only knowledge about the values found at specific locations in the distribution. There is no information regarding the location of values within the quartiles or what the actual values are that are located therein.

With continuous data, each value in the distribution of a variable may be considered and incorporated into a measure of variability and dispersion. Individual values can be described by their deviation. The first mention of this concept came when Francis Galton (1907) discussed a normal "array." In his paper, he described the value of the difference between a line and the median height above the axis as a "deviate" (p. 400). His discussion mirrors our understanding and use of deviations in a normal distribution. He specifically makes note of the fact that in a normal distribution the median and mean are identical. Thus, a deviation is the distance of any individual value from the mean value of a variable.

To calculate a deviation, you use the following formula:

$$X - \overline{X}$$

Figure 5.13 Deviation Equation

where   x = an individual value of a variable

and $\overline{x}$ = the mean value of the variable.

Box 5.9: Example of Deviation

Suppose you were to continue your examination of officer complaints for a local police department. In that hypothetical example, you collected data concerning the number of citizen complaints against officers during their careers. The totals were:

1, 1, 2, 2, 2, 2, 2, 2, 2, 3, 3, 3, 4, 4, 5, 5, 5, 5, 6, 6, 6, 6, 7

What are the deviations of each value of citizen complaints against officers during their careers? In order to answer this, we would first need to calculate the mean. Recall we did this in Box 4.9 Example of the Mean (*Mn*) for Continuous Variables in Chapter 4. The mean value for this data is approximately 3.65. By placing the data in a table, we can see the deviations of each value.

X	$\overline{x}$	$(x - \overline{x})$
1	3.65	−2.65
1	3.65	−2.65
2	3.65	−1.65
2	3.65	−1.65
2	3.65	−1.65
2	3.65	−1.65
2	3.65	−1.65
2	3.65	−1.65
2	3.65	−1.65
3	3.65	−.65
3	3.65	−.65
3	3.65	−.65
4	3.65	.35
4	3.65	.35
5	3.65	1.35
5	3.65	1.35
5	3.65	1.35
5	3.65	1.35
6	3.65	2.35
6	3.65	2.35
6	3.65	2.35
6	3.65	2.35
7	3.65	3.35

Figure 5.14 Deviation Example

If the individual value is less than the mean, the deviation will be negative. This will be seen with all values between the minimum value and the mean. If the individual value is greater than the mean, the deviation will be positive. This will be seen with all values between the mean and the maximum value. If the mean value of the variable is also represented in the data, the deviation will be 0. This indicates there is no difference between the individual value and mean, e.g., no deviation. To examine the deviations of individual values, it may be helpful to put the data into tabular form, as seen in Box 5.9: Example of Deviation. This may be more appropriate with small(er) datasets.

Box 5.10: WHAT WE'VE LEARNED: Deviation

Professors DeFina and Arvanites used deviations in a novel way to examine factors related to crime rates. The researchers were interested in examining, over a nearly 30-year period, the impact of increasing incarceration rates on crime rates. Since they examined so many time periods (1971–1998), they wanted to account for changes in crime rates at the national level. Thus, instead of using the traditional measure of crime rates as their outcome, their dependent variable was the deviation from the national average value for each year (DeFina & Arvanites, 2002). As a result, their outcome was the difference in crime rate between one unit of analysis and the nation. Their units of analysis were states. This is a unique example, as deviation is generally used only as a measure of variability and dispersion for descriptive, not inferential, purposes. The first stage of analysis examined data from 1971–1992. They found that prison rates were significantly and negatively associated with five of the seven crimes they examined. Homicide, robbery, burglary, larceny, and motor-vehicle theft saw effects. The second stage of analysis utilized the full range of data (1971–1998). Here, they found that prison rates have a significant and negative effect on only three of the seven crimes they examined. Burglary, larceny, and motor-vehicle theft showed decreases. There were no effects on homicide, rape, robbery, or assault.

VARIANCE

The use of deviations is not just restricted to measuring variability and dispersion of individual values. Using all deviations, it is possible to obtain a measure of variability and dispersion that would describe the entire distribution, e.g., all observed values of a variable and their *average spread*. To do this we must first calculate the variance. Although the concept had been formulated before his writing, the term variance was first used by Ronald A. Fisher in 1918 in his study of Mendelian heredity.

The variance accounts for all deviations in a distribution by summing them and finding the mean of that value. However, since the deviations represent the difference from the individual values and the mean, the negative values are of equal magnitude to the positive values. Thus, when they are summed, the variance would be 0. A value of 0 would represent absolutely no variability and dispersion. To get around this, we would need to account for only the magnitude of the deviations, not their direction (whether they are negative or positive). To do this, the deviations are squared. Then, the number of cases are controlled to produce an *average* (mean). The following formula reflects this process:

$$\sigma^2 = \frac{\sum (X - \bar{X})^2}{N}$$

Figure 5.15 Population Variance Equation

where σ^2 = variance

and Σ = "the sum of" (Greek letter sigma)

             $(x - \bar{x})$ = deviation from the mean

             N = the number of cases.

This is not the only version of the formula, however. There is an adjusted form of the formula that assumes the data are a sample or that it is small enough where it may not be normally distributed. There is no consensus on what the sufficient number of cases is to make this determination. Some suggest 30 is enough cases while others suggest 100. Some software programs allow the user to specify which formula will be used (such as Excel and R) and others default to one or the other (such as SPSS). For illustrative purposes in this chapter, using 30 or 100 cases as the threshold does not matter since the example data we have been using has less than both of those. Thus, as in our examination, when there are an insufficient number of cases to assume normality, the following formula is used:

$$s^2 = \frac{\sum (X - \bar{X})^2}{n - 1}$$

Figure 5.16 Sample Variance Equation

where s^2 = variance

             Σ = "the sum of" (Greek letter Sigma)

             $(x - \bar{x})$ = deviation from the mean

             n = the number of cases.

When this formula is used, a more conservative estimate of the variance is produced. Besides symbology, e.g., using s^2 instead of σ^2 and n instead of N, the only difference in the equation is the denominator. To create a more conservative estimate, the "–1" is added to reduce the denominator slightly. This results in a slightly larger variance. When the number of cases becomes sufficient (30, 100, etc.), the difference in the variance calculated from both equations becomes negligible, and adherence to the sample formula is observed largely on a theoretical basis.

Box 5.11: Example of Variance

Suppose you were to continue your examination of officer complaints for a local police department. In that hypothetical example, you collected data concerning the number of citizen complaints against officers during their careers. The totals were:

1, 1, 2, 2, 2, 2, 2, 2, 2, 3, 3, 3, 4, 4, 5, 5, 5, 5, 6, 6, 6, 6, 7

What is the variance of the number of citizen complaints against officers during their careers? Using the sample variance formula, you should have come up with approximately 3.42. If you used the first formula, you would have come up with a slightly lower value of 3.27.

STANDARD DEVIATION:
In data analysis, a measure of dispersion that represents the typical deviation from the mean of a variable for all cases in a dataset.

X	$\bar{X}$	$(X - \bar{X})$	$(X - \bar{X})^2$
1	3.65	−2.65	7.02
1	3.65	−2.65	7.02
2	3.65	−1.65	2.72
2	3.65	−1.65	2.72
2	3.65	−1.65	2.72
2	3.65	−1.65	2.72
2	3.65	−1.65	2.72
2	3.65	−1.65	2.72
2	3.65	−1.65	2.72
3	3.65	−.65	.42
3	3.65	−.65	.42
3	3.65	−.65	.42
4	3.65	.35	.12
4	3.65	.35	.12
5	3.65	1.35	1.82
5	3.65	1.35	1.82
5	3.65	1.35	1.82
5	3.65	1.35	1.82
6	3.65	2.35	5.52
6	3.65	2.35	5.52
6	3.65	2.35	5.52
6	3.65	2.35	5.52
7	3.65	3.35	11.22
			$\Sigma = 75.16$

$$\frac{\sum (x - \bar{x})^2}{n-1} = \frac{75.16}{22} = 3.42$$

Figure 5.17 Variance Example

STANDARD DEVIATION

There are two significant issues that arise in the calculation of variance: the unit of measurement and the interpretation of the statistic. In order to have a value that did not sum to 0 due to negative and positive deviations cancelling each other out, the deviations were squared. As a result, the variance represents, in a sense, squared units. Refer back to our hypothetical example of officer complaints of a local police department in Box 5.11: Example of Variance. Regardless of which equation and value we use, the variance will still represent *squared* complaints. This is not an interpretable statistic in its current form (e.g., what is a squared complaint?).

In order to simultaneously account for all deviations in a distribution and have a statistic that can be easily interpreted, one additional step must be taken. Since the variance reflects the sum of squared units—whatever that unit or variable may be—the squaring can be undone by taking the square root. This returns the statistic to the original unit, e.g., from *squared* complaints to complaints. This new statistic is known as the standard deviation.

The term standard deviation was first used in a paper published by Karl Pearson in 1893, though in late 1892 he made notes on the manuscript describing the "standard divergence" (Stigler, 1986). Pearson (1893) notes in his paper that his predecessors had developed measures using the same approach. Carl Gauss had described the "mean error" and George Airy had described the "error of mean square." However, they were different versions of this statistic, similar more so in intent than in calculation. It did not take much time before the measure was lauded by Pearson's contemporaries. Sir George Udny Yule (1911), a British statistician, wrote in his early textbook, "It will be seen from the preceding paragraphs that the standard deviation possesses the majority at least of the properties which are desirable in a measure of dispersion as in an average" (p. 143). The standard deviation is the most commonly reported measure of variability and dispersion for continuous data. To calculate the standard deviation, the following formula is used:

$$\sigma = \sqrt{\frac{\sum (X - \bar{X})^2}{N}}$$

Figure 5.18 Population Standard Deviation Equation

where
σ = standard deviation
$\sum$ = "the sum of" (Greek letter Sigma)
$(x - \bar{x})$ = deviation from the mean
N = the number of cases.

When the number of cases is insufficiently low, the formula for the standard deviation has the same adjustment as the variance formula. To create a more conservative estimate, the "−1" is added to reduce the denominator slightly. Thus, the standard deviation formula is as follows:

$$s = \sqrt{\frac{\sum (X - \bar{X})^2}{n - 1}}$$

Figure 5.19 Sample Standard Deviation Equation

where
s = standard deviation
$\sum$ = "the sum of" (Greek letter Sigma)
$(x - \bar{x})$ = deviation from the mean
n = the number of cases.

Box 5.12: Example of Standard Deviation

Revisit our example found in Box 5.11 Example of Variance, where we examined officer complaints for a local police department. In that hypothetical example, you collected data concerning the number of citizen complaints against officers during their careers. The totals were:

1, 1, 2, 2, 2, 2, 2, 2, 2, 3, 3, 3, 4, 4, 5, 5, 5, 5, 6, 6, 6, 6, 7

What is the standard deviation of the number of citizen complaints against officers during their careers? Using the sample variance formula, you should have come with approximately 1.85. If you used the first formula, you would have come up with a slightly lower value of 1.81.

X	$\bar{X}$	(X − $\bar{X}$)	(X − $\bar{X}$)²
1	3.65	−2.65	7.02
1	3.65	−2.65	7.02
2	3.65	−1.65	2.72
2	3.65	−1.65	2.72
2	3.65	−1.65	2.72
2	3.65	−1.65	2.72
2	3.65	−1.65	2.72
2	3.65	−1.65	2.72
2	3.65	−1.65	2.72
3	3.65	−.65	.42
3	3.65	−.65	.42
3	3.65	−.65	.42
4	3.65	.35	.12
4	3.65	.35	.12
5	3.65	1.35	1.82
5	3.65	1.35	1.82
5	3.65	1.35	1.82
5	3.65	1.35	1.82
6	3.65	2.35	5.52
6	3.65	2.35	5.52
6	3.65	2.35	5.52
6	3.65	2.35	5.52
7	3.65	3.35	11.22
			Σ = 75.16

$$\sqrt{\frac{\sum(X-\bar{X})}{n-1}} = \sqrt{\frac{75.16}{22}} = \sqrt{3.42} = 1.85$$

Figure 5.20 Standard Deviation Example

Recall that the purpose of taking the square root of the variance, to obtain the standard deviation, was to return the statistic to the original unit of analysis and for ease of interpretation. Thus, based on the example in Box 5.12: Example of Standard Deviation, one can explain the value of 1.85 as representing citizen complaints. In this example, the standard deviation of citizen complaints is 1.85. This indicates that across the entire distribution (the 23 cases), the typical case is 1.85 complaints away from the mean (3.65). Essentially, we are averaging the (squared) deviations in the distribution. This is not a precise average, as we generally think of it, since the deviation is squared. A traditional and more precise average would use the absolute value of the deviations. We are calculating an average of the squared deviations, not an average of the deviations. Thus, more weight to the statistic is provided by the extreme values. When the standard deviation is low, the values of the distribution are relatively close together. When the standard deviation is high, the values of the distribution are relatively far apart.

Box 5.13: WHAT WE'VE LEARNED: Standard Deviation

Researcher Patricia M. Harris sought to examine offenders who begin committing crime as adults, or "adult-onset offenders." She studied differences between first-time and repeat offenders (recidivists). In her study, she collected data from more than 3,000 individuals with felony convictions that were placed on probation. Her sample had a mean age of 29.3 years and a standard deviation of 10.3, indicating the values were relatively far apart. The number of prior convictions had a mean of 1.14 and a standard deviation of 1.9, indicating the possibility of outliers. Although the full distribution of values is not provided or displayed, the range (0 to 25 prior convictions) provides support for this. A similar pattern is observed in her sample in which the mean number of prior arrests is 1.91 and the standard deviation is 2.9. Like the data for prior convictions, the range of prior arrests (0 to 32) suggests outliers may be present, resulting in the relatively large standard deviations. Among other findings, she found that older offenders with only adult convictions had a risk of recidivism that was lower than their younger counterparts. This is also the case with first-time offenders. Thus, despite greater dispersion in the age variability, those with positive deviations from the mean tended to fare better (Harris, 2011).

As a measure of variability and dispersion, the standard deviation has several advantages:

1.   Describes all data with one value

2.   Utilizes information from all data

3.   Is fairly easy to calculate

4.   Is least prone to fluctuation due to sampling

5.   Is used in additional analyses

Compared to other measures of variability and dispersion, the standard deviation offers the most advantages when the data are continuous. The standard deviation is the most commonly reported measure of variability and dispersion. This is due to the several advantages it offers. Yule (1911) may have put it best when discussing the properties that make the standard deviation desirable:

It is rigidly defined; it is based on all observations made; it is calculated with reasonable ease; it lends itself readily to algebraical treatment; and we may add, though the student will have to take the statement on trust for the present, that it is, as a rule, the measure least affected by fluctuations of sampling. (pp. 143–144)

SKEWNESS:
In data analysis, a standardized measure of dispersion reflecting the asymmetry of a distribution.

Yule advocates strongly for its use, stating that it should always be used. In practice, that seems to be the case. The standard deviation is the most informative of all measures of variability and dispersion and the most often reported. It is also the most versatile as subsequent chapters will show that it is required for several statistical tests and forms of analysis.

The standard deviation also has several disadvantages, or weaknesses, that may limit its use as the primary statistic for variability and dispersion description:

1. Is moderately difficult to interpret

2. Requires continuous data

3. Can be affected by extreme values

4. Assumes the distribution is normal

Compared to other measures of variability and dispersion, the standard deviation has fewer and less disadvantageous weaknesses. Interpretation of the standard deviation can be difficult for some, particularly those that are not educated in its calculation. It is less intuitive than other statistics, such as measures of central tendency. Like the variance and other statistics that utilize information from all data, the standard deviation can be affected by outliers. The impact of outliers decreases as a distribution becomes more normal and/ or the number of cases increases. If the distribution is not normal, the standard deviation can still be calculated. Conclusions based on its interpretation, however, may be less accurate. If the data are not normal, that is largely a function of outliers. Thus, discussing the standard deviation in terms of "typical distance from the mean" may not accurately represent the entirety of the distribution.

SKEWNESS

The previous measures of variability for continuous data (e.g., the range, quartiles, and the standard deviation) are most appropriate when, and often assume, the data being analyzed are normally distributed. The degree to which a variable is normally distributed can be measured quite easily with two descriptive measures. The first measure is skewness. First used in 1895 by Karl Pearson, the terms skew and skewness were used to describe situations in which data were not normally distributed: they weren't represented with, or as, normal curves, but those that were "asymmetrical" (p. 344). Thus, skewness provides a numerical representation of how asymmetrical a distribution is. Skewness can be measured a variety of ways by incorporating different measures of central tendency into the calculation or by adjusting for the sample size (Tabor, 2010). Perhaps the most common measure of skewness is referred to as the Fisher-Pearson coefficient of skewness, or G_1. This is the measure used by most software programs today, adjusting for the size of the sample (Doane & Seward, 2011):

$$G_1 = \frac{n}{(n-1)(n-2)} \sum \left(\frac{X - \bar{X}}{S} \right)^3$$

Figure 5.21 Fisher-Pearson Skew Equation

Box 5.14: Example of Skewness

Revisit our example found in Box 5.12 Example of Standard Deviation, where we examined officer complaints for a local police department. In that hypothetical example, you collected data concerning the number of citizen complaints against officers during their careers. The totals were:

1, 1, 2, 2, 2, 2, 2, 2, 2, 3, 3, 3, 4, 4, 5, 5, 5, 5, 6, 6, 6, 6, 7

What is the skewness value of the number of citizen complaints against officers during their careers? Using the Fisher-Pearson coefficient of skewness formula, you should have come with approximately .232.

A distribution that is perfectly normally distributed—one that is symmetrical with identical values of the three measures of central tendency—will have a value of skewness equal to 0. This indicates no skewness. If a distribution is asymmetrical at any magnitude, the value of skewness will be greater or less than 0. If the value is less than 0, e.g., a negative value, this indicates that the distribution has a negative skew, meaning the "negative" (left) tail of the distribution is elongated. This provides evidence of relative outliers at the lower range of values. If the value is greater than 0, e.g., a positive value, this indicates that the distribution has a positive skew, meaning the "positive" (right) tail of the distribution is elongated. This provides evidence of relative outliers at the higher range of values.

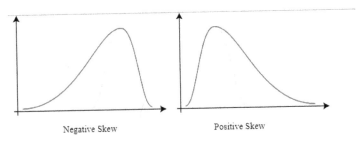

Negative Skew   Positive Skew

Figure 5.22 Distribution Shape and Skew

Opinions differ as to what level of skewness is acceptable in order to treat data as if it were normally distributed. Some suggest that a skewness value less than |2| is appropriate (Trochim & Donnelly, 2006; Gravetter & Wallnau, 2014), while others suggest a more conservative approach in which a skewness value of |1| should be the threshold (Osborne, 2013). Regardless of the threshold chosen, visual inspection and calculation of a variable's skewness is suggested. The example provided in Box 5.14: Example of Skewness found the distribution of number of citizen complaints against officers during their careers has a skewness value of approximately .232. This provides statistical evidence of relative outliers in the higher range of values.

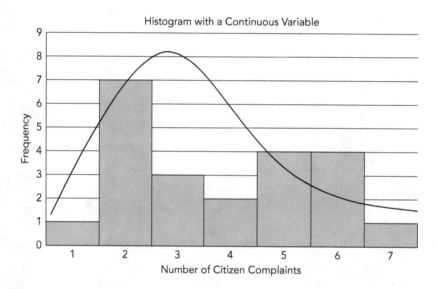

Figure 5.23 Skew Example

Box 5.15: WHAT WE'VE LEARNED: Skewness

Utilizing a self-report survey, Dr. Kyung-shick Choi (2008) gathered data to see if tenets of Routine Activities Theory can explain computer crime victimization. He collected various information concerning the individuals' computer security and online lifestyle and found that college students who "overlook their computer-oriented lifestyle in cyberspace or who neglect the presence of computer-security software" (p. 323) are at greater risk of victimization. Victimization can take many forms: computer virus infection, monetary loss, and hour (productivity) loss. Each of those measures showed very high values of skew. The skewness value for frequency of virus infection was 9.54, monetary loss 6.50, and hour loss 3.89. These all suggest, to varying degrees, a positively or right-skewed distribution in which there is a presence of relative outliers at the higher range of values. Dr. Choi also examined the skew of protective factors, such as the number of computer security programs and the length of time they have had these programs. The skewness value for the number of computer security programs was −1.96, indicating marginal skewness in the negative direction. The skewness value for the length of time computer security programs have been in use was −0.99. Taken with other values, this measure suggests a relatively normal distribution of the variable.

As a measure of variability and dispersion, the skewness value has several advantages:

1. Describes all data with one value

2. Utilizes information from all data

3. Is standardized

4. Is fairly easy to interpret

Measuring skewness has several advantages that make it worthwhile to calculate when analyzing data. Like some of the aforementioned measures of variability and dispersion, the skewness value is a single number that represents all of the variable's values. In its calculation, the skewness value utilizes information from every case. This information includes the individual data values, the mean, and the standard deviation—values we are already familiar with. As a result, the value is a standardized measure that reflects the overall asymmetry of the distribution under study. This allows for ease in interpretation, particularly when a threshold is determined to evaluate its normality.

The skewness value also has several disadvantages, or weaknesses, that may limit its use as the primary statistic for variability and dispersion description:

1. Requires continuous data

2. Is prone to fluctuation due to sampling

3. Is highly dependent on sample size

4. Provides an overview of the distribution

Measuring and using the skewness value as an indicator of variability and dispersion is not without its limits. The value requires continuous data to be calculated. Thus, only for interval and ratio level data can a distribution's skew be measured. Similar to most descriptive measures, skewness can be impacted significantly due to sampling. Different samples may yield drastically different distribution shapes. Related, its value is highly dependent on sample size. There is an adjustment for sample size in the Fisher-Pearson coefficient of skewness formula that is used today in most software programs; however, the value itself may not be accurate in small samples. Accurate or not, the value only provides a broad, and perhaps vague, description of the distribution's shape. It does not allow for the location of specific values like other measures of variability and dispersion do.

KURTOSIS

A descriptive statistic that is often reported with the measure of skewness is the measure of kurtosis. Fittingly, it was Karl Pearson who first described a distribution's kurtosis—at least using those words. In a very sharp rejoinder

KURTOSIS:
In data analysis, a standardized measure of dispersion reflecting the relative "tailedness" and "peakedness" of the distribution.

to scathing criticism of his earlier work on skewness, Pearson (1905) provides description of the "degree of flat-toppedness which is greater or less than that of the normal curve" (p. 173). Essentially, he is describing the difference in a distribution's shape relative to the normal curve, specifically its peak: how flat the top is. Software programs vary in terms of which formula is used to calculate the kurtosis of a distribution. Much of the difference is related to standardization. For illustrative purposes, we will use the formula employed by Excel and SPSS:

$$K = \frac{n(n + 1)\sum(x - \bar{x})^4}{(n - 1)(n - 2)(n - 3)s^4} - \frac{3(n - 1)^2}{(n - 2)(n - 3)}$$

Figure 5.24 Kurtosis Equation

Box 5.16: Example of Kurtosis

Revisit our example found in Box 5.14 Example of Skewness, where we examined officer complaints for a local police department. In that hypothetical example, you collected data concerning the number of citizen complaints against officers during their careers. The totals were:

1, 1, 2, 2, 2, 2, 2, 2, 2, 3, 3, 3, 4, 4, 5, 5, 5, 5, 6, 6, 6, 6, 7

What is the kurtosis value of the number of citizen complaints against officers during their careers? Using the formula provided, you should have come up with approximately −1.35.

This formula standardizes the kurtosis value so that a distribution that is identical to a normal distribution would have a value of 0. This would indicate the distribution is perfectly normal. When a distribution has this characteristic, it is sometimes referred to as being mesokurtic. However, Pearson (1905) notes that, theoretically, not all mesokurtic distributions are normal as we understand them (p. 173). For our purposes, they can be treated analogously. If the kurtosis value was positive, this would indicate that the data are relatively peaked, compared to a normal distribution. This means the peak is leptokurtic, in which the area where the data cluster in the center is "thinner" than that of a normal distribution, and the tails are "lower." This would indicate there are higher frequencies of the middle most values in the distribution and lower frequencies of the outermost values in the distribution. If the kurtosis value was negative, this would indicate that the data are relatively flat, compared to a normal distribution. This means the distribution is platykurtic, in which the area where the data cluster in the center is "wider" than that of a normal distribution, and the tails are "higher." This would indicate there are lower frequencies of the middle most values in the distribution and higher frequencies of the outermost values in the distribution, relative to a normal distribution.

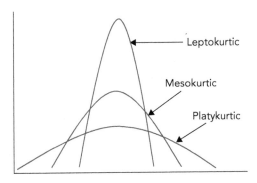

Figure 5.25 Distribution and Kurtosis

Opinions differ as to the level of kurtosis that is acceptable in order to treat data as if it were normally distributed. These suggestions vary widely, much more so than those for skew. Some suggest that a kurtosis value less than |1| is appropriate (Osborne, 2013), while others suggest a threshold as high as |7| (Curran, West, & Finch, 1996). The software program and accompanying equation will affect the threshold chosen, as the value indicating normality may differ, e.g., 0 or 3. Regardless of the threshold chosen, visual inspection and calculation of a variable's kurtosis is suggested. The example provided in Box 5.16: Example of Kurtosis found the distribution of number of citizen complaints against officers during their career has a kurtosis value of approximately −1.35. This provides statistical evidence that the distribution is relatively platykurtic: there are lower frequencies of the middle most values and higher frequencies of the outermost values.

Box 5.17: WHAT WE'VE LEARNED: Kurtosis

Researchers Santtila, Laukkanen, and Zappalà (2007) conducted a study to learn more about the distance offenders travelled from their home to commit violent crime. Specifically, they examined homicide and rape offenses in Finland from the years 1992 to 2000. Measuring the distance between home and crime site, the homicide sample range included distances of 0 to 193.5 kilometers (approximately 121 miles). Nearly all offenses occurred close to home: within less than 5 kilometers (approximately 3.1 miles). There were some outliers, however, which is evidenced by a kurtosis value of 11.73. Since this value is positive, this indicates that most data are clustered around a middle point. As a result, the distribution of the distance between the home of the offender and the victim body location in homicide cases can be described as leptokurtic. The data for rapes were similar, though less kurtotic. Distances ranged from 0.32 to 283.98 kilometers (approximately 0.2 to 177 miles). Like homicides, most occurred close to home, and the majority of the data points were clustered around a middle point. This is evidenced by a kurtosis value of 6.41. As a result, the distribution of the distance between the home of the offender and the point of encounter in rape cases can also be described as leptokurtic.

As a measure of variability and dispersion, the kurtosis value has several advantages:

1. Describes all data with one value

2. Utilizes information from all data

3. Is easy to interpret

The same strengths found in the use of skewness to describe the shape of a distribution can be found in the use of kurtosis. The value of kurtosis is a numerical indicator of the distribution's peakedness or "flat-toppedness," as Pearson would describe it. To calculate this value, information from each case is utilized. This information includes the individual data values, the mean, and the standard deviation—values we continue to see incorporated into more complex calculations. The kurtosis value of a distribution is quite easy to interpret. If the value is positive, the distribution—relative to the magnitude of the value—is leptokurtic. If the value is negative, the distribution is relatively playtkurtic. Values close to or equal to 0 indicate normality, or a distribution that is mesokurtic—though this may depend on the formula used for standardization.

The kurtosis value also has several disadvantages, or weaknesses, that may limit its use as the primary statistic for variability and dispersion description:

1. Requires continuous data

2. Is prone to fluctuation due to sampling

3. Is highly dependent on sample size

4. Can describe multiple distributions

Like their strengths, skewness and kurtosis share many of the same weaknesses. As a descriptive statistic of variability and dispersion, measuring kurtosis also requires the use of continuous data. Thus, only data measured at the interval and ratio levels can have kurtosis calculated. Like skewness, variants of the kurtosis formula account for the sample size in their calculation. Similar to most descriptive measures, kurtosis can be impacted significantly due to sampling. Different samples may yield drastically different distributions. Related, the kurtosis value is highly dependent on sample size and may not accurately reflect the true kurtosis value when a small sample is used. Kurtosis values can be calculated for distributions of many different shapes. The value itself, however, cannot describe or allude to what that shape is. As a result, kurtosis is most appropriately calculated for comparison of, and to, normal distributions.

Measure of Variability and Dispersion	Level of Measurement	Describes
Variation Ratio	Nominal	Difference
Index of Qualitative Variation	Nominal, Ordinal	Difference
Range	Interval, Ratio	Distance
Quartiles	Interval, Ratio	Location
Deviation	Interval, Ratio	Distance
Variance	Interval, Ratio	Cumulative Distance
Standard Deviation	Interval, Ratio	Distance
Skewness	Interval, Ratio	Symmetry
Kurtosis	Interval, Ratio	Peakedness

Figure 5.26 Measures of Variability and Dispersion Summary

SUMMARY

Each measure of variability and dispersion has different assumptions, requires different data, and describes something different. The use of these measures can be highly informative of the difference of individual values and the overall spread of an entire dataset. Knowing when to use each measure requires knowledge of the variables' level of measurement, whether or not the data are normally distributed, and the purpose of the analysis.

For categorical data, the options are rather limited. The VR and the IQV provide some insight into the differences between variable values in a dataset. The former describes the difference of values from the mode, presented in the form of a proportion or a percentage. The latter describes the relative difference of observed values to all possible values of a categorical variable, also presented in the form of a proportion or a percentage. This allows for some ease in interpretation. However, beyond these values, there are few opportunities for variability and dispersion calculation and description. Conversely, continuous data have several ways to measure variability and dispersion.

Continuous data are often analyzed using multiple measures of variability and dispersion. The most simplistic measure, the range, provides an overview of a variable values' bounds, e.g., how spread out the data are overall. For more in-depth description, quartiles can provide the location of specific values by sequentially dividing the data into fourths. This can help in describing where a specific amount (e.g., 25%) of the data lie within the range of values. Perhaps most commonly used, regardless of field or discipline, is the standard deviation. This value provides a measure of spread relative to the distribution's mean. Once the spread of the data is examined, the shape of the distribution can be analyzed using the measures of skewness and kurtosis. These provide, respectively, a measure of asymmetry and peakedness. Taken together, these provide measures of how normally distributed data are. As referenced in Chapter 4, the measure of central tendency that is most appropriate to use for description depends on the distribution's shape. Most often, all three are reported, but when the data are significantly skewed, the median is most appropriate to use. As evidenced here, each descriptive measure can impact the calculation and/or use of another. In order to accurately calculate and interpret measures of variability and dispersion, accurate measures of central tendency much be calculated beforehand.

CHAPTER REVIEW QUESTIONS

1. Explain how a box plot would be created with the hypothetical citizen complaint data. What values would be needed?

2. Explain which measures of variability and dispersion require knowledge of measures of central tendency.

3. Discuss the level of measurement requirements for each measure of variability and dispersion.

4. Which measure of variability and dispersion for categorical variables would you use as a researcher? Explain your position.

5. Which characteristic of a distribution would you find more important as a researcher, its normality or its number of cases? Explain your position.

CHAPTER REVIEW EXERCISES

1. Visit the National Registry of Exonerations website:
https://www.law.umich.edu/special/exoneration/Pages/about.aspx
Select *Using the Registry* and then select *Detailed View*. Based on the variables provided, explain which could be described with a measure of variability and dispersion. Explain which measure is appropriate for which variable and what characteristics of the variable make that so.

2. Covertly observe your class, and identify a measurable variable you can see. Document the values of that variable and calculate an appropriate measure of variability and dispersion. Explain the results.

3. Visit the United Nations Office of Drugs and Crime website: www.unodc.org In the search bar, search the phrase "*International Statistics*". The first result is the report of the International Statistics on Crime and Justice. Which measure of variability and dispersion is discussed in the report? Explain what it is describing.

4. Are there any criminal justice or criminological research questions for which all the measures of variability and dispersion would be desired? Develop a research question and explain the data needed, how the data would be collected, and why the VR, IQV, IQR, range, and standard deviation of particular variables would be of interest.

5. Using your institution's library resources, find a peer-reviewed journal article that is of interest to you that reports on at least one of the measures of variability and dispersion. Discuss the article, the measure(s) of variability and dispersion, and the appropriateness of its use.

REFERENCES

Agresti, A., & Agresti, B.F. (2003). Statistical analysis of qualitative variation. In K. F. Schuessler (Ed). *Sociological methodology* (pp. 204–237). San Francisco, CA: Jossey-Bass.

Beattie, R.H. (1959). Sources of statistics on crime and correction. *Journal of the American Statistical Association, 54*(287), 582–592.

Bernasco, W., & Luykx, F. (2003). Effects of attractiveness, opportunity and accessibility to burglars on residential burglary rates of urban neighborhoods. *Criminology, 41*(3), 981–1002.

Bowley, A.L. (1897). Relations between the accuracy of an average and that of its constituent parts. *Journal of the Royal Statistical Society*, 60, 855–866.

Choi, K. (2008). Computer crime victimization and integrated theory: An empirical assessment. *International Journal of Cyber Criminology, 2*(1), 308–333.

Curren, P.J., West, S.G., & Finch, J.F. (1996). The robustness of test statistics to nonnormality and specification error in confirmatory factor analysis. *Psychological Methods, 1*(1), 16–29.

David, H.A. (1995). First (?) occurrences of common terms in mathematical statistics. *The American Statistician, 49*(2), 121–133.

DeFina, R.H., & Arvanites, T.M. (2002). The weak effect of imprisonment on crime: 1971–1998. *Social Science Quarterly, 83*(3), 635–653.

Doane, D.P., & Seward, L.E. (2011). Measuring skewness: A forgotten statistics? *Journal of Statistics Education, 19*(2). Retrieved from http://ww2.amstat. org/publications/jse/v19n2/doane.pdf

Gorroochurn, P. (2016). *Classic topics on the history of modern mathematical statistics: From Laplace to more recent times.* Hoboken, NJ: John Wiley & Sons, Inc.

Gravetter, F. & Wallnau, L. (2014). *Essentials of statistics for the behavioral sciences (8th Ed.).* Belmont, CA: Wadsworth.

Edgeworth, F.Y. (1892). Correlated Averages, *Philosophical Magazine, 5*(34), 190–204.

Fisher, R.A. (1918). The correction between relatives on the supposition of Mendelian inheritance. *Transactions of the Royal Society of Edinburgh, 52,* 399–423.

Galton, F. (1907). Grades and Deviates. *Biometrika, 5,* 400–406.

Harris, P. M. (2011). The first-time adult-onset offender: Findings from a community corrections cohort. *International Journal of Offender Therapy and Comparative Criminology, 55*(6), 949–981.

Kader, G.D., & Perry, M. (2007). Variability for categorical variables. *Journal of Statistics Education, 15*(2). Retrieved from http://www.amstat.org/publications/jse/v15n2/kader.html

Lexis, W. (1877). *Zur Theorie der Massenerscheinungen in der menschlichen Gesellschaft.* Freiburg, Germany: Wagner.

Lloyd, H. (1848). On certain questions connected with the reduction of magnetical and meteorological observations. *Proceedings of the Royal Irish Academy, 8,* 180–183.

Lombroso, C. (1876). *L'uomo delinquente.* Milan, Italy: Hoepli.

Messner, S.F., Anselin, L., Baller, R.D., Hawkins, D.F., Deane, G., & Tolnay, S.E. (1999). The spatial patterning of county homicide rates: An application of exploratory spatial data analysis. *Journal of Quantitative Criminology, 15*(4), 423–450.

Mueller, J.H., & Schuessler, K.F. (1961). *Statistical reasoning in sociology.* Boston, MA: Houghton Mifflin.

Osborne, J. W. (2012). *Best practices in data cleaning: A complete Guide to everything you need to do before and after collecting your data*. Thousand Oaks, CA: Sage Publications.

Pearson, K. (1893). Contributions to the mathematical theory of evolution. *Philosophical Transactions of the Royal Society of London Series A, 185*, 71–110.

Pearson, K. (1895). Skew variation in homogenous material. *Philosophical Transactions of the Royal Society of London Series A, 186*, 343–414.

Pearson, K. (1905). Das Fehlergestz und seine Verallgemeinerungen durch Fechner und Pearson. A Rejoinder. *Biometrika, 4*, 169–212.

Perry, M. & Kader, G.D. (2005). Variation as unlikeability. *Teaching Statistics, 27*(2), 58–60.

Santtila, P., Laukkanen, M., & Zappalà, A. (2007). Crime behaviours and distances travelled in homicides and rapes. *Journal of Investigative Psychology and Offender Profiling, 4*, 1–15.

Stigler, S.M. (1986). *The history of statistics: The measurement of uncertainty before 1900*. Cambridge, MA: Harvard University Press.

Tabor, J. (2010). Investigation the investigative task: Testing for skewness: An investigation of different test statistics and their power to detect skewness. *Journal of Statistics Education, 18*(2). Retrieved from http://ww2.amstat.org/publications/jse/v19n2/doane.pdf

Toomey, T.L, Erickson, D.J., Carlin, B.P, Lenk, K.M., Quick, H.S., Jones, A.M., & Harwood, E.M. (2012). The association between density of alcohol establishments and violent crime within urban neighborhoods. *Alcoholism: Clinical and Experimental Research, 36*(8), 1468–1473.

Trochim, W.M., & Donnelly, J.P. (2006). *The research methods knowledge base (3rd Ed.)*. Cincinnati, OH: Atomic Dog Publishing.

Truman, J.L., & Morgan, R.E. (2016). *Criminal victimization, 2015*. NCJ 250180. Washington, D.C.: Bureau of Justice Statistics.

Wilcox, A.R. (1973). Indices of qualitative variation and political measurement. *The Western Political Quarterly, 26*(2), 325–343.

Weisberg, H.F. (2004). Variation ratio. In Lewis-Beck, M., Bryman, A.E., & Liao, T.F. (Eds), *The SAGE Encyclopedia of Social Science Research Methods, Volume 3* (p. 1178). Thousand Oaks, CA: SAGE Publications, Inc.

Yule, G.U. (1911). *An introduction to the theory of statistics*. London, UK: Charles Griffin and Company, Limited.

IMAGE CREDIT

SECTION III

INFERENTIAL STATISTICS

This section provides a general discussion of the purpose of moving from statistical description to statistical inference and how sample statistics can be used in the estimation of population parameters. The section will build upon the previous section, explaining the utility of descriptive statistics and their importance in inferential statistics, and provide you with practical examples at each step. Each chapter herein explains, with the use of examples and practical application, the components, uses, and most appropriate times to use particular statistical tests and inferential statistics.

TESTS OF EQUALITY

INTRODUCTION: WHAT'S THE DIFFERENCE?

Lunden (1942) suggests that homicide is a mature man's crime, and auto theft is a young man's offense. The Uniform Crime Reports indicate that in the United States younger and older men tend to be drawn [differently] toward the commission of crimes as indicated ... These differences, though probably reliable, have not yet been shown in the literature to be statistically significant. (Fox, 1946, p. 143)

Dr. Fox asserted, more than 70 years ago, that although official data indicated patterns or trends in criminal activity, those patterns or trends were not yet confirmed. While he indicated that the differences observed in age by offense type may be "reliable," they had not been shown to be "statistically significant." In saying this, Dr. Fox is noting that, although the data may show descriptive differences, they have not been empirically tested for differences that represent patterns or trends observed in the population. The patterns or trends might *look* different, but there are various ways to analyze data to see if data from groups are *statistically significant* in their differences. For example, as we learned in Chapters 4 and 5, there are several descriptive statistics we can calculate from various data. Lunden (1942), for example, had done this for age based on offense type. However, these descriptive statistics from each group were not analyzed further. What might look different in a sample might not be different in a population, and what may be different in a population might not be different in a sample. Consider the following questions:

1.   Does the average length of time to recidivism differ based on offense type?

2.   Does delinquency occur at the same rate between male and female youth?

3.   Are there racial differences in the number of crimes individuals commit?

The processes needed to answer each of these questions involve the statistical comparison of at least two groups. This comparison requires the same descriptive statistics learned in the previous chapters. In Chapter 4, we learned to calculate measures of central tendency, and in Chapter 5, we learned to calculate measures of variability and dispersion. These measures take information from all cases in a dataset to create a single, representative value of a variable in that dataset. However, like the questions above allude to, it is often important to consider differences within the dataset, as values of a variable may differ across individuals, groups, places, etc. Groups within a single dataset may be compared, groups within a single dataset may be compared across multiple time periods, and entire datasets may be compared by analyzing their respective descriptive statistics to see if the groups under study are statistically different or, more appropriately, if there is enough evidence to say they are not equal. In doing so, findings from a sample can be generalized to a population. This chapter examines the histories, calculations, and uses of various tests of equality.

LEARNING OBJECTIVES

By the end of this chapter, students will be able to:

1: Identify the most common tests of equality

2: Discuss the level of measurement requirements of each test of equality

3: Explain the difference between alpha and p-values

4: Evaluate the reciprocity of Type I and Type II errors

5: Assess the advantages and limitations of statistical significance

KEY TERMS

ALPHA VALUE

DEGREES OF FREEDOM

LEVEL OF CONFIDENCE

LEVEL OF SIGNIFICANCE

NULL HYPOTHESIS

P VALUE

RESEARCH HYPOTHESIS

SIGNIFICANCE

TYPE I ERROR

TYPE II ERROR

STATISTICAL SIGNIFICANCE

To understand the nature of tests of equality, we need only revisit the preceding chapters. Many of the assumptions inherent in many contemporary data analysis techniques can also be found in the practice of research. The primary assumption, particularly in the context of descriptive statistics, is that cases were selected and data were obtained from a sample—not the population. As a result, if/when inferences are to be made, they are made relating the calculated sample statistics to the hypothesized (or expected) population parameters. When data are analyzed to make inferences, values observed in a sample are analyzed and "tested" to make conclusions about those findings with respect to the population. Data from a sample are used to estimate what would be found in the population. Results from small-scale studies

SIGNIFICANCE:
In data analysis, the condition that the results of a statistical test are unlikely to be the result of chance or error.

can be examined and extrapolated to describe the population at large. When results, like the "reliable" differences in Fox's quote, appear to show patterns in a sample, data analysis techniques can determine if these patterns would also be observed in the greater population. This would indicate the patterns in the data are *real*. When patterns, such as differences, associations, relationships, effects, etc. are found in sample data and are statistically inferred to be present in the population—with a high degree of likelihood and certainty—we refer to these results as *significant*. This likelihood, or chance, is a fundamental element in determining and reporting statistical significance.

SIGNIFICANCE

The concept of statistical significance, like many other data analysis concepts, is one that predates its practical development. In fact, its conceptual development began more than 200 years before statisticians developed the formulae to test it. In a 1710 paper, Scottish physician and mathematician John Arbuthnot discussed the sex ratio (the split of males and females born or "christened") as being—save for a small chance—constant. While not statistically sophisticated, he notes, by showing 22 years of data, that the number of born males is greater than the number of born females. More than 50 years later, Reverend John Michell (1767) calculated the probability, or chance, that the stars he was observing—the Pleiades—were clustering due to chance as 1 in 500,000. His calculations found there was little to no difference in the distance between stars of the cluster when measured repeatedly, indicating their location was relatively fixed—perhaps the result of gravity. Subsequent tests would be conducted for similar purposes, including those by Laplace (1823) on barometric changes and moon phases, and Pearson (1900) on the calculation of errors that can occur as a result of sampling.

However, the foundation of the concept and application of tests of significance as it relates to the majority of data analysis in criminal justice and criminology lies elsewhere. Francis Y. Edgeworth (1885) contributed a paper that was relatively ignored in the statistics community, perhaps as a result of his temperament (Aldrich, 2010). In this paper, Edgeworth focused on methodology and how a comparison of means can be conducted and interpreted to determine statistical significance. He presented the position that one of the main problems with the "science of means" was "to find how far the difference between any proposed Mean is accidental" (1885, p. 182). In essence, he suggests a fundamental issue in statistics lies in the ability to determine if a difference of means between groups is the result of chance, e.g., a result of sampling, or is accurate and can be found in the larger population. But, perhaps his most important contributions to the field of statistics by way of statistical significance lie in his written correspondence to and with Karl Pearson and Francis Galton. It was through these remote interactions, specifically those with Pearson, that led to the development of some of the statistical significance concepts, assumptions, and criteria we use today.

HYPOTHESIS TESTING AND SIGNIFICANCE

When analyzing data, the determination that findings are significant is often directly related to the hypotheses of the study. Hypotheses have been tested, statistically, since at least the 13th century (Stigler, 1999). Recall that a hypothesis is a statement that clarifies and explicitly describes what the researcher expects to find. In criminal justice and criminological data analysis, there are two approaches used to test for significance that involve, and require, hypotheses (Huberty, 1993). These are sometimes referred to as the Fisher significance testing approach (or the p-value approach) and the Neyman-Pearson hypothesis testing approach (or the fixed-alpha approach). They are quite similar to one another and need not be differentiated, as the steps involved are nearly identical. The first step in both of these approaches is the statement of hypotheses. First, the null hypothesis is stated. The null hypothesis is formulated based on what statistical test is being conducted. Even tests of the same kind, such as those described in this chapter, will have different null hypotheses based on the assumptions of the test, the type of data, and—like most tests—the variables under study.

Generally, in tests of equality, the null hypothesis states that the groups under study are equal or any observed difference is the result of chance. Researchers begin with the assumption of equality. Statistical tests, then, offer the possibility of empirical proof to refute that assumption. This possibility is often explicitly stated in the form of a research, or alternative, hypothesis. This type of hypothesis specifies what the researcher expects to find, according to theory or prior studies (recall the research cycle in Chapter 2). In tests of equality, the research hypothesis states that the groups under study are not equal, with respect to the descriptive statistic under study. When presented, the null hypothesis is denoted by the symbol H_0, and the research hypothesis is denoted by the symbol H_1. In studies with multiple research hypotheses, the subscript number will increase, e.g., H_1 to H_2 and so forth. For research hypotheses with related predictions, the subscript number will not change, and a letter will be added, e.g., H_{1a} and H_{1b}.

CRITERIA FOR SIGNIFICANCE

Statistical significance is the result of comparing results to predetermined, and perhaps somewhat arbitrary, criteria. These criteria can be traced numerically back to the early works of Pearson (1900) and conceptually all the way back to the 17th century (David, 1962, as discussed in Cowles & Davis, 1982). However, for tests of equality, R.A. Fisher (1925) led the way in suggesting that a specific threshold should exist. In his early textbook *Statistical Methods for Research Workers*, Fisher noted Pearson's (1900) work on the chi-square test, which does not assume the data are normally distributed (We'll learn about chi-square tests of association in Chapter 7 and chi-square tests of inequality

NULL HYPOTHESIS:
In data analysis, a hypothesis that states no significant findings are expected and that any observed findings are the result of chance, e.g., sampling error.

RESEARCH HYPOTHESIS:
In data analysis, a hypothesis that states expectations of a study and that any observed findings are real and not the result of chance, e.g., sampling error.

P VALUE:
In data analysis, this value represents the probability that the null hypothesis is true, that the observed results could occur by chance alone.

Box 6.1: WHAT WE'VE LEARNED: Hypotheses Testing and Significance

In a recent article by Lee, Eck, and Corsaro (2016), the researchers sought to synthesize a body of research spanning more than 40 years to clarify the relationship between the size of a police force and crime. The authors conducted a systematic review in which they covered results from 62 studies, published between 1971 and 2013. From these studies, a total of 229 findings related to police force size and crime were found. The researchers' null hypothesis in this study was for "nonsignificant findings" (p. 439). This means that the assumption before the study was that there was no significant relationship between police force size and crime. Thus, the assumption of equality suggests that changes in police force size have no effect on crime. Alternatively, the research hypothesis would suggest that changes in police size do affect crime. The researchers derived their specific research hypothesis, in part, from Becker (1968), who suggested that increasing police force size reduces crime. Of the 62 studies, individually, about half (32) found statistically significant support for this hypothesis, while the other half (30) did not. Lee et al. reviewed all 62 studies together to conduct a single test of significance. Ultimately, they found no support for the research hypothesis, concluding that "the overall effect size of police force size is negative, small, and statistically not significant" (p. 445).

---

in this chapter). Regardless of the type of chi-square test, a non-normal (the chi-square) distribution is used to determine significance. He notes, that "it is a convenient convention to take ... the corresponding limit P = 0.05" (p. 113). This value has also become more conservative in some disciplines (P = 0.01 or P = 0.001). Fisher's textbook may be perhaps the most influential textbook in statistics. Dozens of introductory and graduate-level textbooks, in addition to an innumerable number of dissertations, research reports, journal articles, and books, utilize the "convenient convention" Fisher mentions (Huberty, 1993). It is unlikely that those using a P = 0.05 even know *why* they do so.

The convention Fisher noted is a traditional threshold that has since been referred to as the *p* value. This value has been computed numerous ways since the 18th century and was first described as the *p* value by Deming (1943). It represents *"the probability of the observed result, plus more extreme results, if the null hypothesis were true"* (Goodman, 2008). With respect to hypothesis testing, the *p* value has come to be understood, albeit not entirely accurately, as the probability that the null hypothesis is true; that alternative findings would be the result of chance, e.g., out of 100 studies, the results would happen 5 times as the result of sampling (error), if Fisher's value was used.

Since Fisher's (1925) text, nearly all criminal justice and criminological research has used the threshold of P = 0.05. In fact, this by itself may be an issue as the question arises, "What if P is exactly 0.05?" As a result, the threshold has come to be slightly more conservative, P < 0.05. When results are tested for their significance and the p value is less than 0.05, the results suggest significant findings. In the present context, a p value less than 0.05 would suggest that the groups under study are not equal. If the p value is greater than or equal to 0.05, the results suggest findings that are not significant. In the present context, a p value greater than or equal to 0.05 would suggest that the groups are equal. These are often referred to as null findings, as they result in support for the null hypothesis. In significance tests, precise p values are calculated.

Due to these assumptions, the use of, and ubiquitous adherence to, the threshold value of 0.05 represents an important facet of hypothesis testing and the determination of "significance." The predetermined value, whether it be 0.05 or the more stringent value of 0.01, represents what is called the alpha value. The alpha value is typically chosen before research has begun—or at least before the analysis stage of a study. The alpha value is also referred to as the level of significance. This value provides the threshold by which a decision can be made when reporting results: are there significant findings or not? The complement to the level of significance is the level of confidence. When the level of significance is 0.05, the level of confidence will be 0.95. When the level of significance is 0.01, the level of confidence will be 0.99 (However, they are often interpreted as percentages). As probabilities, the levels of significance and confidence must sum to 1.0 (like proportions in Chapter 3). When statistical significance is found, based on the calculation of the p value and its comparison to the predetermined alpha value, the level of confidence refers to the probability that the results found are not the result of chance and would also be found in the population. In the context of this chapter, the level of confidence represents the percentage to which the researcher is confident that an observed difference is *true* and found in the population.

TYPE I ERROR

The alpha value also represents the allowable probability of committing a Type I error. A Type I error is made when significant results are found and the null hypothesis is rejected in favor of the alternative hypothesis, but incorrectly. When the alpha value is determined to be 0.05, for example, the researcher is allowing for a probability of 0.05, or a 5% chance, of incorrectly rejecting the null hypothesis based on the results of the study. In the case of a test of equality, there would be a 5% chance of finding significant differences of a statistic between groups when, in fact, there are not. In addition, since the alpha value represents only a threshold used to determine statistical significance, the specific p value is likely to be different. If the p value is found to be 0.03, for example, the actual probability of committing a Type I error is 3%. In cases in which there were not

ALPHA VALUE:
In data analysis, this value represents the probabilistic threshold that the observed results could occur by chance alone, by which the determination of statistical significance is made. The probability of making a Type I error.

LEVEL OF SIGNIFICANCE:
In data analysis, analogous to the alpha value, the probability that the observed results could occur by chance alone, by which the determination of statistical significance is made.

LEVEL OF CONFIDENCE:
In data analysis, as the complement to the level of significance, the probability that the observed results in a test of significance are not the result of chance and are represented in the population.

TYPE I ERROR:
This type of error occurs when a researcher rejects the null hypothesis when, in fact, it is true. Results suggest statistical significance exists when it really does not: a false positive.

significant findings, the p value would represent a high chance of Type I error, e.g., if $p = 0.28$, the probability of committing a Type I error is 28%.

TYPE II ERROR

Type II error, then, involves the opposite circumstance. This type of error is made when results are not found to be significant, and the null hypothesis is supported incorrectly. In a test of equality, this would occur if the results suggested that the groups under study are equal when, in fact, they are not. The most common way to limit the occurrence of a Type II error is to increase the sample size. By providing more cases, two things happen. First, as you will see in subsequent formulae, the increase in n will be quite influential, particularly in the various tests of significance. Second, and perhaps substantively clearer, an increase in the sample size inherently brings the number of cases being studied closer to the total number of cases in the population. Thus, it can be assumed that a larger sample will more closely resemble, and be representative of, the population. As a result, greater confidence in the findings may be had when larger samples are utilized.

Decision	Null Hypothesis is True	Null Hypothesis is not True
Reject Null Hypothesis	Type I Error	Correct Decision (no error)
Accept Null Hypothesis	Correct Decision (No Error)	Type II Error

Figure 6.1 Decision and Error Chart

INTERPRETING ALPHA, *P*, AND ERROR TYPE

The discussion of alpha, p, and the two types of errors can seem very abstract. Even the most educated and experienced researchers differ on their understanding, interpretation, and even use of these concepts (Goodman, 2008). To further clarify their meanings, refer back to the initial chapters. For example, in Chapter 2, we discussed the cyclical nature of research. Fisher (1925), himself, noted that the conventional alpha value (0.05) is determined for, and the p values are calculated from, experiments conducted with sample data. Thus, they would not be needed if population data were used in a study, because there would be no need for inferential tests, e.g., generalizations, since *all* the data are available.

Fisher (1925) was suggesting that the p value, while providing a probability to be used in hypothesis testing, should impact future research. Fisher's contention was that statistically significant findings of one "experiment" are not definitive. Research should build upon itself through additional studies for a greater degree of certainty in findings, a perspective clearly embodying the research cycle. As such, he later stated that "scientific fact should be regarded as experimentally established only if a properly designed experiment rarely fails to give (this level of) significance" (1026, p. 504). What Fisher is saying is that the 0.05 alpha value is a starting point for future research. Only with repeated studies, and those that find similar and statistically significant results, can results be treated as "fact." Thus, while some may explain the p value in the context of being *right*, Fisher's stance may have been more focused on the prospect of being *wrong*.

Fisher (1926) stated that the P = 0.05 value was one of "preference" and that it was a rather "low" standard, while suggesting that the line could be drawn at any value, such as 0.02 or 0.01 (p. 504). Others, such as Kendall and Yule (1950) suggest that the determination is "a matter of personal taste" (p. 472). Thus, the alpha value—the allowable probability of Type I error—is one of choice. It is somewhat arbitrary (Huberty, 1993). When testing hypotheses by conducting inferential tests, the researcher often weighs the subject under study and the impact of a Type I error to determine what alpha value will be used.

Type I error in criminal justice and criminology research may have relatively minor (negative) consequences. For example, if research found a treatment program to have a significant effect on inmates who participated, the treatment program would have empirical support for its continuation. If, in fact, there was not a significant effect, this would ultimately prove to be of little consequence (unless the program produced a negative outcome). However, in other fields, this may have more dire consequences. For example, if research found an experimental drug had a significant effect on patients who used it as part of their treatment, the drug would have empirical support for its continuation as well. But, these "false positives" could result in patients continuing to take a medicine in place of one that *is* effective that has no effect on their treatment. Similar considerations can be made for a Type II error, in which a treatment may be effective, but research does not find significant results. Here, it is unlikely inmates would have the opportunity to continue a positively impactful program and patients would not be provided a treatment that does, in fact, help.

CATEGORICAL VARIABLES

Much like the measures of central tendency (Chapter 3) and measures of variability and dispersion (Chapter 4), there are specific tests of equality available to variables that are categorical and continuous. Furthermore, there are specific tests within those groups. There are tests of equality for nominal data, tests for ordinal data, and tests that may be conducted on both levels of measurement. Since the data are categorical, each test operates—at minimum—with the same assumptions of the level of measurement being analyzed. Nominal data are categorical groups that are mutually exclusive, exhaustive, and without an ascending or descending hierarchy. There is no "order." That additional element of categorical data is represented in ordinal level data.

DIFFERENCE OF PROPORTIONS TEST

One of the most common tests of equality, as found in nearly all criminal justice and criminology statistics textbooks, is the difference of proportions test. This test examines a characteristic of two groups to determine if their respective proportions are significantly different. Alternatively, the test can be described with percentages. The difference of proportions tests can determine if the percentages of two groups with a given characteristic are significantly different. For example, a difference of proportions can be used to help answer Question #2 provided in the Introduction to this chapter: *Does juvenile delinquency occur at the same rate between male and female youth?* This question can be answered differently depending on operationalization. If juvenile delinquency is measured as a proportion (or percentage), a difference of proportions test can be used. The following formulae are used in determining if there is a significant difference of proportions between two groups:

$$z = \frac{P_1 - P_2}{S_{p1-p2}}$$

$$S_{p1-p2} = \sqrt{P^*(1-P^*)\left(\frac{N_1 + N_2}{N_1 N_2}\right)}$$

$$P^* = \frac{N_1 P_1 + N_2 P_2}{N_1 + N_2}$$

Figure 6.2 Difference of Proportions Equations

where N_1 = the size of group one
   N_2 = the size of group two
   P_1 = the proportion of group one
   P_2 = the proportion of group two.

Box 6.2: Example of Difference of Proportions Test

Recall the examples from Chapters 4 and 5. Suppose you were to continue your examination of officer complaints for a local police department. In addition to the data collected previously, you also asked questions to obtain demographic information and information concerning the officers' educational background. From these questions, you found that of the 23 officers, 17 were male and 6 were female. With respect to their educational background, 12 males earned a college degree, while all 6 females did. Thus, the proportion of male officers with a college degree is approximately 0.71, and the same proportion for female officers is 1.0.

Is the proportion of officers with a college degree significantly different between males and females? Using the various formulae, you ultimately should arrive at a z value of approximately −1.52 (see equation below)

$$z = \frac{P_1 - P_2}{S_{p1-p2}} \qquad P^* = \frac{17(.71) + 6(1.0)}{17 + 6} = .79$$

$$S_{p1-p2} = \sqrt{P^*(1-P^*)\left(\frac{N_1 + N_2}{N_1 N_2}\right)} \qquad S_{p1-p2} = \sqrt{.79(1-.79)\left(\frac{17+6}{(17)(6)}\right)} = .19$$

$$P^* = \frac{N_1 P_1 + N_2 P_2}{N_1 + N_2} \qquad z = \frac{-.29}{.19} = -1.52$$

Figure 6.3 Difference of Proportions Example

In Box 6.2: Example of Difference of Proportions Test, we were looking to compare the educational attainment of male and female officers in a local department. Using the proportions of 0.71 and 1.0, respectively, and the formulae required, we calculated a z value of -1.52. By itself, this will not tell us if the difference of proportions is statistically significant. It must be compared to a "critical" z value that corresponds to the predetermined alpha value: the threshold at which we determine statistical significance.

Since criminal justice and criminology research utilizes the alpha value of 0.05 most frequently, the corresponding critical z value is 1.96. The critical z value will never change, assuming a consistent level of significance. If a researcher conducts test of equality using an alpha value of 0.05, the critical z value will always be 1.96. If s/he uses an alpha value of 0.01, the critical z value will always be 2.58. The values can be viewed in terms of their absolute value. Both positive and negative values are treated and interpreted the same way.

In our example, we calculated a z value of –1.52. Comparing the absolute value (1.52) to the critical z value of 1.96, we see our value is *smaller*—or, closer to 0. One way to view this, albeit not entirely conceptually and statistically accurate, is to consider values closer to 0 as representing proportions that are closer in value—or, similar proportions of few cases. For example, if the proportion of male officers increased to 0.88 (15 of male 17 officers earned a degree), the z value we would calculate would be approximately –0.89. This value is closer to 0 than that of our example and statistically indicates what we can see: 0.88 is closer to 1.0 than 0.71 is to 1.0. Also, the number of cases is important. If the local police department had the same proportions found in Box: 6.2 Example of Difference of Proportions Test, but had twice as many officers, the z value would be approximately –2.12, an absolute value *larger* than the critical z value of 1.96. Thus, in our example with 17 male and 6 female officers with their respective proportions, we do not have: 1) a large enough difference between our groups and/or 2) enough cases to say the proportion of officers with a college degree is significantly different between males and females.

Steps

1. Calculate descriptive statistics
2. Calculate standard error
3. Calculate the test statistic
4. If needed, determine degrees of freedom
5. Compare test statistic with critical value

Figure 6.4 General Steps to Testing Hypotheses

Box 6.3: WHAT WE'VE LEARNED: Difference of Proportions Test

A recent study conducted by Dixon and Williams (2015) sought to quantify the representation of race and crime on network and cable news, as well as to empirically test to see if what is reported through that medium is significantly different than what occurs in society. The authors state that misrepresentation of racial and ethnic groups in televised media can impact public perception by way of creating or reinforcing bias, and it may also affect public policy. This may be of particular interest today with "racialized" issues, such as those related to immigration and, albeit mistakenly, religious fanaticism and terrorism (p. 35). To see if a significant difference existed between the representation of various racial/ethnic groups and their respective representations in official statistics, Dixon and Williams conducted difference of proportions tests. The first test examining the difference in representation of all violent perpetrators found there was no difference for white perpetrators, significantly less representation for black perpetrators, and significantly more representation for all other races and ethnicities. The second test examining the difference in representation of homicide victims found greater representation of white victims (though this was *just* non-significant), significantly less representation of black victims, and significantly more representations of all other races and ethnicities. Additional tests found Latino immigrant suspects are significantly overrepresented in the news, while non-Latino immigrant suspects are significantly underrepresented. The same pattern was present for undocumented immigrants and Muslim terror suspects, who are significantly overrepresented in the news, while non-Muslim terror suspects are significantly underrepresented.

MCNEMAR TEST

Named after its creator, Quinn McNemar (1947), the McNemar test is a test of equality that is often used to examine differences in characteristics over time. This is common in studies with pre- and post-test experimental designs. There are several restrictions, however. First, the test can only be applied to data that can be arranged in a two by two cross-tab. Thus, the second restriction is that the single variable tested must have only two values. As a result of having only two values, the McNemar test does not assume the distribution of variable values is normal (it can not be). Thus, an alternative distribution—the chi-square distribution—is used to test for statistical significance. In order to calculate the McNemar test value, the following table and updated formula (Edwards, 1948) are used:

	"0" or "−"	"1" or "+"
"0" or "−"	A	B
"1" or "+"	C	D

$$\chi^2 = \frac{(B-C)^2}{B+C}$$

Figure 6.5 McNemar Equation

Box 6.4: Example of a McNemar Test

Let us conduct a McNemar test by continuing our example of the inquiry into citizen complaints against police officers. The police chief, upon seeing your initial results, asked you to learn more about the officers' perceptions of the incidents. You ask the officers, "*Knowing a complaint was filed, would you change how you handled the incident(s) in question?*" Of the 23 officers, 8 said "Yes" and the remaining 15 said "No." The chief decides to provide additional training for his staff on community relations and a refresher on department procedures. After the training, you ask the same officers the same question. You notice a difference in the data. Of the eight officers that said "Yes" initially, two changed their response to "No." None of the officers that said "No" initially changed their answer.

Is the division of answers significantly different after the additional training? Using the table and formula, you would ultimately arrive at a χ^2 value of 2.

	"0" or "−"	"1" or "+"
"0" or "−"	A	B
"1" or "+"	C	D

$$\chi^2 = \frac{(B-C)^2}{B+C}$$

	"0" or "−"	"1" or "+"
"0" or "−"	15	0
"1" or "+"	2	6

$$\chi^2 = \frac{(0-2)^2}{0+2} = 2$$

Figure 6.6 McNemar Example

In Box 6.4: Example of a McNemar Test, we were looking to compare the number of individuals that answered "Yes" or "No" on a survey question before and after additional training. Using the McNemar test table and formula, we found that there were six officers that said "Yes" both times, while two that said "Yes" initially said "No" the second time. There were zero officers that changed from their initial answer of "No." Based on these frequencies, we calculated an unadjusted χ^2 (chi-square) value of 2. Like the difference of proportions test, this value must be compared to a critical χ^2 value that corresponds to the predetermined alpha value. The critical χ^2 value, when tested at the 0.05 level of significance, is 3.84. When tested at the 0.01 level of significance, the critical value is 6.63. These values will always be the critical values when choosing an alpha value of 0.05 or 0.01, respectively, in a McNemar test. To say the answers were different before and after training, the value we calculated must exceed 3.84 (or 6.63). Clearly, the value of 2 does not. Thus, there was not a significant change in answers after the training was implemented.

Box 6.5: WHAT WE'VE LEARNED: McNemar Test

In 2014, researchers Uggen, Vuolo, Lageson, Ruhland, and Whitham examined the effects of low-level criminal records on employment. To do so, the researchers matched pairs of African-American and White men and sent them to apply for 300 entry-level jobs. In each pair, one member reported a disorderly conduct arrest that did not result in a criminal conviction. Thus, they were examining differences based on arrest records in each racial group, not differences based on race. White individuals that did not report an arrest received the highest rate of callbacks from the employers (38.8%), while White individuals that did report an arrest received the second highest rate of callbacks (34.7%). The pattern was similar for the African-American men, however with lower rates. For example, those that did not report an arrest were called back 27.5% of the time, while those that did report an arrest were called back 23.5% of the time (p. 637). The McNemar test examined if the callback rates between the experimental (arrest record) and control group (no arrest record) were equal or if the 4% difference was statistically significant. Ultimately, though the researchers stated a "modest but nontrivial" effect was found, the McNemar tests did not result in a significant finding (p. 627).

MANN-WHITNEY *U* TEST

A similar test of equality to the McNemar test is the Mann-Whitney *U* test. While also used for continuous data, this test is available to data that are measured at the ordinal level. The Mann-Whitney *U* test requires that there be only two groups for comparison. Unlike the McNemar test, however, the Mann-Whitney *U* test is used to compare two independent, e.g., different, groups. One of the test's assumptions is that the two groups differ with respect to the cases: cases in one group are not found in the other group. Thus, a comparison of groups such as in a pre- and post-test experimental design cannot be conducted with this test.

A form of this specific test was first put forth by Frank Wilcoxon (1945), a chemist who eventually became a very prominent statistician of the first half of the 20th century, developing several popular techniques of data analysis. Wilcoxon's test was refined shortly thereafter by mathematicians Henry Mann and Donald Whitney (1947). The 1947 paper has been described as one of the most widely cited papers in statistics and the test itself "the most widely used non-parametric statistic for two-sample tests" (Hern, 2013, p. 1). Practically, the test allows for the comparison of two groups with respect to their medians by ranking values when the data are not normally distributed: an assumption when the number of cases is <20. To do so, the following formulae may be used:

$$U_1 = n_1 n_2 + \frac{n_1(n_1 + 1)}{2} - R_1$$

$$U_2 = n_1 n_2 + \frac{n_2(n_2 + 1)}{2} - R_2$$

Figure 6.7 Mann Whitney U Equation

where R_1 = the sum of the ranks in sample 1
R_2 = the sum of the ranks in sample 2
n_1 = the number of cases in group 1
n_2 = the number of cases in group 2.

Box 6.6: Example of the Mann-Whitney *U* Test

Let us conduct a Mann-Whitney test by continuing our example of the inquiry of citizen complaints against police officers. You seek to test equality across sex. In your survey of the officers before their additional training, you asked, "*How much training do you receive on community relations?*" Available answers included "Not enough," "Somewhat adequate amount," "Adequate amount," "Somewhat excessive amount," and "Excessive amount." Let the first answer be labeled "1" and the final answer "5." The remaining answers are labeled accordingly. All answers are ranked (see table). These rankings are required to compare the median values between the two groups. The lowest *U* value, as well as a critical *U* value, is used to determine significance.

Case	Score	Rank
F #1	1	1
F #2	2	4
F #3	2	4
F #4	2	4
F #5	2	4
F #6	2	4
M #1	3	10.5
M #2	3	10.5
M #3	3	10.5
M #4	3	10.5
M #5	3	10.5
M #6	3	10.5
M #7	3	10.5
M #8	3	10.5
M #9	4	17.5
M #10	4	17.5
M #11	4	17.5
M #12	4	17.5
M #13	4	17.5
M #14	4	17.5
M #15	5	22
M #16	5	22
M #17	5	22

Figure 6.8 Mann Whitney U Example

Is the answer significantly different between males and females? Using the Mann-Whitney U test formula, you should have come up with a U_1 value of 102 and a U_2 value of 0. This is called complete separation, where there is no overlap or "ties" between the groups: the smallest U value is 0 and the largest U value is the product of the group size ($n_1 n_2$).

$$U_1 = 6(17) + \frac{6(6+1)}{2} - 21 = 102$$

$$U_2 = 6(17) + \frac{17(17+1)}{2} - 255 = 0$$

Figure 6.9 Mann Whitney U Example #2

In Box 6.6: Example of the Mann-Whitney U test, we were looking to compare ordinal-level answers to see if they were significantly different between male and female officers with respect to the median. Unlike the difference of proportions and McNemar tests, there is no consistent critical value used to determine significance. For the Mann-Whitney U test, like others we will soon learn, the critical value is based on n_1 and n_2—the number of cases in each group. When one group has 17 cases and the second group has 6 cases, such as in our hypothetical example, the critical value (with a corresponding 0.05 level of significance) is 22. Also unlike the previous tests, to be statistically significant, the U value must be less than the critical value. In our case, the lower U value of 0 provides evidence that the answers to the question, *"How much training do you receive on community relations?"* are significantly different between male and female officers.

Box 6.7: WHAT WE'VE LEARNED: Mann-Whitney U Test

Utilizing data from the Orange County Community Correction Department (OCCD) in Florida, Dr. Laurie Gould (2010) surveyed community correctional officers to see how gender might influence classification and supervision of offenders. Dr. Gould used the Mann-Whitney U test to see if there were differences for male and female offenders based on perceived risk. In her survey, she provided four scenarios to which the respondents would identify what their course of action would be for handling the situation. The responses availed to the community correctional officers varied with each scenario; however, all included options ranging from lower severity, e.g., a warning, to options of higher severity, e.g., filing for an arrest warrant. She hypothesized that the officers would recommend a more lenient course of action for female offenders than for male offenders. Her results found "that there were no statistically significant differences in the proposed course of action for male and female offenders" (p. 334), indicating that gender does not influence the supervision of offenders. Gould does note that some officer responses allude to a practice of taking needs into account when making a course of action decision. For example, a female offender is more likely to be a caregiver or need assistance, confounding the gender-decision relationship.

WILCOXON SIGNED-RANKS TEST

When the groups under study in a categorical test of equality are not independent from one another, like in a pre- and post-test experiment design, the Wilcoxon Signed-Ranks test can be used. This test was also put forth by Wilcoxon in his seminal 1945 paper. Future statisticians (see Siegel, 1956) developed alternative versions of this test, and those with minor improvements (see Pratt, 1959) account for some of its disadvantages. As an inferential test, the data are assumed to be selected randomly.

The Wilcoxon Signed-Rank test is based on the calculation of differences between paired cases, or their differences before and after some point in time, such as a treatment or other intervention. If the values of the variable are different from one time to the other, values of one would be consistently larger than the other. Values in either the before or after groups would have differences that are consistently positive or consistently negative. If the differences in values between groups were positive and negative, represented fairly evenly across the pairs, there would be no difference between groups. As a result, this test of equality uses both the direction (negative and positive) and the rank ordering of the differences to test for significance. To test the equality of a paired sample with ordinal data, the following formula can be used:

$$z = \frac{W_s - \frac{n(n+1)}{4}}{\sqrt{\frac{n(n+1)(2n+1)}{24}}}$$

Figure 6.10 Wilcoxon Signed Rank Test Equation

where n = the number of pairs with a non-zero difference
         w_s = the smaller absolute value of ranked sums.

The Wilcoxon Signed-Rank test, luckily, need not be calculated by hand. With the help of statistical software, the data can be (nearly instantly) analyzed to test equality. However, there are several considerations that must be made. Most importantly is what to do with "ties" when the differences in value rank equal 0. Different software programs have different default settings, so this example will use data without any ties for illustrative purposes.

Since this test of equality utilizes the z distribution, the same critical values we used in the difference of proportions test apply here as well. Thus, using data from Box 6.8, at neither the 0.05 or 0.01 levels of significance can we reject the null hypothesis that the answers changed. We cannot say the answers were significantly different before and after the officers' training. The officers' training did not significantly change their perceptions of their training with respect to community relations.

Box 6.8: Example of the Wilcoxon Signed-Rank Test

Using the data from Box 6.6: Example of the Mann-Whitney Test, the table in Figure 6.11 contains the answers and their respective ranks as provided by officers before their training session. In an effort to see if more training resulted in a difference of officer perception of their training, you asked the same question with the same available answers: "*How much training do you receive on community relations?*" Available answers included "Not enough," "Somewhat adequate amount," "Adequate amount," "Somewhat excessive amount," and "Excessive amount." The first answer was labeled "1" and the final answer "5." The remaining answers were labeled accordingly.

Case	Score #1	Score #2	|Difference|	Rank
F #1	1	3	−2	−18.5
F #2	2	3	−1	−8
F #3	2	3	−1	−8
F #4	2	5	−3	−22.5
F #5	2	3	−1	−8
F #6	2	1	1	8
M #1	3	2	1	8
M #2	3	2	1	8
M #3	3	5	−2	−18.5
M #4	3	2	1	8
M #5	3	1	2	18.5
M #6	3	2	1	8
M #7	3	4	−1	−8
M #8	3	2	1	8
M #9	4	2	2	18.5
M #10	4	3	1	8
M #11	4	5	−1	−8
M #12	4	5	−1	−8
M #13	4	3	1	8
M #14	4	5	−1	−8
M #15	5	3	2	18.5
M #16	5	2	3	22.5
M #17	5	3	2	18.5

Figure 6.11 Wilcoxon Signed Rank Test Example

Is the answer significantly different before and after the officers' training? Using the Wilcoxon Signed-Rank test, you should have come up with a z value of approximately −0.683.

$$z = \frac{115.5 - \dfrac{23(23+1)}{4}}{\sqrt{\dfrac{23(23+1)((2(23)+1))}{24}}} = -.683$$

Figure 6.12 Wilcoxon Signed Rank Example #2

> **Box 6.9: WHAT WE'VE LEARNED: Wilcoxon Signed-Rank Test**
>
> In 2011, Winstock and Barratt distributed an anonymous online survey to compare the patterns of use and effect profile between synthetic cannabis and natural cannabis. The researchers were able to obtain data from a large sample: approximately 15,000 respondents provided information. These respondents came from around the world: about half from the U.K., a quarter from the U.S., with other sizable contingents from Canada, Australia, and Ireland. The median age was 26, and nearly all (91.5%) identified as White. To compare synthetic and natural cannabis, Winstock and Barratt (2013) conducted Wilcoxon Signed-Rank tests of paired samples—approximately 900 similarly situated individuals, different only on the basis of their cannabis use. Their survey provided data from which measures of speed of onset, time to peak effect, and duration of peak effect were created. These three variables were measured at the ordinal level. Results showed that "the speed of onset for synthetic and natural cannabis was almost the same" (p. 109). However, the second test of equality found that synthetic cannabis had a significantly shorter time until peak effect was reached, compared to natural cannabis. Finally, the synthetic cannabis users reported to have a significantly shorter duration of effect than natural cannabis users.

KRUSKAL-WALLIS *H* TEST

While the Mann-Whitney *U* test may be conducted to compare two groups, the Kruskal-Wallis *H* test is designed to accommodate multiple groups, e.g., two or more groups. Thus, when there are several groups for which you want to test for equality, the Kruskal-Wallis *H* test is most appropriate. Like the Mann-Whitney test of equality, the observations must be independent. The test was named after its developers, William Kruskal and W. Allen Wallis. Kruskal was a mathematician and statistician, as was Wallis, though Wallis is perhaps equally known amongst political circles as an economist and presidential advisor (Pace, 1998).

Kruskal and Wallis (1952) calculate the test's *H* value using statistics similar to previously discussed tests of equality. Each group under study has its variable values ranked and summed. These sums are also weighted, accounting for the sample size. This is particularly advantageous as some groups—particularly those examined in criminal justice and criminological research—are likely to be unequal in size. Common examples include age groups, races/ethnicities, and offense types, just to name a few. To calculate the *H* statistic, the following formula is used:

$$H = \frac{12}{N(N+1)}\left(\frac{R_1^2}{n_1} + \frac{R_2^2}{n_2} + \ldots + \frac{R_k^2}{n_k}\right) - 3(N+1)$$

Figure 6.13 Kruskal Wallis H Test Equation

where R_1 = sum of ranks in group 1

R_2 = sum of ranks in group 2

n_1 = size of group 1

n_2 = size of group 2

R_k = sum of ranks in group *k*

N_k = sum of group *k*

N = total number of cases.

Box 6.10: Example of the Kruskal-Wallis H Test

The police chief believes that there may be differences in the officers' perceptions based on when they work. As a result, you are tasked with comparing the officers' perceptions across the three shifts. The chief provides you with this information, and you choose the officers' perceptions before they underwent additional training to test for equality. Each shift is simply grouped by their traditional shift number, e.g., "1" for first shift, "2" for second shift, and "3" for third shift. Since there are more than two groups, and the cases are independent of one another, the Kruskal-Wall H test is appropriate.

Case	Shift	Score	Rank
F #1	1	1	1
F #2	1	2	4
F #3	1	2	4
F #4	1	2	4
F #5	1	2	4
F #6	1	2	4
M #1	1	3	10.5
M #2	1	3	10.5
M #3	2	3	10.5
M #4	2	3	10.5
M #5	2	3	10.5
M #6	2	3	10.5
M #7	2	3	10.5
M #8	2	3	10.5
M #9	2	4	17.5
M #10	2	4	17.5
M #11	2	4	17.5
M #12	3	4	17.5
M #13	3	4	17.5
M #14	3	4	17.5
M #15	3	5	22
M #16	3	5	22
M #17	3	5	22

Figure 6.14 Kruskal Wallis H Test Example

Are the pre-training answers significantly different between shifts? Using the Kruskal-Wallis H test, you should have come up with an H value of approximately 15.89.

$$H = \frac{12}{N(N+1)}\left(\frac{R_1^2}{n_1} + \frac{R_2^2}{n_2} + \ldots + \frac{R_k^2}{n_k}\right) - 3(N+1)$$

$$H = \frac{12}{N(N+1)}\left(\frac{1764}{8} + \frac{13,340.25}{9} + \ldots + \frac{14,042.25}{6}\right) - 3(N+1)$$

$$H = \frac{12}{23(23+1)}(220.5 + 1,482.25 + 2,340.375) - 3(23+1)$$

$$H = \frac{12}{23(23+1)}(220.5 + 1,482.25 + 2,340.375) - 3(23+1) = 15.89$$

Figure 6.15 Kruskal Wallis H Test Example #2

Like the Wilcoxon Signed-Rank test, the Kruskal-Wallis H test need not be calculated by hand. With the help of statistical software, the data can be (nearly instantly) analyzed for equality. However, there are several considerations that must be made. Most importantly is what to do with "ties" when the differences in value rank equals 0. This is a consideration in all tests of equality that use rankings. Different software programs have different default settings. As a result, what could be calculated by hand can (and probably will) be slightly different when calculated with a program.

H values are not normally distributed; thus, the chi-square distribution is used—just like we observed in the McNemar test. In addition, the same practice of comparing the test statistic, in this case the H value, to a critical value is conducted. When there are three groups and the level of significance is 0.05, the critical value is 5.99. When there are three groups and the level of significance is 0.01, the critical value is 9.21. As a result, we can be 99% confident that the answer to the question, *"How much training do you receive on community relations?"* is significantly different between shifts. The null hypothesis that the perceptions of community relations training is equal across shifts is rejected: this perception does significantly vary by shift.

Box 6.11: WHAT WE'VE LEARNED: Kruskal-Wallis H Test

A very important facet of criminal investigation is the suspect interview. Researchers McDougall and Bull (2014) were interested in seeing how the revelation of evidence and the amount of delay affect the "quality" of statements, i.e., the difference between truthful and false statements. To conduct this study, the researchers enlisted the help of 42 high school students. The students took part in a mock crime scenario in which they role-played. The students were randomly assigned the role of a liar or a truth-teller. Next, they were interviewed about their role and "activities." McDougall and Bull conducted multiple Kruskal-Wallis H tests. The first tests were conducted to see if there was a significant effect on the statement length based on the veracity of statements, how gradual evidence was introduced, or the interview type. Initially, there were no significant findings. However, subsequent tests did find significant differences in statement-evidence consistency based on interview style. Further, there were significant differences in statement-evidence consistency based on the delay of evidence (p. 8). Finally, there were found to be significant differences in within-statement consistency based upon interview style. These results suggest that gradual discloser in interviews could benefit interviewers by increasing their accuracy in the determination of truth.

CONTINUOUS VARIABLES

The use of tests of equality is more frequently seen with continuous variables. This is due to the fact that continuous variables, generally, have many more statistical tests and techniques of data analysis available to them. With these variables, then, the comparison of groups is not of frequencies but of continuously measured descriptive statistics, such as means and variances. Data measured at the interval or ratio level have several tests of equality that are used, based on what characteristic the researcher is intending to compare between groups, the value(s) that s/he wishes to test, and the number of groups. An additional consideration, one that most statistical tests using continuous data must make, is that of the distribution's normality. Some tests assume the data are normally distributed and, like tests of equality for categorical variables, some do not.

DIFFERENCE OF MEANS TEST (Z)

There are two types of tests of equality that compare the means of groups to see if they are significantly different. The first of which are referred to as z tests, as they use the z distribution, a normal distribution first described by Fisher (1925). This normal distribution is referred to as the z distribution because of its additional assumptions, most notably the variability and dispersion of data at specific locations, or z scores. By assuming normality and the relative dispersion of values of a z distribution, the z test should be conducted on data with a sufficient number cases. A common rule of thumb is to use the z test with data that contain more than 30 cases (or 100 cases—there is no consensus), those of which were randomly sampled. The difference of means test (z) can determine if the mean values of two groups with a given characteristic is significantly different. For example, a z test can also be used to help answer Question #2 provided in the Introduction section of this chapter: *"Does delinquency occur at the same rate between male and female youth?"* If delinquency is measured by the number of offenses that males and females commit, a z test could be used—assuming there is a sufficient number of cases that were randomly sampled and the population parameters were known. The following formula is used in determining if there is a significant difference of means between two groups:

$$z = \frac{\bar{X}_1 - \bar{X}_2}{\sqrt{\dfrac{\sigma_1^2}{N_1} + \dfrac{\sigma_2^2}{N_2}}}$$

Figure 6.16 Difference of Means Equation (Z test)

where $\bar{X}_1$ = the sample mean of group one
   $\bar{X}_2$ = the sample mean of group two
   n_1 = the size of group one
   n_2 = the size of group two
   σ_1^2 = the population variance of group one
   σ_1^2 = the population variance of group two

As we learned previously, much of criminal justice and criminological research is conducted using samples. Thus, several values in Figure 6.16: Difference of Means Equation (Z test) are unknown. The population variances of both groups cannot be input into the formula. As a result, an alternative formula—and an alternative distribution—is used.

STUDENT'S *T* TEST

When population parameters, such as the variance, are unknown, a *t* test can be conducted. This test may also be preferable when there is a small sample size, such as less than 30 (or 100), due to the unlikelihood the data will be normally distributed. Although work on the concept of comparing means, or making inferences with small groups, had long been a focus of mathematicians (such as Laplace), it was not until the early 1900s that a solution was proposed.

In the late 1890s, the Guinness brewery in Dublin began to hire first-class chemists from Oxford and Cambridge University (Box, 1987). In their experimentation, which seemingly was a precursor to, or early version of, quality control, the brewers had difficulty interpreting any findings, because every sample was small. Central to their interpretations were two questions. First, the chemists needed to know how much error should be allowed when using estimated values of the mean and standard deviation based on samples, and at what level of probability are results significant? Others would approach the second question later, while William S. Gosset calculated the allowable error. This error can be thought of as the difference between sample and population values, as well as the resultant difference between the distribution of the sample and the normal, *z* distribution. As an employee of Guinness, the brewery encouraged him to use a pseudonym per its regulations; either "Pupil" or "Student." He chose the latter and Student's (1908) paper became a cornerstone of data analysis, albeit only later through application by R.A. Fisher.

The *t* test is a test of equality that can be used to see if the mean values of two (small) groups are significantly different. Since population parameters are unknown, sample statistics are used in their place. Additionally, a standard error value is calculated to account for the unknown variation between the means of the two groups. This results in two equations being used to calculate the *t* value. The resultant *t* value, then, accounts for the difference of means between the two groups under study and the variation of the differences, accounting for the size of the samples. The following formulae can be used to calculate *t*:

$$S\bar{x}_1 - \bar{x}_2 = \sqrt{\left(\frac{N_1 S_1^2 + N_2 S_2^2}{N_1 + N_2 - 2}\right)\left(\frac{N_1 + N_2}{N_1 N_2}\right)}$$

Figure 6.17 Standard Error of the Difference Between Means Equation

where N_1 = the number of cases in group 1
           N_2 = the number of cases in group 2
           S_1^2 = the variance of group 1
           S_2^2 = the variance of group 2

$$t = \left| \frac{\bar{x}_1 - \bar{x}_2}{S\bar{x}_1 - \bar{x}_2} \right|$$

Figure 6.18 t value Equation

where $\bar{x}_1$ = the sample mean of group one
           $\bar{x}_2$ = the sample mean of group two
           $S\bar{x}_1 - \bar{x}_2$ = the standard error of the difference between means

Box 6.12: Example of Student's *t* Test

At this point, you have clearly shown your statistical prowess; thus, the police chief would like you to examine his officers further. Review Box 6.6: Example of the Mann-Whitney U Test. Since the chief knows there are differences in the perceptions across gender, he would now like to know if there are differences in the number of complaints between male and female officers, too. The 6 female officers had an average of 2.67 citizen complaints and a variance of 2.27. The 17 male officers had an average of 4.00 citizen complaints and a variance of 3.5.

Is the mean number of citizen complaints significantly different between male and female officers? Using the two formulas, you should have calculated a *t* value of approximately 1.50.

$$S\bar{x}_1 - \bar{x}_2 = \sqrt{\left(\frac{6(2.27)+17(3.5)}{21}\right)\left(\frac{6+17}{6(17)}\right)} = .89$$

Figure 6.19 Standard Error of the Difference Between Means Example

$$t = \left|\frac{2.67-4}{.89}\right| = 1.50$$

Figure 6.20 t value Example

Thus far, we have used the *z* distribution, the chi-square distribution, and the Mann-Whitney *U* critical values table to determine significance. Now, the *t* value is compared to a critical value that is selected based on two criteria: the level of significance (0.05 or 0.01, for example) and the number of cases. When the level of significance is 0.05 and there are 23 cases, such as in our example, the critical value is 2.08. The corresponding value for the 0.01 level of significance is approximately 2.52. By comparing our *t* value with the critical value(s), we conclude that the mean number of complaints does not significantly differ between male and female officers. While the values of 4.00 and 2.67 are different, the difference is not substantial enough and/or there are not enough cases to make the inference that—in the population—the mean number of complaints is significantly different between the groups: male and female officers.

T tests can also be conducted on dependent samples—the same sample measured twice. This test of equality can be used to see if the mean value of a group is significantly different at a second point in time. This type of *t* test is often used in experimental research where a treatment or intervention has taken place. For this test, three formulas are used. The first formula estimates the variation of the difference between values. The second formula estimates the standard error of that difference, and the final formula calculates the *t* value.

$$D = (x_1 - x_2)$$

$$Sd = \frac{\sqrt{\frac{\sum D^2}{N} - (\bar{x}_1 - \bar{x}_2)^2}}{\sqrt{N-1}}$$

$$t = \frac{(\bar{x}_1 - \bar{x}_2)}{Sd}$$

Figure 6.21 t test for Dependent Samples Equations

where N = the number of cases

D^2 = the sum of squared differences

$\bar{x}_1$ = the mean at time one

$\bar{x}_2$ = the mean at time two

Sd = the standard error of the difference between means

Box 6.13: WHAT WE'VE LEARNED: Student's t Test

Researchers Marcum, Higgins, Freiburger, and Ricketts (2014) were recently interested in examining cyberbullying. Of particular interest was the victim-offender relationship. The data obtained for this study were drawn from sample data gathered through online surveys. The respondents were students at a "large, southeastern public university" (p. 542). However, the response rate of 5.9% resulted in a sample size of only 1,139 students. The first stage of analysis involved conducting t tests on several measures. The tests were conducted to see if there were gender differences in age, race, residency, parental attachment, school commitment, self-control, the number of hours spent on social networks, the number of social network friends, use of gossip, and whether or not the student had ever posted on Facebook to hurt someone. From their t tests, they found that, in their sample, the distribution of race was significantly different across gender: a larger proportion of the male respondents were white. There were also significant differences found in parental attachment, school commitment, self-control, the number of hours spent on social networks, the number of social network friends, and the use of someone else to post gossip. Ultimately, the researchers concluded that lower levels of self-control are associated with an increased likelihood of cyberbullying.

ONE-WAY ANOVA

Tests of equality for categorical variables are quite similar to one another, such as the Kruskal-Wallis H test, which is an extension of another test—the Mann-Whitney U test. While the latter can only test equality of two groups, the former can test equality of multiple groups. For continuous variables, a specific analysis of variance, or ANOVA, test is used. The one-way analysis of variance can test equality of multiple groups. This specific ANOVA test can test if there are any significant differences between the means of one (independent) variable from three or more groups. The two-way analysis of variance test, then, can test if there are any significant differences between the means of two (independent) variables from three or more groups. This form of ANOVA could provide evidence of an "interaction," the assumption that both independent variables impact the dependent variable—specifically its mean, which is being tested for equality across groups. There are many other ANOVA tests (we will see this again in Chapter 9).

The analysis of variance, as both a concept and practice, can be traced back to the early 1800s. Early discussions of these tests—or tests that resembled ANOVA—are seen in the works of Legendre (1805), Gauss (1809), and Quetelet (1835). Later, statisticians would continue to develop the methods that would ultimately be the analysis of variance (see Searle, 1989, and Stigler, 1986, for a discussion). The term "analysis of variance" can be found in the early work of R.A. Fisher (1918), specifically a paper in which he discusses variation among humans. Fisher (1925) would continue his work on the analysis of variance but perhaps only out of necessity. Stigler (2008) notes that, because Fisher and Pearson were by no means collegial, Fisher had to compute his own statistical tables. These tables were needed, because Fisher was introducing ANOVA to a broader audience, and he needed to be able to test the concept he described. Thus, like the proliferation of significance levels and *p*, Fisher (1925) was most directly responsible for the widespread use of analysis of variance tests.

Since ANOVA tests involve several groups, there are several formulae required to calculate its resultant statistic, the *F* ratio. Thus, ANOVA tests are sometimes referred to as *F* tests. To obtain *F*, six formulae are needed.

$$SS_{total} = \sum (x - \bar{X}_{total})^2$$

$$SS_{within} = \sum (x - \bar{X}_{group})^2$$

$$SS_{between} = \sum N_{group} (\bar{X}_{group} - \bar{X}_{total})^2$$

Figure 6.22 Sum of Squares Equations (F test)

where $\bar{X}_{total}$ = the mean of all groups

$\bar{X}_{group}$ = the mean of a group

N_{group} = the number of cases of a group

These three formulas represent various "sum of squares," e.g., the total variation of, the variation between, and the variation within groups. Just as the *t* test incorporated the variance of two groups into its formula, the *F* test incorporates the variation of and amongst all groups, thus resulting in multiple formulae.

$$MS_{between} = \frac{SS_{between}}{df_{between}}$$

$$MS_{within} = \frac{SS_{within}}{df_{within}}$$

Figure 6.23 Mean Squares Equations (F test)

where $df_{between} = k - 1$

$df_{within} = N_{total} - k$

These two formulas represent various "mean squares," e.g., the average sum of squares according to the sample sizes. Recall in Chapter 5 the calculation of variance involved the sum of squares (in that case, the sum of squared deviations from the mean) divided by the number of cases. These formulae operate similarly.

$$F = \frac{MS_{between}}{MS_{within}}$$

Figure 6.24 F ratio Equation

DEGREES OF FREEDOM:
A value that represents a compensation for differences in statistics due to sampling. In statistical tests, degrees of freedom may be based on measures such as the sample size or the number of variable values.

This final formula is where the F ratio is calculated. Like z and t values, the larger the F ratio, the higher the likelihood of rejecting the null hypothesis. Also like the z and t values, a critical value is needed for comparison, provided by the F distribution. The critical value is determined by establishing a level of significance and knowing the corresponding degrees of freedom.

Box 6.14: Example of One-Way ANOVA

The final test of equality the police chief would like you to conduct is a one-way ANOVA test to see if there is a significant difference in initial officer perceptions of training (pre-training scores) across the three shifts. You first examine the groups and see the first shift has the lowest mean perception score (2.13), followed by second shift (3.33), and then third shift (4.50). The overall mean, accounting for all 23 officers, is approximately 3.22.

Is the mean perception of training score significantly different between the first, second, and third shifts? Using the six formulas, you should have calculated an F value of approximately 30.65 (with rounding).

$$SS_{total} = 25.91$$

Figure 6.25 Sum of Squares Example

$$SS_{within} = 6.38$$

Figure 6.26 Sum of Squares Example #2

$$SS_{between} = 19.54$$

Figure 6.27 Sum of Squares Example #3

$$MS_{between} = 9.77$$

Figure 6.28 Mean Squares Example

$$MS_{within} = .32$$

Figure 6.29 Mean Squares Example #2

$$F = 30.65$$

Figure 6.30 F ratio example

The analysis of variance test uses yet another different distribution and corresponding table of critical values to determine statistical significance. In the case of the F distribution, the degrees of freedom required are both the $df_{between}$ ($k - 1$) and the df_{within} ($N_{total} - k$). In Box 6.14: Example of One-Way ANOVA, these values are 2 and 20, respectively. As a result, the critical F value needed to determine statistical significance at the 0.05 level of significance is 3.49. At the 0.01 level of significance, the critical value is 5.85. With an F value of 30.65, far exceeding both critical values, we conclude that the mean perception of training scores are significantly different between the first, second, and third shifts and not the result of chance or (sampling) error. Remember, in this example, the perception score was measured ordinally. Likert-type scales are in a "gray area". There are conflicting opinions concerning if ANOVA could/should be used for such variables; thus it may be beneficial to use multiple tests in these instances.

Box 6.15: WHAT WE'VE LEARNED: One-Way ANOVA

A recent study by Sherretts, Boduszek, Debowska, and Willmott (2017) sought to test the assumption that murderers differed from recidivistic and first-time incarcerated offenders on psychopathy and criminal social identity measures. The researchers selected nearly 500 offenders incarcerated across three prisons under the supervision of the Pennsylvania Department of Corrections. There were 94 murderers, 266 recidivistic offenders, and 118 first-time incarcerated offenders in the sample. The data were obtained via an anonymous questionnaire, completed individually by the inmates. To examine differences across the three offender groups, ANOVA tests were conducted on a variety of measures. Several significant differences emerged, including scores on cognitive centrality, in-group ties, erratic lifestyle, anti-social behavior, and interpersonal manipulation. Interestingly, murderers had significantly lower scores on a variety of measures compared to the other groups. The remaining two measures, in-group affect and callous affect did not show any significant differences across the three groups. The researchers, in explaining these findings, suggest that career criminals (recidivists) may develop cognitive structures that impact their identity as a criminal. Murderers, alternately, often commit crimes alone, thus the interaction with other criminals may not impact their cognitive structure. As a result, murderers have significantly lower scores of psychopathy measures, contrary to previous research and current theoretical premises.

THE "OTHER OVAS"

In addition to the one-way analysis of variance (ANOVA), there are also statistical tests that can compare multiple groups *and* multiple variables simultaneously. For example, the two-way analysis of variance tests for equality of means between groups that have been partitioned by a second categorical (independent) variable. The two-way ANOVA tests three things. First, it tests the means of the first (independent) variable for significant differences. Second, it tests the means of the second (independent) variable for significant differences. Finally, it tests if there is an interaction effect between the variables. An interaction effect would signify that the effect of one independent variable on the dependent variable is contingent on the value of the other independent variable. In the example highlighted throughout this chapter, a two-way ANOVA could test the mean values of pre-training scores across shifts and by gender. The test would examine if the mean values are significantly different across shifts, by gender, and if the values of one are dependent on the other. For example, the mean value for males may be dependent on the shift they are working.

The multivariate analysis of variance (MANOVA) is an extension of the one-way ANOVA test. This test of equality tests the difference in means across multiple groups *and* across multiple outcomes. Stated differently, MANOVA tests the differences in the mean value of one independent variable across groups *and* across dependent variables. A MANOVA test adds an additional dependent variable (or more) to an ANOVA test. Review Box 6.14: Example of One-way ANOVA. In that example, a one-way ANOVA test examined the mean value of initial officer perception across the three shifts. A one-way MANOVA test could examine the mean values of initial officer perception and the mean values of officer perception following training across the three shifts. The test would examine if the mean values of both dependent variables are equal across the three shifts.

Finally, there are also tests of equality that serve the same functions as ANOVA and MANOVA tests, but do so while controlling for covariates. These types of tests are called analysis of covariance (ANCOVA) and multiple analysis of covariance (MANCOVA) tests, respectively. These are extensions of the aforementioned tests of equality. They differ by statistically controlling for variables that may be impacting the relationship under study, e.g., the mean values of a dependent variable across groups. The example highlighted throughout this chapter is suited well for these types of tests, as ANCOVA and MANCOVA are often used in pre- and post- test experimental designs. For example, it is highly likely the officers' perception pre-training scores are related to their respective post-training scores. As a result, if we wanted to extend our inquiry found in Box 6.14: Example of One-Way ANOVA to examine the differences in post-training scores, we could do so by accounting for the individuals' pre-training scores by conducting an ANCOVA test.

Test of Equality	Level of Measurement
Difference of Proportions	Nominal
McNemar	Nominal
Mann-Whitney U	Ordinal
Wilcoxon Signed-Ranks	Ordinal
Kruskal-Wallis H	Ordinal
Difference of Means (Z)	Interval, Ratio
Student's (t)	Interval, Ratio
ANOVA	Interval, Ratio

Figure 6.31 Tests of Equality Summary

SUMMARY

Just as we saw in previous chapters, and will continue to see in subsequent chapters, there are different assumptions and requirements of data when conducting different statistical tests. Tests of equality are no different. The appropriateness of a test is contingent upon a variety of factors: the level of measurement of the independent variable(s), the level of measurement of the dependent variable(s), the number of independent and dependent variables, and, like all statistical tests, the purpose of the analysis, e.g., what the researcher is hoping to learn.

Compared to measures of central tendency and variability and dispersion, there are several options available to examine categorical data with respect to tests of equality. Data that are measured at the nominal and ordinal levels can be tested for equality in pre- and post-test experimental designs, such as in the McNemar test or the Wilcoxon-Signed Ranks test. Tests that require independence of groups, where cases are not found in both groups, are also available. These include the Mann-Whitney U test and the Kruskal-Wallis H test. Finally, perhaps the most common test of equality for categorical variables, the difference of proportions test, can be conducted on data collected from a variety of research designs—highlighting its versatility.

Continuous data also have several ways in which it can be tested for equality. Most frequently, difference of means tests are employed to examine group differences of the mean value of an independent variable. The Student's t test is the most frequently used of these tests and, like other tests of equality, it is used across disciplines and fields of study—not exclusively in criminal justice and criminology. In addition to the more traditional difference of means test, there are several other tests of equality that examine differences in mean values. These tests differ, primarily, based on the number of groups and/or the number of variables under examination. Some tests, such as the one-way ANOVA and ANCOVA, can test differences in the mean values of one dependent variable across several groups. Other tests, such as the one-way MANOVA and MANCOVA, can test differences in the mean values of multiple dependent variables across several groups. Finally, two-way tests can test differences in the mean values of one dependent variable across several groups and multiple independent variables. Though each may differ in their formulae and interpretations, when a test of equality is conducted it is dependent on the available data and the intent of the analysis.

CHAPTER REVIEW QUESTIONS

1. Explain why the t distribution is often used instead of the z distribution in a difference of means test.

2. Explain which tests of equality can be conducted on more than two groups.

3. Discuss the difference between Type I and Type II error.

4. What is the difference between the alpha value and the p value? Explain how they, together, help determine statistical significance.

5. What does "statistical significance" represent? Can you describe what that phrase means differently?

CHAPTER REVIEW EXERCISES

1. Visit the National Gang Center's Survey Analysis website:
https://www.nationalgangcenter.gov/Survey-Analysis
Identify as many tests of equality as possible that can be conducted based on the available data.

2. Revisit Question #2 from the Chapter Review Exercises in Chapter 5. Conduct a test of equality based on the variable(s) and data you collected. Explain the results.

3. Visit the Study of Terrorism and Responses to Terrorism website: http://www.start.umd.edu/publications
Using the search bar, type in "Border Crossings," and select *Apply*. Open the publication by clicking on its title. Next, click *Visit Website*. Find the discussion of the one-way ANOVA test. Were the results of the test significant? What do the results suggest?

4. Develop a criminal justice or criminological research question that could test the difference of proportions and the difference of means between groups. Explain which difference of means test you would use, based on the data, and what variables and groups would be under study.

5. Using your institution's library resources, find a peer-reviewed journal article that is of interest to you that reports on at least one of the tests of equality discussed in this chapter. Discuss the article, the test of equality, and what the researcher(s) found.

REFERENCES

Aldrich, J. (2010). Mathematics in the London/Royal Statistical Society 1834–1934. *Electronic Journal for History of Probability and Statistics, 6*(1), 1–33.

Arbuthnot, J. (1710). An argument for Divine Providence. *Philosophical Transactions, 27*, 186–190.

Box, J.F. (1987). Guinness, Gosset, Fisher, and small samples. *Statistical Science, 2*(1), 45–52.

Cowles, M. & Davis, C. (1982). On the origins of the .05 level of statistical significance. *American Psychologist, 37*(5), 553–558.

David, F.N. (1962). *Games, gods, and gambling.* New York, NY: Hafner.

Deming, W.E. (1943). *Statistical adjustment of data. New York: John Wiley and Sons.*

Dixon., T.L., & Williams, C.L. (2015). The changing misrepresentation of race and crime on network and cable news. *Journal of Communication, 65,* 24–39.

Edgeworth, F.Y. (1885). Methods of statistics. *Jubilee Volume of the Statistical Society,* 181–217.

Edwards, A.L. (1948). Note on the "correction for continuity" in testing the significance of the difference between correlation proportions. *Psychometrika, 13*(3), 185–187.

Fisher, R.A. (1918). The causes of human variability. *Eugenics Review, 10,* 213–220.

Fisher, R.A. (1925). *Statistical methods for researchers.* Edinburgh, UK: Oliver and Boyd Ltd.

Fisher, R.A. (1926). The arrangement of field experiments. *Journal of the Ministry of Agriculture, 33,* 503–513.

Fox. V. (1946). Intelligence, race, and age as selective factors in crime. *Journal of Criminal Law and Criminology, 37*(2), 141–152.

Gauss, C.F. (1809). *Theoria motus corporum celestium.* Hamburg, Germany: Perthes et Besser.

Goodman, S. (2008). A dirty dozen: Twelve *p*-value misconceptions. *Seminars in Hematology, 45,* 135–140.

Gould, L.A. (2010). Risk and the female offender: An analysis of classification and supervision issues. *Women & Criminal Justice, 20*(4), 323–342.

Hern, T. (2013). *D. Random Whitney.* Retrieved from http://sections.maa.org/ ohio/ohio_masters/whitney.pdf.

Kruskal, W.H., & Wallis, A.W. (1952). Use of ranks in one-criterion analysis of variance. *Journal of the American Statistical Association, 47*(260), 583–621.

Laplace, P.S. (1823). De l'action de la lune sur l'atmosphere. *Annales de Chimie et de Physique, 24,* 280–294.

Legendre, A.M. (1805). *Nouvelles méthodes pour la determination des orbites des cométes.* Paris, France: Courcier.

Lee, Y., Eck, J.E., & Corsaro, N. (2016). Conclusions from the history of research into the effects of police force size on crime—1968 through 2013: A historical systematic review. *Journal of Experimental Criminology, 12,* 431–451.

Lunden, W.A. (1942). *Statistics on crime and criminality*: A handbook of primary data. Pittsburgh, PA: Stevenson and Foster Company. *The Annals of Mathematical Statistics, 18*(1), 50–60.

Mann, H.B., and Whitney, D.R. (1947). On a test of whether one of two random variables is stochastically larger than the other. *Annals of Mathematical Statistics, 18*(1), 50–60.

Marcum, C.D., Higgins, G.E., Freiburger, T.L., Ricketts, M.L. (2014). Exploration of the cyberbullying victim/offender overlap by sex. *American Journal of Criminal Justice, 39,* 538–548.

McDougall, A.J., & Bull, R. (2015). Detecting truth in suspect interviews: The effect of use of evidence (early and gradual) and time delay on criteria-based content analysis, reality monitoring and inconsistency within suspect statements. *Psychology, Crime & Law, 21*(6), 514–530.

McNemar, Q. (1947). Note on the sampling error of the difference between correlated proportions or percentages. *Psychometrika, 12*(2), 153–157.

Michell, J. (1767). An inquiry in the probably parallax, and magnitude of the fixed stars, from the quantity of light which they afford us, and the particular circumstances of their situation. *Philosophical Transactions, 57,* 234–264.

Pace, E. (1998, October 14). W. Allen Wallis, 85, Economist and President of U. of Rochester. *The New York Times.* Retrieved from http://www.nytimes.com/1998/10/14/us/w-allen-wallis-85-economist-and-president-of-u-of-rochester.html

Pearson, K. (1900). On the criterion that a given system of deviations from the probable in the case of a correlated system of variables is such that it can be reasonably supposed to have arisen from random sampling. *Philosophical Magazine, 5*(50), 157–175.

Pratt, J. (1959). Remarks on zeros and ties in the Wilcoxon signed rank procedures. *Journal of the American Statistical Association, 54*(287), 655–667.

Quetelet, A. (1835). *Sur l'homme et le développement de sus facultés, ou Essai de physique sociale.* Paris, France: Bachelier.

Searle, S. (1989). Variance components—Some history and a summary account of estimation methods. *Journal of Animal Breeding and Genetics, 106*(1–6), 1–29.

Sherretts, N., Boduszek, D., Debowksa, A., & Willmott, D. (2017). Comparison of murderers with recidivists and first time incarcerated offenders from U.S. prisons on psychopathy and identity as a criminal: An exploratory analysis. *Journal of Criminal Justice, 51*, 89-92.

Siegel, S. (1956). *Non-parametric statistics for the behavioral sciences.* New York, NY: McGraw-Hill.

Stigler, S.M. (1986). *The history of statistics: The measurement of uncertainty before 1900.* Cambridge, MA: Harvard University Press.

Stigler, S.M. (1999). *Statistics on the table: The history of statistical concepts and methods.* Cambridge, MA: Harvard University Press.

Stigler, S.M. (2008). Fisher and the 5% level. *Chance, 21*(4), 12.

Student. (1908). The probable error of a mean. *Biometrika, 6*(1), 1–25.

Uggen, C., Vuolu, M., Lageson, S., Ruhland, E., & Whiteham, H.K. (2014). The edge of stigma: An experimental audit of the effects of low-level criminal records on employment. *Criminology, 52*(4), 627–654.

Yule, G.U. & Kendall, M.G. (1950). *An introduction to the theory of statistics* (14th ed). London, UK: Griffin.

Wilcoxon, F. (1945) Individual comparison by ranking methods. *Biometrics Bulletin, 1*(6), 80–83.

Winstock, A.R., & Barratt, M.J. (2013). Synthetic cannabis: A comparison of patterns of use and effect profile with natural cannabis in a large global sample. *Drug and Alcohol Dependence, 13*, 106–111.

TESTS OF ASSOCIATION

7

INTRODUCTION: MAKING CONNECTIONS

When respectable research reemerged in the fifties, it focused on the causes of crime suggested by leading sociological theories—such as group membership and social class—but it was not restricted to such 'causes'. In fact, in many ways it resembled the presociological multiple factor approach, and therefore its 'findings' resembled those of earlier periods. The traditional correlates of crime—age, sex, ethnicity, low social position, low intelligence, urban residence, family disruption, and poor school performance—were discovered. (Hirschi & Rudisill, 1976, p. 22)

Still seen to this day is the examination and discovery of factors related to the genesis, continuation, and cessation of criminal activity. These factors are observed across several disciplines, including, but not limited to, psychology, biology, and sociology (Hirschi & Rudisill, 1976). In fact, 40 years after Hirschi and Rudisill's 100-year summary, the Federal Bureau of Investigation (FBI) summarized these factors in an annual bulletin published in conjunction with the Uniform Crime Reports (UCR). In addition to the factors quoted above, the FBI states that the factors related to the "volume and type of crime occurring from place to place" include density and the urbanization of an area, population composition, residential mobility, infrastructure, economy, culture, climate, the size of law enforcement agencies, the practices of law enforcement agencies, the practices of other criminal justice agencies and institutions, the attitudes and perceptions of crime, and—with respect to measurement—the reporting practices of the public (FBI, 2013). To conclude that these factors are related to criminal activity, specific empirical tests of association must be conducted.

Consider the following questions:

1. Is student victimization related to lifestyle choices, such as illicit drug use?

2. Is an offender's criminal history related to the provision of bail?

3. Is an offender's criminal history related to the provision of bail, while accounting for their age?

The processes needed to answer each of these questions involve the statistical examination of at least two variables. This examination requires the same types of values, e.g., descriptive statistics learned in the initial chapters and seen utilized in Chapter 6, as testing equality between groups. Tests of association are attempting to determine if two variables are significantly related to one another. If two variables are significantly related to one another, you can—with a specific degree of certainty—predict the value of one variable based on the value of the second variable. Different data must be analyzed in different ways. Some tests require lower, categorical levels of measurement that rely on frequencies. While other tests require higher, continuous levels of measurement that rely on the raw values, means, and deviations from the mean. With new tests, different values are not needed, just different formulae. This chapter examines the histories, calculations, and uses of various tests of association.

LEARNING OBJECTIVES

By the end of this chapter, students will be able to:

1: Identify the most common tests of association

2: Discuss the level of measurement requirements of each test of association

3: Explain the utility of measures of association

4: Evaluate the difference between correlation and partial correlation

5: Assess the advantages and limitations each test of association's test statistic

KEY TERMS

CORRELATION

CORRELATION COEFFICIENT

DIRECTION

EFFECT SIZE

EXPECTED FREQUENCY

LINEAR

NONPARAMETRIC

OBSERVED FREQUENCY

PARAMETRIC

POWER

CATEGORICAL VARIABLES

In the preceding chapter (Chapter 6), you learned about several tests of equality by which you can test for statistical significance. Statistical significance, in these cases, refers to the finding that there are differences between groups that, with a predetermined degree of certainty, are not the result of chance and are believed to be real and exist in the population. Like those tests of equality, tests of association function similarly.

Based on the characteristics of the data and the purpose(s) of the research, data analysts have several tests of association to which they are availed. For categorical variables, there are several tests of association that can see if variables are related to one another or are independent of one another—where the likelihood of having one characteristic is unrelated to the likelihood of having another.

CHI-SQUARE

The tests of the difference of means examined in Chapter 6 employed the use of the t value and the F ratio when examining data for statistical significance. Tests of significance using t or F rely on the assumptions that the distribution of the population is (at least relatively) normal, the sample is relatively small, and the data are measured at the interval or ratio level. Combined, we refer to this type of analysis as a parametric test. At times, a researcher may have a small sample, may not be able to assume normality, or may have data that is not measured at least at the interval level. When this occurs, the researcher will use a different distribution, and subsequent test statistic, to conduct analysis.

As seen in the McNemar test in Chapter 6, a chi-square distribution may be used to analyze categorical data. This analysis is an example of a nonparametric test. Nonparametric tests, generally, have less power than parametric tests. In data analysis, the power of a test refers to, and is reflected by, the probability that significant findings are found correctly, e.g., the null hypothesis is correctly rejected. Nonparametric tests all vary with respect to power, and the most powerful tests have the most strict requirements. Thus, nonparametric tests, with less strict requirements than parametric tests, are generally weaker in power. While there are various measures that do not utilize the value in calculation (see Cohen, 1988), in most cases, the easiest way to increase the power of a test is to increase the sample size.

The most common tests of association for categorical variables, as found in nearly all criminal justice and criminology statistics textbooks, are chi-square tests. The formative basis for the chi-square test has been traced, by some, to 1811 (Plackett, 1983). During the early part of the 19th century Pierre-Simon Laplace (1811:1820) was interested in distributions, but only peripherally for the purpose of his primary area of study—the theory of errors. It was not until Pearson (1900) developed the "goodness of fit" test by coalescing, correcting, and refining decades of work that the chi-square test was created. The newly defined chi-square test was derived from the z test (see Chapter 6). In fact, the critical values are closely related. The critical values of the chi-square statistic, denoted by χ^2, are the squares of the critical values for the z statistic at the same levels of significance with one degree of freedom.

Chi-square tests utilize frequencies in their analysis. In a one-way chi-square test, a variable's values are tested to see if they are significantly different with respect to their frequencies. In essence, the frequencies are tested to see if the variable's values are distributed evenly. For example, a one-way chi-square

PARAMETRIC:
In data analysis, the type and quality of a statistical test in which the assumption that the population is normally distributed is made.

NONPARAMETRIC:
In data analysis, the type and quality of a statistical test in which the assumption that the population is normally distributed is not made.

POWER:
In data analysis, the probability that significant findings are found correctly or that the null hypothesis is correctly rejected.

test could test to see if a class has an even distribution of students based on a categorical variable, such as *class standing* or *major*. This may also be interpreted as testing the relationship between a variable's values and its incidence in a dataset, as measured by frequencies. The following formulae are used when conducting a one-way chi-square test:

$$\chi^2 = \frac{\sum (f_0 - f_e)^2}{f_e}$$
$$df = k - 1$$

Figure 7.1 One-way Chi-Square Test Equations

where f_0 = observed frequency of a category

f_e = expected frequency of a category.

Box 7.1: Example of One-Way Chi-Square

As you continue to present your findings to the police chief, as you did from skills learned in previous chapters, they are presented to the town's mayor and council. After discussion, some recommendations are made to prevent and reduce the number of complaints against officers by citizens. One recommendation is that there should be additional training provided to officers, and those that are recruited to work for the agency should be college educated. The chief believes that his agency is represented by many college graduates—and they are educated at different, increasing levels. However, he is unsure and would like you to conduct an analysis. You decide to conduct a one-way chi-square test to see if there is an even distribution of college education present in the agency. Your demographic data show nine officers have not graduated college, six have an Associate of Science (A.S.), six have a Bachelor of Science (B.S.), and two have a Master of Science (M.S.) degree.

Is the agency equally divided in its education levels? Using the chi-square formula, you should have come up with a chi-square value of approximately 4.30.

Education Level	f_0	f_e	$f_0 - f_e$	$(f_0 - f_e)^2$	$\dfrac{(f_0 - f_e)^2}{f_e}$
No college	9	5.75	3.25	10.5625	1.84
A.S.	6	5.75	.25	.0625	.01
B.S.	6	5.75	.25	.0625	.01
M.S.	2	5.75	−3.75	14.0625	2.45
					$\chi^2 = 4.30$

Figure 7.2 One-way Chi-Square Test Example

In order to determine if the calculated chi-square value represents significance, it must be compared to a critical chi-square value. Significance in the case of a one-way chi-square test represents an unequal distribution of values of a single categorical variable. Since the variable is categorical, the values are represented by frequencies. In Box 7.1: Example of One-Way Chi-Square, you were testing to see if there is an unequal distribution of the level of college education across the 23 officers surveyed. If the calculated chi-square value of 4.30 is *less* than the critical value, the null hypothesis—that there is an equal distribution—is accepted or retained. If the value is *more* than the critical value, the null hypothesis is rejected and—with some level of certainty—it may be concluded that there is a significantly unequal distribution of the level of college education. The critical value is determined by the degrees of freedom (*df*), calculated by *k* − 1 where *k* is the number of variable values, and the alpha value (α)—the level of significance. With a *df* of three and an α of 0.05, the critical value is 7.815. As a result, it may be concluded that the agency is not unequally divided in the distribution of their education levels.

The chi-square test is more commonly used to examine the paired occurrences across two categorical variables. This test of association can be conducted on categorical data that are arranged in a contingency table, e.g., a cross-tabulation. When data are examined using a two-way chi-square test, the χ^2 value is calculated identically to the one-way test. However, the expected frequency (f_e) and *df* values are calculated differently. The f_e values, in a two-way chi-square test, are calculated based on the individual probabilities of having each characteristic in a paired occurrence, which aligns with the null hypothesis that the two variables are independent of one another. In a two-way chi-square test, the *df* still reflects the number of values but takes into consideration the second variable.

$$\chi^2 = \frac{\sum(f_o - f_e)}{f_e}$$

$$df = (r-1)(c-1)$$

Figure 7.3 Two-way Chi-Square Test Equations

where   *r* = the number of rows (or values of the row variable)
       c = the number of columns (or columns of the column variable).

Box 7.2: Example of Two-Way Chi-Square

The police chief, upon seeing the results from Box 7.1: Example of One-Way Chi-Square, requests additional tests be conducted. You present several sub analyses that show statistical significance. One finding you present to the chief is an Analysis of Variance (ANOVA) test that shows there is a significant difference in the number of citizen complaints across the three shifts. The chief would like you to try to uncover other related factors to help explain those differences. The chief suggests that the significant difference in the number of complaints by shift may be attributed to differences in education levels. Education may provide officers with additional knowledge when responding to an incident. As a result, you decide to conduct a two-way chi-square test to see if the education level of officers is independent of the shift they work.

OBSERVED FREQUENCY:
The frequency of each characteristic or paired occurrence as found in the data.

EXPECTED FREQUENCY:
The frequency of each characteristic or paired occurrence when the null hypothesis is true.

Shift Education Level	First	Second	Third	
No college	2	4	3	9
A.S.	3	2	1	6
B.S.	2	2	2	6
M.S.	1	1	0	2
	8	9	6	23

Figure 7.4 Two-way Chi-Square Test Example

Is the education level of officers independent of the shift they work? Using the chi-square formula, and constructing a cross-tabulation (see Figure 7.4), you should have come up with a chi-square value of approximately 2.20.

Education Level by Shift	f_o	f_e	$f_o - f_e$	$(f_o - f_e)^2$	$\dfrac{(f_o - f_e)^2}{f_e}$
No college First	2	3.13	−1.13	1.28	.41
No college Second	4	3.52	.48	.23	.07
No college Third	3	2.34	.66	.44	.19
A.S. First	3	2.09	.91	.83	.40
A.S. Second	2	2.35	−.35	.12	.05
A.S. Third	1	1.57	−.57	.32	.21
B.S. First	2	2.08	−.08	.01	.00
B.S. Second	2	2.35	−.35	.12	.05
B.S. Third	2	1.57	.43	.18	.12
M.S. First	1	.70	.30	.09	.13
M.S. Second	1	.78	.22	.05	.06
M.S. Third	0	.52	−.52	.27	.52

$$\chi^2 = 2.20$$
$$df = (3 - 1)(4 - 1) = 6$$

Figure 7.5 Two-way Chi-Square Test Example #2

Just like the one-way chi-square test, the two-way chi-square test requires the calculated chi-square value to be greater than the corresponding critical value to claim statistical significance. In Box 7.2: Example of Two-Way Chi-Square, the critical value when df equals 6 and α equals .05 is 12.592. Since the calculated chi-square value in the test is less than the critical value, the null hypothesis is retained. As a result, the officers' education level and the shift they work are independent of one another, e.g., they are not associated with, or related to, one another.

One of the disadvantages to nonparametric tests like the one-way and two-way chi-square test lies in the value that is calculated. The chi-square statistic, by itself, is not very informative or interpretable. It relies on, and is heavily influenced by, the sample size and the number of variable values, in addition to the degree of (in)dependence. There are several ways in which the chi-square value has been standardized to improve interpretation and, in a sense, evaluate the magnitude of a present association. This magnitude is known as the effect size. While effect sizes are also available for tests of equality, they may be more helpful for tests of association, particularly those with categorical variables where the relationship is difficult to assess on the surface. Since tests of association rely on raw values and frequencies, significance tests alone may not be too informative. As a result, standardized values to quantify associations are often sought.

Two such standardized values that are used specifically for the analysis of nominal data are the phi coefficient and Cramér's V. The phi coefficient and Cramér's V are individual values representing the effect size, standardized with a range of values from 0.0 through 1.0, to assess the strength of the association between categorical variables. The phi coefficient has been credited to Pearson by some (see Cramér, 1946), but more often, it is discussed as a development of his former student, Yule (1912). The phi coefficient, denoted by ϕ or r_ϕ, can only be calculated for dichotomous variables—those in which there are only two values. The phi coefficient can be calculated using the following formula:

	Value 1	Value 2
Value 1	A	B
Value 2	C	D

$$\phi = \frac{AD - BC}{\sqrt{(A+B)(C+D)(A+C)(B+D)}}$$

Figure 7.6 Phi Coefficient Equation

Cramér's V is also known as Cramér's Phi, denoted by ϕ_c, since it is an extension of the phi coefficient for two by two cross-tabulations. This measure of effect size is utilized when the cross-tabulation is greater than two by two: at least one of the variables has more than two values. The formula for Cramér's V alters the phi coefficient slightly to account for the increased number of categories:

$$V = \sqrt{\frac{\chi^2}{N * \min(r-1, c-1)}}$$

Figure 7.7 Cramer's V Equation

An additional measure of effect size for tests of association that examine nominal data is the contingency coefficient (Pearson, 1904). The contingency coefficient, provides an adjustment for different sample sizes:

$$C = \sqrt{\frac{\chi^2}{n + \chi^2}}$$

Figure 7.8 Contingency Coefficient Equation

EFFECT SIZE:
In data analysis, a quantitative measurement of the magnitude or strength of the phenomena under study.

Box 7.3: WHAT WE'VE LEARNED: Two-Way Chi-Square

Though the phenomenon has been documented for years, since at least the 19th century, school shootings have only recently become incidents garnering scholarly attention. In 2016, a study was published detailing the work of a group of researchers from the United Kingdom. Gerard, Whitfield, Porter, and Browner (2016) sought to provide descriptive statistics concerning school shootings, discover any patterns or themes across the incidents, and test for the association of age and various incident characteristics. The researchers used two-way chi-square tests to see if there was an association of age and personal characteristics and offense characteristics. By aggregating cases collected from Internet, database, and media sources, Gerard et al. compiled a sample of 27 cases of shooting incidents that occurred in a school setting over a 22-year period (1988–2009), the majority of which happened after 1996 and/or occurred in the United States. The chi-square tests found several statistically significant associations. Age was found to be associated with offenders' depression, the location of the incident, and whether or not the offender was linked to the school where the incident took place. With respect to the association of age and offense characteristics, age was associated with whether or not the offender committed suicide, whether or not they made threats, and whether or not they stole weapons to be used in the incident.

GOODMAN AND KRUSKAL'S GAMMA

In addition to the chi-square test that can be used to test associations of nominal and ordinal variables, there are some tests specifically designed for ordinal data. The first of which is the Goodman and Kruskal gamma test. Sometimes called Goodman and Kruskal's correlation, the statistician-duo developed this test, and the resulting statistic, over the course of nearly 20 years (Goodman & Kruskal, 1954;1959;1963;1972). In order to use this test, both variables must be measured at the ordinal level. The test is similar to the chi-square test in that it results in a specific value (here, γ) that may be compared to a critical value to determine statistical significance. Gamma (γ) can be found using the following formula:

$$\text{Gamma}(G \text{ or } \gamma) = \frac{N_s - N_d}{N_s + N_d}$$

Figure 7.9 Goodman and Kruskal's Gamma Equation

where N_s = the number of concordant pairs
N_d = the number of discordant pairs (ties are dropped).

To test for significance, the Goodman Kruskal gamma test may use the z or the t distribution. Since the data are unlikely to be normally distributed, a t value is often calculated. The following formula is used to calculate t:

$$t = G\sqrt{\frac{N_s + N_d}{N(1 - G^2)}}$$

Figure 7.10 t value for Gamma Test Equation

where N = the number of pairs.

The value of gamma can range from −1.0 to +1.0, with |1| indicating perfect prediction of one ordinal variable's value based on knowing the other, with respect to direction. This is also more commonly referred to as a perfect association (or relationship). A significant finding from a gamma test would suggest that the ordinal variables are not independent of one another. Knowing the value of one variable significantly increases the accuracy of predicting the value of the other variable to the proportional extent of γ.

DIRECTION:
In data analysis, the characteristic of a phenomenon (either positive or negative) that indicates the relative change, e.g., increase or decrease, of one variable based on the value of another variable.

Box 7.4: WHAT WE'VE LEARNED: Goodman and Kruskal's Gamma

Recently, a group of psychologists was interested in the memory of adults, specifically older adults. The research team of Dahl, Allwood, Scimone, and Rennemark (2015) compared event memory metacognition in "old adults" and "very old adults" (p. 764). The authors suggest that memory is an important area of study, particularly concerning older adults, as memory performance tends to decrease with age, and an aging population is likely to be called upon more often in coming years to serve as a witness in criminal trials. The "old adult" group consisted of 66-year old adults, and the "very old adults" consisted of 87-year-old or 90-year-old adults. The researchers compared each group to see if age was significantly related to the accuracy of memory and metamemory performance. Using Goodman and Kruskal's gamma as a relative measure of confidence accuracy, the researchers obtained some interesting results. There was a significant difference between each group with respect to the gamma values. The very old group had a negative value, while the old had a positive value of approximately the same magnitude. The researchers concluded that memory ability may be impaired in advanced age. Further evaluation focused on the age difference. The researchers calculated the effect size and found it to be 0.60, representing a substantial proportional reduction of error in the memory tests.

KENDALL'S τ

Credited to the work of statistician Maurice Kendall (1938), Kendall's τ (tau) is a set of measures of association: τ_a, τ_b, and τ_c. These tests require that two ordinal variables be paired observations. Paired observations concern data from one set of cases measured multiple times. Kendall's development of these measures stem from the earlier works of Fechner (1897), Lipps (1905), and Deuchler (1909;1914). All three τ measures have nearly the same numerator in their formula, with the denominator being different to account for different elements of the data. For example, τ_a is the first version that fails to make adjustment for ties. The tau statistic has the same interpretation as gamma and nearly the same range of values: tau-a can never equal |1| if there are ties in the data, and tau-b and tau-c can equal |1| if the cross-tabulation is presented in a square, i.e., the two variables have the same number of values. Tau-a can be calculated with the following formula:

$$\tau_a = \frac{N_s - N_d}{\left(\dfrac{N(N-1)}{2}\right)}$$

Figure 7.11 Tau-a Equation

The second version, τ_b, which includes an adjustment for ties, is best suited for when the cross-tabulation is a square. This version, along with the third version, are the most commonly calculated and reported in research and by software programs. Tau-b can be calculated with the following formula:

$$\tau_b = \frac{N_s - N_d}{\sqrt{\left(\dfrac{N(N-1)}{2} - \dfrac{t_j(t_j-1)}{2}\right)\left(\dfrac{N(N-1)}{2} - \dfrac{u_k(u_k-1)}{2}\right)}}$$

t_j = number of tied x values
u_k = number of tied y values

Figure 7.12 Tau-b Equation

The third and final version of Kendall's tau, τ_c, has the same elements of the tau-b statistic; however, it is best suited when the cross-tabulation is a rectangle, i.e., the two variables have a different number of values. Tau-c can be calculated with the following formula:

$$\tau_c = \frac{2(N_s - N_d)}{n^2 \dfrac{(m-1)}{m}}$$

m = minimum (lowest) number (row or columns)

Figure 7.13 Tau-c Equation

When testing for statistical significance, increasingly complex formulas to calculate a z statistic are utilized. These need not be calculated by hand. Data analysis software provide significance results nearly instantly and provide corresponding p values for interpretation.

SPEARMAN'S CORRELATION

Another frequently used nonparametric test of association for ordinal variables, though it may be used for continuous variables as well, is Spearman's rank-order correlation. Charles Spearman was a psychologist whose experimental work drove him to find better ways to analyze its data. Spearman's (1904) seminal paper provided a nonparametric complement to the statistical procedure of correlation refined by Pearson just a few short years prior. Denoted by ρ (rho), the Spearman correlation statistic can

Box 7.5: WHAT WE'VE LEARNED: Kendall's τ

Those involved with the criminal justice system have long been associated with other, related negative outcomes. One set of outcomes that has garnered increased attention in recent years is that of inmate and former inmate health. A group of public health scholars recently examined the smoking behaviors and other cancer-related outcomes among males involved with the criminal justice system. Specifically, the researchers narrowed their inquiry to urban, middle-aged, and older males with a history of incarceration (Valera, Anderson, Cook, Wylie-Rosett, Rucker, & Reid, 2015). Using survey data from 259 males age 35–67 that were formerly incarcerated in New York City, the researchers used Kendall's τ to quantify the association between a Cancer Knowledge and Prevention (CKP) score, calculated by a series of questions about the participants' knowledge of cancer-related activities, and various smoking behaviors. Results showed that CKP scores were significantly associated with the number of cigarettes an individual smoked per day. The negative τ value indicated that the greater the knowledge of cancer-related activities one has, the fewer number of cigarettes the individual smoked per day. There was not a significant association between the CKP score and the "intent to quit smoking" (p. 91).

take a value between −1.0 and +1.0, with a value of |1| indicating a perfect monotonic relationship. A monotonic relationship is one in which the relationship between variables is consistent in one direction (positive or negative), despite being nonlinear.

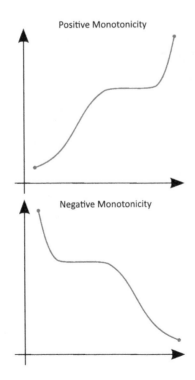

Figure 7.14 Positive Monotonic and Negative Monotonic

Specifically meant for when there are no ties of rank in the data, the following formula can be used to calculate ρ:

$$\rho = 1 - \frac{6 \sum d_i^2}{n(n^2 - 1)}$$

Figure 7.15 Spearman's Rank Correlation Equation

where d_i = the difference between the ranks of an observation.

The formula in Figure 7.15 is commonly used, and some data analysis software may use it, regardless of ties. Others may not compute rho if there are ties in the data. When rho is computed, the interpretation of the value is considered more clear than other measures of association for categorical variables. The closer the value to |1|, the stronger the relationship between the two variables is, e.g., the monotonicity of each variable approaches the other. The closer to 0, the weaker the relationship, and the values of each variable are not related to the values of the other. Once rho is calculated, there are several ways to test for statistical significance—the most common of which being based on the t distribution with df equal to $n - 2$:

$$t = \rho \sqrt{\frac{n-2}{1-\rho^2}}$$

Figure 7.16 t-value for Spearman's Rank Correlation Equation

Box 7.6: WHAT WE'VE LEARNED: Spearman's Correlation

British researchers Newton, Partridge, and Gill (2014) recently conducted a study to assess the risk of crime within and around major transit systems, specifically those that are underground, e.g., the subway. While their research was based in London, the results offer interesting insights that may apply elsewhere. Their study analyzed both traditional, aboveground offenses and those that occur underground. Data were gathered at four points. The first two points were considered aboveground. Those were offenses that occurred outside of the station and inside of the station while still aboveground and before gate-fare had been paid. The second two points were considered belowground. These offenses were those that occurred below the ground inside the station and after gate-fare had been paid, and inside the station while in transport. Using Spearman's rank-order correlation, the researchers measured the association between the crime counts (e.g., frequencies) and rates for three offenses that occurred at the station and those that occurred near the station. For counts, only theft from persons at the station was significantly associated with offenses near the station: shoplifting, other thefts, and theft from persons were found to have significant associations. For rates, only theft from persons at the station and theft from persons near the station were significantly associated. Additional results found significant associations between the time of day and offense rates (pp. 9–10).

CONTINUOUS VARIABLES

Data that are measured at increasingly higher levels of measurement also have a greater number of tests of association with which they can be examined. Unlike categorical data—which are measured at the nominal or ordinal level—continuous data provide variable values that are measured numerically. Interval and ratio level data, then, inherently provide two characteristics of a relationship when a test of association finds statistical significance: direction and strength. As a result, like tests of association for categorical variables, tests of association for continuous variables can see if variables are related to one another and how strong the relationship is, but also whether the relationship is negative or positive.

PEARSON'S CORRELATION

Ubiquitous across disciplines, the concept of correlation is one that is mentioned frequently but done so correctly only sparingly. While correlation *is* a measurement of two variables' relationship and *does* reflect the characteristic of that relationship numerically, it is often mentioned colloquially with respect to any type of variable or level of measurement. In the strict statistical sense, correlation is a measurement of two continuous variables' relationship and the numerical description of that relationship. Nominal and ordinal variables can be *related* or *dependent*; however, they cannot be *correlated*, as that alludes to the specific value that is calculated from numerical data.

Correlation, by some, has its roots in the work of Bravais (1846), from a paper he read before the Institut de France. In this paper, he presented perhaps the first theoretical discussion of correlation theory. However, formulaic expression and discussion of a single value (or term) that is comparable to what is used today may be traced back further to Laplace (1811) and Plana (1813), in which the "probability of the simultaneous occurrence of two variables" was then discussed (Walker, 1929).

Despite these early discussions of the theory of correlation, it would be some time later until the ideas of early mathematicians were refined into applicable formulae. In fact, the term "correlated" does not appear in the statistical literature until Galton (1875) began his work in the area. More than a decade later (1888) he first used the term "correlation" (David, 1995). Following Galton's (1889) "discovery" of correlation, he returned to his primary area of interest —heredity and the measurement of physical traits—which was spurred by the work of his cousin, Charles Darwin. Work in the area of correlation, or the measurement of bivariate relationships, was then taken on by Pearson (Stigler, 1986). Ultimately, it is from Pearson's (1896) work that the present-day correlation coefficient is derived. The correlation coefficient is the numerical value that represents the direction and strength of the relationship between two continuous variables.

The relationship of two continuous variables can be displayed using a scatter plot (see Figure 7.17) with a best fit line. This line summarizes the relationship between the two variables, represented as a slope. A line with no slope indicates no relationship. Thus, the more horizontal the best fit line is, the weaker the relationship. A line with a steep slope indicates a strong relationship.

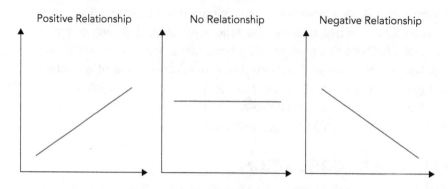

Figure 7.17 Slope of Relationships Comparison

Denoted by *r* and referred to as Pearson's *r*, the correlation coefficient ranges in value from −1.0 to +1.0. Thus, a negative relationship indicates that as the *x* variable—often describing an independent variable—increases, the *y* variable— or the dependent variable—decreases. A positive relationship indicates that, as the *x* variable increases, the *y* variable increases. Unlike Spearman's correlation, Pearson's *r* measures linear relationships. Regardless of the direction (negative or positive) and strength of the relationship, those characteristics are assumed to be equal across all values of the variables. With respect to strength, *r* values of |1| indicate a perfect relationship. A perfect relationship signifies the ability to determine the value of one variable from the value of the second variable with 100% accuracy. Thus, the closer to |1| *r* becomes, the stronger the relationship is. The closer to 0 *r* becomes, the weaker the relationship is.

Correlation Value	Interpretation
.00 < .25	Weak relationship
.25 to < .50	Moderate relationship
.50 to < .75	Moderately strong relationship
.75 to 1.0	Strong relationship

Figure 7.18 Correlation Value Interpretation

To calculate Pearson's *r*, the following formula is used:

$$r = \frac{N\left(\sum xy\right) - \left(\sum x\right)\left(\sum y\right)}{\sqrt{\left[N\left(\sum x^2\right) - \left(\sum x\right)^2\right]\left[N\left(\sum y^2\right) - \left(\sum y\right)^2\right]}}$$

Figure 7.19 Pearson's Correlation Equation

where   N = the number of cases.

Box 7.7: Example of Correlation

The police chief, upon seeing the results from Box 7.2: Example of Two-Way Chi-Square, requests additional tests be conducted. Specifically, the chief would like you to try to uncover additional factors that may be related to the number of citizen complaints an officer receives. Anecdotally, the chief states that he notices younger, less experienced officers receiving more complaints. As a data analyst, this would suggest a negative correlation between experience and complaints. Thus, you decide to calculate the correlation coefficient for the years of experience on the job and the number of citizen complaints an officer receives.

Experience (Years)	Number of Citizen Complaints
12	1
5	2
12	2
13	2
11	2
14	3
8	3
20	3
18	4
13	5
4	5
20	5
3	6
16	6
33	6
30	6
6	7
20	1
6	2
15	2
9	2
4	4
2	5

Figure 7.20 Pearson's Correlation Example

What is the correlation coefficient for the years of experience on the job and the number of citizen complaints an officer receives? Is the chief's belief that there is a negative relationship between the variables supported by the data? Using the r formula, you should have come up with a correlation coefficient of approximately 0.13.

$$.13 = \frac{23(1117) - (294)(84)}{\sqrt{[23(5224^2) - (294)^2][23(382^2) - (84)^2]}}$$

Figure 7.21 Pearson's Correlation Example #2

In Box 7.7: Example of Correlation, the r value that was calculated is very close to zero. A correlation coefficient of 0.13 indicates two things: the direction of the relationship is positive, and the strength of the relationship is very weak. Thus, the years of experience on the job and the number of citizen complaints an officer receives have a very weak, positive relationship. Knowing the r value is not fully indicative of a relationship's characteristics. A positive yet very weak relationship, for example, may not be statistically significant. The determination of statistical significance is especially important for "strong" relationships. This is due to the nature of the null hypothesis in a test of significance for correlation. The null hypothesis states the correlation value is equal to zero, meaning there is no relationship between the variables under study. In Box 7.7: Example of Correlation, the r value of 0.13 is already quite close to zero, indicating a very weak relationship exists. Substantively, it may be interpreted that this relationship is not much different from having "no relationship," or having an r value of zero. If r was 0.90, the relationship could be interpreted as being far from equal to zero. If so, at least on the surface, one may be apt to reject the null hypothesis. Thus, a significance test is required.

A significance test for Pearson's r utilizes the t distribution and can be found using the following formula:

$$t = \frac{r\sqrt{N-2}}{\sqrt{1-r^2}}$$

$N =$ number of pairs

Figure 7.23 t value for Pearson's Correlation

Using this formula, the t value is approximately .60. Corresponding critical values, where df is equal to $N - 2$, are 2.080 when $\alpha = 0.05$ and 2.831 when $\alpha = 0.01$. As a result of the t value being less than the critical values, the relationship—albeit a very weak one—is not statistically significant. The null hypothesis would be accepted, and the chief would be informed that there is not a relationship between the years of experience on the job and the number of citizen complaints an officer receives.

Box 7.8: WHAT WE'VE LEARNED: Correlation

A recent study by Wang, Kifer, Graif, and Li (2016) investigated how emerging technologies may help to collect data and provide new ways to view and understand the commission of crime. The authors collected demographic, point-of-interest (POI), and taxi flow data to describe the characteristics of Chicago neighborhoods. Pearson's r values were calculated for 18 different bivariate relationships, though only six were found to be statistically significant. Found to be significantly related to crime rate were a neighborhood's poverty index, disadvantage index, ethnic diversity, percentage of residents that are Black, and percentage of residents that are Hispanic. Of these, the poverty index, disadvantage index, and percentage of residents that are Black were positively related to the crime rate. The strongest positive relationship was found to be between the percentage of residents that are Black and the crime rate ($r = 0.67$). The remaining two relationships, ethnic diversity and the percentage of residents that are Hispanic, shared a negative relationship with the neighborhood crime rate. The strongest negative relationship was found to be between ethnic diversity and the crime rate ($r = -0.55$). With respect to POI correlations, only one of the 10 relationships examined was found to be statistically significant. The number of "professional" POIs in a neighborhood was positively related to the neighborhood crime rate ($r = 0.32$).

PARTIAL CORRELATION

As we will discuss in greater detail in the subsequent chapters, the relationship between two variables can be affected by external forces, e.g., another variable. Thus, the correlation coefficient as calculated in the previous section may not be the most accurate representation of the variables' relationship. Recall the third question in the Introduction to the chapter: *Is an offender's criminal history related to the provision of bail, while accounting for their age?*

	Criminal history (# of prior arrests)	Bail (# of dollars)	Age
Criminal history (# of prior arrests)	1.0		
Bail (# of dollars)	.9	1.0	
Age	.8	.8	1.0

Figure 7.23 Correlation Matrix

Suppose a positive and strong relationship was found to exist between the number of prior arrests, or *x*, and the number of dollars required to post bail, or *y*, (see Figure 7.23). Suppose also that a positive and strong relationship was found to exist between the age, or *z*, of the accused and the number of dollars required to post bail, *y*. It is possible that the initial relationship may be impacted by the second. To more accurately quantify the relationship between *criminal history* and *the provision of bail*, age can be statistically accounted for. This process would result in a partial correlation coefficient, computed by examining all three possible bivariate correlations. To calculate the partial correlation coefficient, the following formula is used:

$$r_{xy.z} = \frac{r_{xy} - r_{xz}\,r_{yz}}{\sqrt{1 - r_{xz}^2}\,\sqrt{1 - r_{yz}^2}}$$

Figure 7.24: Partial Correlation Equation

where r_{XY} = the correlation between *x* and *y*
r_{XZ} = the correlation between *x* and *z*
r_{YZ} = the correlation between *y* and *z*.

By accounting for the third variable and calculating the partial correlation coefficient, the bivariate relationship between *criminal history* and the *provision of bail* is shown to be slightly weaker than originally thought. The correlation value, interpreted identically as before, decreases from 0.90 to 0.72. The partial correlation coefficient is a helpful statistic to more closely examine the bivariate relationship between continuous variables. However, in practice, partial correlations are not calculated very frequently. Alternative data analysis techniques are available to account for the effects of categorical variables, as well, and for the effects of several variables. These techniques will be discussed beginning in Chapter 8.

Box 7.9: WHAT WE'VE LEARNED: Partial Correlation

Researchers Glaser and Denhardt (2010) gathered data from more than 500 police officers working in the Midwest to see if and how the practice of community policing may create a greater sense of purpose for all of those exposed to it: the officers, the citizens, the neighborhoods, and organizations. As part of their data analysis, the two researchers calculated partial correlation coefficients for 15 bivariate relationships, all of which were positive and statistically significant. The third variable, z, was the number of years of departmental service. The strongest relationships found were between different outcomes, e.g., dependent variables. The strongest partial correlation coefficient ($r = 0.80$) was found for an index created to represent a co-produced flow of information and an index to represent an improved co-production climate. The second strongest partial correlation coefficient ($r = 0.72$) was found between an index representing the tailoring of community police to the neighborhood and the aforementioned flow of information index. The tailoring index was equally (partially) correlated to reduced fear. The weakest relationship was found to be between the flow of information index and a measure representing conflict between self-interest and community well-being ($r = 0.22$). The second weakest relationship was found to be between the tailoring index and the measure representing conflict between self-interest and community well-being ($r = 0.29$).

Test of Association	Levels of Measurement
Chi-Square	Nominal, Ordinal
Goodman and Kruskal's Gamma	Nominal, Ordinal
Kendall's Tau	Ordinal
Spearman's Correlation	Ordinal, Interval, Ratio
Pearson's Correlation	Interval, Ratio
Partial Correlation	Interval, Ratio

Figure 7.25: Tests of Association Summary

SUMMARY

Tests of association allow a researcher to determine—with a particular degree of certainty—whether variables are independent of one another or if they are related. Each test has different requirements, examines independence differently, and has findings that result in different interpretations. Knowing what type of data one has and the intent of the research is paramount to conducting the correct statistical test. To choose the appropriate test of association, one must know the level(s) of measurement, the number of variables, and the number of values across the variables under study.

Like the tests of equality discussed in Chapter 6, there are several tests of association available to data analysts when data are categorical. When data are measured at the nominal level, a chi-square test is often employed, utilizing the χ^2 distribution. Ordinal data have multiple statistical tests available due mostly to the added characteristic of having a hierarchy across the variables' values, i.e., there is an ascending or descending order. These tests include what are known as the Goodman and Kruskal gamma test, the Kendall τ tests, and Spearman's rank-order correlation. Sometimes these tests are referred to strictly based on their resultant test statistic, that which is compared to a critical value to determine significance: γ (gamma), τ (tau), and ρ (rho), respectively. The critical value to which the calculated statistic is compared is derived using different formulae and distributions—either the z or t distribution—based on the normality of the data and the specific test employed. Each new test discussed began to more closely resemble the test of association used for continuous data: Pearson's correlation.

At times, Spearman's rank-order correlation is used to test the association between continuous variables. This is most likely done when the relationship is not linear. Simple scatter plots can provide evidence of such a pattern. However, when the relationship appears to be linear and the data are continuous, Pearson's correlation is used. Like some of the tests for categorical data, Pearson's correlation provides a numerical value that quantifies the direction and strength of the relationship between two continuous variables. This allows for clear interpretation and aids in prediction. Knowing the value of one variable may help predict the value of the second variable, depending on the strength (and significance) of the relationship. An advantage of being able to calculate the correlation value for continuous variables is the ability to account for a third variable that may be affecting the primary relationship of interest. By calculating a partial correlation coefficient, a clearer understanding of two variables' relationship can be had. If there are additional variables that one would like to account for, or those additional relationships are between or including categorical variables, alternative tests are required. These will be discussed in Chapters 8 through 10.

CHAPTER REVIEW QUESTIONS

1. Explain why Spearman's rank-order correlation may be used for continuous data instead of Pearson's correlation.

2. Explain which tests of association can be conducted with more than two variables.

3. Discuss the differences between a one-way and a two-way chi-square test.

4. What are the differences between the three different Kendall τ tests?

5. What can some tests of association for ordinal variables and all tests of association for interval/ratio variables provide that tests of association for nominal variables cannot?

CHAPTER REVIEW EXERCISES

1. Visit the United Nations Office of Drugs and Crime website: www.unodc.org In the search bar, search the phrase *International Statistics*. The first result is the report of the International Statistics on Crime and Justice. Find Figure 2 on page 56. Based on this scatter plot, how would you describe the relationship between drug trafficking and drug-related crime with respect to direction and strength? Explain.

2. Collect information, anonymously, from your classmates concerning the number of hours a week they study, their GPA, and the number of hours a week they work. Conduct a correlation between study time and GPA, and a partial correlation when accounting for work hours. Explain your results.

3. As an extension of Question #2, collect categorical data from your classmates. Perform a one-way or two-way chi-square test of association. Explain the results.

4. Develop a criminal justice or criminological research question that could test the partial correlation between two variables, while accounting for a third.

5. Using your institution's library resources, find a peer-reviewed journal article that is of interest to you that reports on at least one of the tests of association discussed in this chapter. Discuss the article, the test(s) of association, and what the researcher(s) found.

REFERENCES

Cohen, J. (1988). *Statistical power analysis for the behavioral sciences* (2nd Ed.). Hillsdale, NJ: Lawrence Earlbaum Associates.

Cramér, H. (1946). *Mathematical methods of statistics*. Princeton, NJ: Princeton University Press.

Dahl, M., Allwood, C.M., Scimone, B., & Rennemark, M. (2015). Old and very old adults as witnesses: Event memory and metamemory. *Psychology, Crime, and Law, 21*(8), 764–775.

David, H.A. (1995). First (?) occurrence of common terms in mathematical statistics. *The American Statistician, 49*(2), 121–133.

Deuchler, G. (1909). Beiträge zur erforschung der reaktionsformen. *Psychologische Studien, 4,* 353–430.

Deuchler, G. (1914). Über die methoden der korrelationsrechnung in der paidagogik and psychologie. *Zeitschrift fur Padagogische Psychologie und Experimentelle Padagogik, 15,* 114–131; 145–159; 229–242.

Fechner, G. (1897). *Kollektivmasslehre*. Leipzig, Germany: Verlag Von Wilhelm Engleman.

Federal Bureau of Investigation. (2013). *Variables affecting crime (Caution Against Ranking)*. U.S. Department of Justice. Retrieved from https://ucr.fbi.gov/nibrs/2013/resources/variables-affecting-crime/at_download/file

Galton, F. (1875). *English men of science*. New York, NY: Appleton.

Galton, F. (1888). Co-relations and their measurement. *Proceedings of the Royal Society of London, 45*, 135–145.

Gerard, F.J., Whitfield, K.C., Porter, L.E., & Browne, K.D. (2016). Offender and offence characteristics of school shooting incidents. *Journal of Investigative Psychology and Offender Profiling, 13*(1), 22–38.

Glaser, M.A., & Denhardt, J. (2010). Community policing and community being: A case study of officer perceptions. *The American Review of Public Administration, 40*(3), 309–325.

Goodman, L.A., & Kruskall, W.H. (1954). Measures of association for cross classification. *Journal of the American Statistical Association, 49*(268), 732–764.

Goodman, L.A., & Kruskall, W.H. (1959). Measures of association for cross classification II: Further discussion and references. *Journal of the American Statistical Association, 54*(285), 123–163.

Goodman, L.A., & Kruskall, W.H. (1963). Measures of association for cross classification III: Approximate sampling theory. *Journal of the American Statistical Association, 58*(302), 310–364.

Goodman, L.A., & Kruskall, W.H. (1972). Measures of association for cross classification IV: Simplification of asymptotic variances. *Journal of the American Statistical Association, 67*(338), 415–421.

Hirschi, T., & Rudisill, D. (1976). The great American search: Causes of crime 1876–1976. *The Annals of the American Academy of Political and Social Science, 43*, 14–22.

Laplace, P.S. (1811). Mémoire sur les intégrales definies, et leur application aux probabilites, et spécialement à la recherche du milieu qu'il faut choisir entre les résultats des observations. *Mgm. Inst. Imp. France Annie 1810*, 279–347.

Laplace, P.S. (1820). *Théorie analytique des probabilitiés*. Paris, France.

Lipps, G.F. (1905). Die bestimmung der abhängigkeit zwischen den merkmalen eines gegenstades. *Berichte über die Vorhadlundgen der Königlich Sachsischen Gesellschaft der Wissenschaften zu Leipzig, Mathetmatisch-Physische Klasse, 57*, 1–32.

Newton, A.D., Partridge, H., & Gill, A. (2014). Above and below: Measuring crime risk in and around underground mass transit systems. *Crime Science, 3*(1), 1–14.

Pearson, K. (1896). Regression, heredity, and panmixia. *Philosophical Transactions of the Royal Society of London, Series A, 185*, 71–110.

Pearson, K. (1900). On the criterion that a given system of deviations from the probable in the case of a correlated system of variables is such that it can be reasonably supposed to have arisen from random sampling. *Phil. Mag.*, *(5)*50, 157–175.

Pearson, K. (1904). *On the theory of contingency and its relation to association and normal correlation.* London: Dulau & Co.

Plackett, R.L. (1983). Karl Pearson and the Chi-squared test. *International Statistical Review, 51,* 59–72.

Plana, G. (1813). Mémoire sur divers problémas de probabilité. *Mémoires de l'Académie Impériale de Turn, pour les* Années 1811–1812, 355–498.

Spearman, C. (1904). General intelligence: Objectively determined and measured. *The American Journal of Psychology, 15*(2), 201–292.

Stigler, S.M. (1986). *The history of statistics: The measurement of uncertainty before 1900.* Cambridge, MA: Harvard University Press.

Valera, P., Anderson, M., Cook, S.H., Wylie-Rosett, J., Rucker, J., & Reid, A.E. (2015). The smoking behaviors and cancer-related disparities among urban middle aged and older males involved in the criminal justice system. *Journal of Cancer Education, 30*(1), 86–93.

Yule, G.U. (1912). On the methods of measuring the association between two variables: The first identification of the phi-coefficient. *Journal of the Royal Statistical Society, 75*(6), 579–652.

Walker, H.M. (1929). *Studies in the history of statistical method: With special reference to certain educational problem.* Baltimore, MD: The Williams & Wilkins Company.

Wang, H., Kifer, D., Graif, C., & Li, Z. (2016). Crime rate inference with big data. In *Proceedings of the 22nd ACM SIGKDD International Conference on Knowledge Discovery and Data Mining* (pp. 635–644).

IMAGE CREDITS

- Fig. 7.14a: Source: https://commons.wikimedia.org/wiki/File:Monotonicity_example1.png.
- Fig. 7.14b: Source: https://commons.wikimedia.org/wiki/File:Monotonicity_example2.png.

INTRODUCING REGRESSION ANALYSIS

INTRODUCTION: PHYSICAL SCIENCE VS. SOCIAL SCIENCE

Few problems in criminology present as many difficulties as the causes of criminal behavior. A fundamental examination of the meaning of "cause" as applied to crime will obviate some of these difficulties. The concept of cause as used in natural and physical sciences cannot be applied in exactly the same sense in the social sciences. (Cantor, 1932, p. 854)

As the sociologist Cantor (1932) stated nearly 90 years ago, determining the "cause" of crime is difficult for several reasons. First, *cause* as a concept must be explicated with respect to its meaning. Without a concept being clearly defined, it cannot be objectively measured. Furthermore, a "cause," as is generally understood, is viewed differently in the physical sciences than in the social sciences—such as criminal justice and criminology. In the physical sciences, experiments and studies can be conducted in a vacuum, so to speak. Those in disciplines such as biology, chemistry, and physics can conduct studies in controlled environments where (at least nearly) all conditions are created, regulated, and/or measured. In the social sciences, conditions cannot be controlled so readily. Researchers in disciplines such as sociology, criminal justice and criminology, and psychology do their best to control, or account for, all conditions—but it is just not possible. The study of these areas, specifically criminal justice and criminology, occurs in the *real world* and, if/when an experiment is conducted, not all conditions can be controlled, regulated, and/or measured. Thus, social scientists can never *really* determine causation, they can only provide empirical support for it.

Consider the following questions:

1. Is the amount of money embezzled related to an offender's sentence length, accounting for his/her age?

2. Is the number of hours a child plays violent video games related to misconduct in school, accounting for the level of parental supervision?

3. Are crime rates related to the size of the population, accounting for employment rates?

As an extension of the previous chapter, the processes needed to answer each of these questions involve the statistical examination of at least three variables. By increasing the number of variables under examination, compared to the analyses learned in previous chapters, social sciences can approach the requirements needed to determine causation. While the physical sciences can account for (at least nearly) all conditions in an experiment, social sciences account for as many relevant conditions as possible. These conditions are often derived from theory or from previous research, exemplifying the deductive and inductive research processes, and are measured accordingly when data are available. The group of tests by which several variables are tested with respect to their relationship to another, dependent variable is known as regression. This chapter examines the history, calculation, and basics of regression analysis.

LEARNING OBJECTIVES

By the end of this chapter, students will be able to:

1: Identify the assumptions of regression analysis

2: Discuss the level of measurement requirements of regression analysis

3: Explain the notation of the regression equation

4: Evaluate the advantages and limitations of regression analysis

5: Interpret the results of a regression analysis

KEY TERMS

B COEFFICIENT

BETA COEFFICIENT

CAUSATION

CONFIDENCE INTERVAL

ERROR TERM

OMITTED VARIABLE BIAS

ORDINARY LEAST SQUARES

REGRESSION

RESIDUAL

Y-INTERCEPT

PURPOSE OF REGRESSION

The term regression refers to a group or class of data analysis techniques in which several (independent) ...les are analyzed to predict or estimate the value of another (dependent) variable. Defined, the term ...sion alludes to the return to something. In statistics and data analysis, "return" is in reference to ...ean value, specifically that of the dependent variable. Incorporating data from several independent variables allows for the estimation of a mean based on those aforementioned characteristics. While there is likely to be variation in a variable, its mean (as discussed in Chapter 4) is its best representation in a linear regression model, based on its assumptions. The variation of the dependent variable is analyzed based on the variation of the independent variables. Thus, variation of data allows for the "return" to the mean value by way of estimation, incorporating all of the different values in the dataset to predict the average effect of independent variables on the dependent variable. There are several types of regression techniques, with an inordinate number of variants therein. The most basic and easily understood technique is linear regression, also known as ordinary least squares (OLS) regression.

Regression, as the OLS namesake shows, has its formative basis in the analysis, or method, of least squares. The method of least squares is the "procedure to determine the best-fit-line to data" (Miller, 2017, p. 1). In essence, this type of analysis takes data from all cases under study to calculate one summary statement about their combined, i.e., simultaneous, effects—specifically of the effects of the independent variables on the dependent variable. Least squares, as a concept, refers to the statistical procedures by which the sum of squares are minimized to produce the line of best fit. The sum of squares refers to the square of the difference, or distance, between each data point and the line of best fit. The data point represents the observed value, and the line of best fit represents the predicted value. The difference between the two is known as the residual. Since there is variation among the variables' values, the line of best fit is determined by reducing the difference between each value and the predicted value, e.g. the residuals. This line, ultimately, represents the one summary statement that shows the combined effects of independent variables on the dependent variable. This statement is often shown with an equation.

The concept of least squares did not appear in statistical literature until 1805 (Smith, 1929; David, 1995). In the early 19th century, Adrien-Marie Legendre was studying astronomy using mathematical applications. His discussion of the method of least squares is found in work that seeks to determine the orbits of comets (Legendre, 1805). At the time, he proposed the method out of convenience, though he makes notes that a practical use would be one based on the arithmetic mean (Merriman, 1877). Its history may go back slightly further, as Gauss stated that he had been using the principle a decade earlier (Smith, 1929; Stigler, 1986). Soon thereafter, the first mathematical proofs were derived; the first by Adrain (1808) and then Gauss (1809) himself, followed by several others. The development of the method of least squares was a monumental step, one that was required to develop the group of regression techniques decades later into the techniques we know and use today.

Nearly all discussions of the origins of regression attribute its genesis to Galton in the 1880s. While some credit is given to others, such as to R.J. Adcock and his work in the 1870s (see Finney, 1996), it was Galton who began to apply

REGRESSION:
In data analysis, a statistical technique that examines the simultaneous effects of multiple independent variables on one dependent variable.

ORDINARY LEAST SQUARES (OLS):
Also known as simple linear regression, this statistical technique examines the simultaneous linear effects of multiple independent variables on one continuous dependent variable.

RESIDUAL:
In data analysis, the difference between the observed value and the predicted value.

the theoretical concept of regression to actual data. As early as 1875, Galton began experimenting with sweet peas. His work was specifically focused on determining how successive generations of peas inherited their size. Every time he produced a new batch of seedlings, he noticed that the characteristics were, on the whole, similar to previous seedling batches, while individually, the seedlings resembled the seed from which it came. Galton decided he needed more data, so he distributed seedling packets to seven friends who harvested them and returned them to him. From those packets, he compared the weight of the returned seedlings to their parent seeds. He found that the median weights of the seedlings from a particular size of a parent seed could be plotted with a relatively straight and positively sloped line (Stanton, 2001). This line of best fit, e.g., line of regression (Yule, 1897), was first presented during a lecture in 1877 at the Royal Institution. In fact, this was when regression was first referred to, though Galton used the term *reversion* at this point in time (Walker, 1929). It would not be until 1885 that the concept of regression was seen in the statistical literature. And, it would not be until the turn of the century that Yule (1899) would utilize social data to conduct a regression analysis.

CORRELATION VS. CAUSATION

Regression analysis is a step beyond bivariate tests of association as it allows researchers to determine the extent to which the independent variable predicts the dependent variables, while controlling for other variables, not just whether they are significantly related. Generally, there are two types of regression analysis under which all forms fall: bivariate regression and multiple (sometimes inappropriately referred to as multivariate) regression. This chapter will initially discuss bivariate regression analysis—that which examines one independent variable and one dependent variable—before discussing multiple regression. Chapters 9 and 10 will discuss different forms of multiple regression—that which examine at least two independent variables and one dependent variable.

As an extension of correlation, regression allows for the pursuit of determining if a linear relationship is causal. In order to determine causation, there are at least three criteria that must be met:

1. Temporal Precedence

2. Covariation

3. Non-spuriousness

The first two criteria are very easily determined. Temporal precedence refers to the chronological order in which conditions are observed. If an independent variable is presumed to *cause* a change in the dependent variable, it must come before it. For example, if a researcher is analyzing data to see if participation in a correctional program results in a change of behavior, participation in the program (the independent variable) must come before the behavior change (the dependent variable). Covariation refers to the finding of a statistically significant relationship between the independent variable and the dependent variable. As the value of the independent variable changes, so too must the value of the dependent variable. Thus, if participation in a correctional program is presumed to *cause* a change in behavior, there must be observed changes in behavior across levels of participation. The third criterion is where social sciences depart from physical sciences in their ability to determine causation. A spurious relationship is one that appears to be valid on the surface but does not actually exist. Thus, non-spuriousness refers to the characteristic of an observed relationship that exists in actuality and is not the product of something else. A spurious relationship would show a relationship between two variables which is either the product of another variable or is masking another, true relationship. Thus, if participation in a correctional program is presumed to *cause* a change in behavior, all other factors must be controlled for. While many factors can be controlled for, social science experiments and the environments in which they are conducted cannot be created, regulated, and/or measured like those of the physical sciences, e.g., labs. Thus, criminal justice and criminological studies can provide support for causation but can never, with 100% confidence, claim it exists.

This is exemplified in Yule's (1899) study, as well as a subsequent and ardent critique by A.C. Pigou (1910). In his critique, Pigou explicitly refuted the notion that regression analysis can be used as a process to determine causality, particularly in social science research. The inability of a researcher to account for and control all possible related factors renders causality impossible. Mistaking regression results as support for causation was of grave concern. Yule, too, noted this when discussing the bias that can result from omitting variables from analysis. As a result, omitted variable bias may occur, resulting in inaccurate findings of the effects of the factors that were included in the model.

OMITTED VARIABLE BIAS: The characteristic of inaccurate findings of the effects of factors in a statistical model as a result of misspecification, e.g., the exclusion of relevant variables.

Box 8.1: WHAT WE'VE LEARNED: Correlation vs. Causation

Using data from the National Survey of Adolescents (NSA), researchers Lin, Cochran, and Mieczkowski (2011) examined how violent victimization, vicarious victimization, and dual victimization are related to both juvenile crime perpetration and drug use. Utilizing the General Strain Theory (GST) framework, the researchers examined the mediating and moderating effects of depression, low social control, and association with delinquents on the victimization-delinquency relationship. The authors hypothesized that victimization of any type would have a positive effect on delinquency, dual victimization would have a greater effect than the other forms of victimization, the effects of victimization are mediated by GST factors, and the effects of victimization on delinquency are moderated by GST factors. Generally, the hypotheses were supported by the results; however, the researchers explicitly caution against interpreting the relationships as causal. In effect, the authors were able to find associations, or relationships, between variables, but not state the relationships were causal in nature. The survey, as they note, was cross-sectional. Thus, the first criterion, temporal precedence, could not be met. The same can be said for the third criterion, non-spuriousness. As a result, establishing a causal relationship from this specific study is not possible. However, the results were found to be similar to those found in several longitudinal studies (p. 218), indicating reliability of the findings.

VARIABLES

In regression analysis, there are several assumptions related to the variables included in the statistical model(s). These assumptions, or the characteristics of the variables included in the models, differ based on the type of regression analysis being conducted. Each type of regression analysis requires the variables included be operationalized at a specific level of measurement. Generally, this is more important and impactful when considering the characteristics of the dependent variable(s) and deciding which type of regression analysis is most appropriate. The requirements of independent variables can be relaxed to some extent.

DEPENDENT VARIABLE

The type of regression analysis that is conducted is related to the characteristics of the dependent variable. When the dependent variable is "quantitative, continuous, and unbounded" (Berry, 1993, p. 12), the most common type of regression analysis conducted is a linear regression. This type of regression analysis will be discussed in this chapter and explained more thoroughly, by example, in Chapter 9. When the dependent variable is discrete and has only two possible outcomes, the most common type of regression analysis conducted is a logistic regression. This type of regression analysis will be discussed in Chapter 10. There are also types of regression analysis that can analyze a dependent variable that is discrete and has more than two possible outcomes (see Box 2.4: WHAT WE'VE LEARNED: Ordinal, for an example). In addition, there are various types of regression analysis that can analyze a quantitative dependent variable that is discrete (see Box 2.5: WHAT WE'VE LEARNED: Count Data, for an example). There are numerous variants of each of these types of regression analysis. These involve additional, or at least different, assumptions and are more complex. In this chapter, our discussion of regression analysis will first be restricted to general assumptions, and then the linear model.

INDEPENDENT VARIABLE(S)

As stated previously, the assumptions of the independent variables included in a regression model can be more relaxed than the assumptions and requirements of the dependent variable. As Berry (1993) mentions when discussing these assumptions, "All independent variables ... are quantitative or dichotomous ..." (p. 12). However, this is not always the case. It is not uncommon to see independent variables operationalized at the ordinal level of measurement included in a regression analysis. Ordinal variables are neither quantitative nor dichotomous (having just two categories). Some data analysts, however, choose to treat ordinal variables with several categories as if they are measured continuously. A second requirement of independent variables, regardless of the type of regression analysis conducted, is that they have a variance that is not equal to zero. This ensures variability in the variable. If a variable has no variability, e.g., a variance of zero, it is unnecessary to include it in the statistical model. Independent variables, remember, are included for theoretical or statistical reasons to help predict or estimate the value of the dependent variable. If an independent variable has no variability, all cases have the same value, and it will add no predictive value to the statistical model. For example, if a team of researchers gathered data from prisoners incarcerated in a male prison, there would be no need to have a *gender* or *sex* variable, since there would be no variability. The *gender* or *sex* of an individual would have no impact on findings because everyone has the same value of that variable.

THE REGRESSION EQUATION

The basic equation for a linear regression is:

$$y = \beta_{0} + \beta_{1}X_{1} \dots + \varepsilon_{1}$$

Figure 8.1: Linear Regression Equation

where Y = the value of the dependent variable
β_{0} = the y-intercept
β_{1} = the slope of the line (i.e., coefficients)
X_{1} = the value of the independent variable
ε_{1} = the value of the error term.

This equation represents the model for the underlying population, inferred from sample statistics. The equation for a linear regression has several components. However, each component and corresponding symbol can be interpreted fairly easily. Ultimately, the value of the dependent variable (Y), which is on the *left* side of the equation, is estimated by the *right* side of the equation: the values of the y-intercept (β_{0}), the products of the coefficients and the independent variable values ($\beta_{1}X_{1}\dots$), and the value of the error term (ε_{1}). This is a more advanced version of the traditional linear equation seen in "slope and y-intercept" form, which may be familiar to you: $y = mx + b$. The equation for a linear regression may also be expressed as:

$$y = b_{0} + b_{1}x_{1}\dots + e_{1}$$

Figure 8.2 Linear Regression Equation #2

where y = the value of the dependent variable
b_{0} = the y-intercept
b_{1} = the slope of the line (i.e., coefficients)
x_{1} = value of the independent variable
e_{1} = the value of the error term.

ASSUMPTIONS

Like all statistical tests discussed thus far, regression analysis has its own set of assumptions and requirements. These extend beyond just the characteristics of the variables involved in the analysis. Some of these assumptions are more complex than others and will be discussed in detail in Chapter 9. There is a substantial amount of literature that documents, displays, and explains the various assumptions of regression. According to Berry (1993), the following assumptions must be taken into consideration when conducting a regression analysis (though more specific assumptions also apply):

ERROR TERM:
In data analysis, the numerical representation of the combined effect of all omitted variables and measurement error.

Y-INTERCEPT:
In regression analysis, the value of Y when X is equal to 0.

1. There is an absence of multicollinearity

2. The error term is uncorrelated with the independent variables

3. The mean of the error term is equal to 0

4. The error term is normally distributed

5. There is homoscedasticity

6. There is an absence of autocorrelation

7. There is measurement without error

On the surface, there appears to be many assumptions—possibly too many to meet when conducting data analysis. However, there are a variety of ways to detect and correct for the violation of these assumptions. In addition, some of the assumptions are difficult to detect. Thus, correction may not be required (or even possible).

The first assumption of regression is that there is an absence of multicollinearity. Multicollinearity simply refers to the condition of a statistical model that includes independent variables that have built in linearity or are a linear combination of one another. For example, multicollinearity would exist if the variables *age* and *year* were both simultaneously input into a regression model. As age increases by one year, so too would the year—and vice versa. Multicollinearity would also exist if the variables *number of offenses as a juvenile*, *number of offenses as an adult*, and *number of overall offenses* were all simultaneously input into a regression model. The third variable, *number of overall offenses*, is a linear combination (e.g., it is the sum) of the previous two variables: *number of offenses as a juvenile* and *number of offenses as an adult*.

Box 8.2: WHAT WE'VE LEARNED: Multicollinearity

Recently, researchers Walfield, Socia, and Powers (2017) studied the topic of religiously motivated hate crime. Of specific interest to the researchers were reporting to law enforcement and outcomes of those specific types of cases. Using data from both the National Crime Victimization Survey (NCVS) and the National Incident-Based Reporting System (NIBRS), the research team examined the effects of a variety of factors, including victim, offender, and incident-related characteristics. Results showed that more than 40% of religious hate crimes are not reported to law enforcement. Furthermore, when the incident is violent, less than a quarter (22.2%) of the incidents result in an arrest. Only a few factors were related to reporting and case outcomes, though the factors that were related to reporting and case outcomes showed a large effect size, i.e., those factors were strongly related to the dependent variables. Due to multicollinearity, a total of three variables were excluded from the various analyses. The variables *injury*, *juvenile offender*, and *weapon* were omitted from analysis. This is often seen in research utilizing these datasets, as *injury* may be related to *weapon use* or *offense type* (e.g., the difference between a simple and aggravated assault may be the use of a weapon), among other things. Factors related to reporting to law enforcement included if medical care was required, if the victim was a juvenile, if they had a college degree, and if there were prior victimizations. Factors related to arrest included the type of religious motivation (e.g., anti-Christian), if there were multiple victims, if it occurred at a religious institution, if there was an injury, and the geographic location of the incident(s).

The second, third, and fourth assumptions that deal with the error term in a regression model are more complex than the first assumption (and later assumptions, too). In a regression model, the error term simply represents the combined effect of all variables that are related to the dependent variable, but for various reasons are not included in the analysis. In essence, the error term represents the effects of the omitted variables and what is not captured as the result of sampling procedures. If the second assumption is not met, there is a problem with endogeneity. This means that there is something that is related to the dependent variable and perhaps the independent variable(s), but it is not included in the analysis. There are multiple ways to test this assumption, often by way of the statistical software used for the analysis. The third assumption, that the mean of the error term is equal to 0, is conceptually and statistically straightforward. Since the error term represents, in a sense, the unmeasured factors in a regression analysis, the residuals should sum, and average, to zero—assuming a correct line of best fit has been estimated. Positive residuals (observed values higher than the predicted values) should *cancel out* negative residuals (observed values lower than the predicted values). This is analogous to the sum of deviations discussed in Chapter 5. To check for normality, the residuals can be plotted in the form of a histogram.

Box 8.3: WHAT WE'VE LEARNED: Error Term Assumptions

Weisburd, Wooditch, Weisburd, and Yang (2016) discussed the problems associated with violating error term assumptions in their study examining stop, question, and frisk (SQF) practices and deterrence. In their study, they explored the impact of SQFs on the number of criminal incidents, both daily and weekly, in New York City. Their analysis examined the effects of SQFs at the microgeographic level, as previous research suggested that the SQFs were mostly found in hot spots throughout the city. Weisburd et al. noted that, in estimating the deterrent effect of SQFs, there is likely to be a correlation between the error term and the SQFs that occurred during the previous week. To address this concern, the researchers included controls based on the street segment. The theory behind this practice is that a biased estimate of the deterrent effect of SQFs may occur if, for example, an omitted variable such as the level of police deployment is actually the deterrent. Their results showed a significant, albeit modest, deterrent effect on crime as the result of SQFs. The researchers caution that although a reduction in crime may be observed, it may not be cost-efficient or a practice that garners public support.

The fifth assumption of regression is what is known as homoscedasticity, first described by Pearson (1905). Its opposite, heteroscedasticity, also spelled as heteroskedasticity (Valavanis, 1959), is problematic. Homoscedasticity refers to the condition of the dependent variable (or error term) when the variability/variance is equal or constant across all values of an independent variable. This would suggest that the effect of an independent variable is equal regardless of its value, i.e., the relationship is linear. This can be detected by examining the residuals, or plotting the individual data points against the line of best fit. Statistical software also provide various tests to detect this potential problem. Homoscedasticity would be found if the distance between the observed values and the predicted values is at least fairly equal across all values. Violation of this assumption can bias the estimated effects of variables and lead to inaccurate results found in significance tests.

CONFIDENCE INTERVAL:
A range of values, based on a specific degree of certainty, where the population value is located.

The sixth assumption of regression is the absence of autocorrelation, first described by Wold (1938). Autocorrelation occurs when the error term of one observation is correlated with the error term of the next observation. This is particularly important in geography-based research and time-series research as, "Variables that change 'incrementally' over time will tend to be autocorrelated" (Berry, 1993, p. 67). Clearly, this would be a problem in the criminal justice and criminological fields when longitudinal and spatial research is conducted, such as the examination of crimes rates over time or across space. For example, it is likely that yearly changes in crime rates or crime rates in adjacent neighborhoods will be quite similar, e.g., autocorrelated. When autocorrelation exists, significance tests and coefficient estimates by way of confidence intervals will be unreliable. Detection of autocorrelation is typically done through a series of statistical tests included in most statistical software.

Box 8.4: WHAT WE'VE LEARNED: Homoscedasticity and Autocorrelation

A recent study by Rosenfeld and Levin (2016) sought to examine the relationship between economic indicators and criminal activity. Specifically, the researchers studied whether price inflation increases crime rates motivated by monetary gain. Using data from 1960 through 2012 obtained from the Uniform Crime Reports (UCR), the primary offenses of interest were robbery, burglary, larceny, and motor vehicle theft. Data for the economic indicators were gathered from several sources, including the Bureau of Labor Statistics, the Census Bureau, and surveys conducted by the University of Michigan and Thomson Reuters (pp. 433–434). The researchers tested for heteroscedasticity and, since they analyzed several decades of data, autocorrelation. Results indicated that there was no first-order autocorrelation. This means that the error terms of consecutive years were not correlated—meeting that regression assumption. Similarly, tests showed equal or constant variance in the residuals indicating homoscedasticity—meeting that regression assumption. Results indicated that inflation had both short- and long-term effects on yearly change in acquisitive crime rates. Rosenfeld and Levin suggest that incorporating economic indicators such as inflation into studies of crime should be pursued in the future. They note that this is but one study and only through cumulative research can substantively meaningful conclusions be made (just as Fisher suggested).

The seventh assumption, that there is measurement without error, can be interpreted in several ways. More generally, measurement error may be viewed as occurring when a true value is measured with an indicator, e.g., with a proxy. This occurs when variables are measured subjectively. Objective measures are those in which consensus exists with respect to its measurement. For example, if a researcher were to measure *length of incarceration* for prisoners, an objective measurement would be "number of years (or months)." There would be little disagreement with the operationalization of the concept *length of incarceration*. Concepts, such as those that represent beliefs, feelings, or perceptions, are more likely to have several forms of operationalization. As a result, the data captured in the variable may not be the truest measure of the concept. Furthermore, error can result from the actions of the data analyst, such as the miscoding or collapsing of data (e.g., making an interval/ratio variable an ordinal variable). Error in measurement can result in the variance of a variable being different than the true variance: often it is greater, because there is more error introduced into the model. It can also lead to biased estimates of the effects of independent variables on the dependent variable. This bias can be upward or downward, indicating a difference in strength from the true value. This can become more problematic as additional variables are included in the regression analysis. Ultimately, more measurement error results in a reduction in the explanatory power of a regression model, e.g., there is more uncertainty in prediction and estimation.

Box 8.5: WHAT WE'VE LEARNED: Measurement Error

Many studies have examined the effects of law enforcement practices, visibility, and staffing on crime—particularly in large cities. A more recent analysis of data attempted to improve upon previous studies by improving the precision of estimates obtained by mismeasurement. Professors Chaflin and McCrary (2012) used panel data from medium to large cities in the United States from the years 1960 to 2010 to confirm that police reduce violent crime significantly more than property crime. The researchers note that there is a "surprisingly high degree of measurement error" (p. 2) in the UCR, which is the most commonly used data source concerning crime. Of note, they show that even the enumeration of *number of officers* in a police department is subject to measurement error, as evidenced by discrepancies between administrative data and the UCR. With adjusted estimates, they found year-to-year changes in police staffing, operationalized as *police per capita*, are independent of demography, economic and budgetary factors, social disorganization measures, and crime rate changes. Further, their results show that every dollar spent on police is associated with approximately a $1.60 reduction in victimization costs. This suggests that medium to large cities may not be employing enough police officers currently.

INTERPRETING RESULTS

When conducting a regression analysis there are several important calculations from which one may interpret the results. Each software program used in data analysis may report results differently and may also report different results. Statistical software programs like *R*, Stata, SAS, or SPSS (just to name a few) provide results in different formats, some by default and others that are defined by the user. In addition, not all software programs will report identical results. The primary reason for this is that the algorithms or formulae that a program uses in calculations may differ from another program. Often, these default algorithms can be changed and specified by the user. In some instances, however, the

B COEFFICIENT:
In regression analysis, an unstandardized coefficient that represents the effect of an independent variable (IV) on a dependent variable (DV): specifically, the average change in the DV as the result of a one-unit increase in the IV, controlling for the other IVs.

program may treat variables differently than others would. For example, in some forms of data analysis, SPSS will treat categorical data as continuous data and standardize the scores. Thus, when comparing results across software, such as between SPSS and *R*, the results may slightly differ. In other instances, a software program may just not have the ability to produce a test statistic or value that another program can. This can be because one program requires add-ons or additional features, or it simply has not been configured to produce the desired result. Regardless of the statistical software program used, there are specific test statistics that are needed to interpret regression results. In this chapter, we will focus on coefficients, standard error, significance, confidence intervals, and the coefficient of determination.

	b	Std. Error	a	t	Sig.	Lower 95.0 %	Upper 95.0 %
Constant	4.751	2.375		2.000	.059	−.204	9.706
Years of Experience	.043	.054	.191	.801	.433	−.069	.156
Salary ($1,000s)	−.036	.054	−.156	−.655	.520	−.149	.078
Dependent Variable = Number of Citizen Complaints							

Figure 8.3 Linear Regression Results

COEFFICIENTS

The first test statistics provided in the results of a regression analysis, regardless of the statistical software used, are the coefficients. In the regression equation, *b* denotes the coefficients, and β denotes the beta coefficients. These are also referred to as the partial slope coefficients. They are considered *partial*, because each slope, e.g., variable, affects and contributes to the estimation of the line of best fit. The *slope* refers to the steepness of the regression line and is a measure of the change in the dependent variable produced by a one-unit increase in the independent variable. Each independent variable in the equation has its own slope, measured in its own unit of analysis, contributing to the statistical model.

Initially, Galton referred to the slope coefficients with the symbol *r*, which meant *reversion*. Subsequently, he used *w* (1886), and then reverted to using *r* when he used the concept *regression* (1888). The symbol *r* was used for several years. It wasn't until Yule (1907) described a new notation that *b* became the symbol used for regression coefficients.

The *b* coefficients are the coefficients that are provided by all statistical software programs. These partial slope coefficients are unstandardized, meaning the values associated with them are presented in their original units of analysis. For example, if the variables *crime rate per 100,000* and *average*

age of population are included in a regression analysis, their *b* coefficients will be expressed in their respective metrics: rate per 100,000 and age, likely measured by number of years. This may prove difficult to compare the strength of the effects if both, or others, are found to be significantly related to the dependent variable.

To address this dilemma, some software programs also provide β coefficients (e.g., SPSS), while others require additional commands or calculations to produce them (e.g., R and STATA). These coefficients are standardized by calculating the z score for each *b* coefficient. Z scores have a distribution with a mean equal to 0 and a standard deviation equal to 1. A benefit to the standardization of coefficients (i.e., converting *b* values to β values) is the subsequent ability to compare effects. When standardized, the absolute values of each β can be compared to assess their relative strength, or effect, on the dependent variable. In the above example, if the *crime rate per 100,000* has a β value of -0.5 and the *average age of the population* has a β value of 0.7, the *average age of the population* has a stronger effect compared to the *crime rate per 100,000*. The direction of the relationship (negative or positive) is irrelevant to the comparison of strength. Standardization is done by multiplying the *b* coefficient by the standard deviation of the independent variable (*x*), and dividing by the standard deviation of the dependent variable (*y*). A downside to the use of standardized coefficients is the difficulty in interpreting their meaning, as they are not in their original units. Instead, they represent standard deviations of a variable.

$$B = \frac{b(s_x)}{(s_y)}$$

Figure 8.4 Coefficient Standardization (Z score) Equation

STANDARD ERROR

The second test statistic that is provided in the results of a regression analysis, regardless of the statistical software used, is the standard error of the coefficient. In the results of a regression analysis, the standard error can be denoted by a variety of symbols and abbreviations: se, SE, Std. Error, etc. Sometimes, such as when provided in a report or journal article, the standard error of the coefficient is not denoted by a symbol or abbreviation. Instead, it may be provided parenthetically beside or underneath the coefficient values. The standard error of the coefficient represents how precise the *b* (or β) coefficient is. Since each independent variable in the equation has its own coefficient, it also has its own standard error.

As a concept, the origins of the standard error are less clear than other test statistics. Astronomers had long made reference to error with respect

β COEFFICIENT:
In regression analysis, a standardized coefficient that represents the effect of an independent variable (IV) on a dependent variable (DV): specifically, the average change in the DV as the result of a one-unit increase in the IV, controlling for the other IVs, expressed as a z-score.

to sample measurements and population estimates. However, the type of error, what it describes, its calculation, and its interpretation varied for quite some time (Walker, 1929). In the 18th and 19th centuries, several scholars proposed several equations to measure *error* with relatively few similarities with respect to calculation and purpose. It was not until Galton (1877) that the standard error of the coefficient (also called the standard error of the estimate) was developed formulaically. He discussed this in the same lecture he presented on hereditary, much of which was the product of his study of peas. This standard error was created and used for correlation. Yule's (1897) work helped to further develop and introduce the concept to the application of regression analysis. The general formula to calculate the standard error of coefficients is:

$$\text{Std. Error} = \sqrt{\frac{\sum (Y - Y^1)^2}{N}}$$

Figure 8.5 Standard Error of Coefficients Equation

where Y = the observed DV value
   Y^1 = the predicted DV value.

The difference between Y and Y^1 represents the individual error in estimation. Thus, the pooled (or summed) values, divided by the number of cases, represents the precision of the coefficient. A more conservative estimate of the standard error of coefficients is often employed. This version of the formula provides a relatively higher value as the result of employing the use of a smaller denominator. N is replaced with $N - 2$, since the slope and the y-intercept were included in the sum of squares procedure.

$$\text{Std. Error} = \sqrt{\frac{\sum (Y - Y^1)^2}{N-2}}$$

Figure 8.6 Standard Error of Coefficients Equation #2

SIGNIFICANCE

The third test statistic that is provided in the results of a regression analysis, regardless of the statistical software used, is the *p* value. The symbolic representation of the *p* value varies based on the statistical software used by the data analyst. Some programs will explicitly title the values as "P values" (e.g., Excel), some will refer to it as the indicator of significance, such as "Sig." (e.g., SPSS), and others title the values in reference to both the *p* value and the distribution from which it is calculated, such as "P > |t|" (e.g., SAS, STATA, and R). Regardless of the symbolic representation, the numerical representation is the same. The *p* value has the same interpretation as discussed previously, beginning in Chapter 6. The lower the value, specifically if lower than the predetermined alpha value, the greater confidence the researcher has that, controlling for the other factors included in the regression, the independent variable is significantly related to the dependent variable.

The *t* distribution is used in regression analysis for the same reason, among others, that it is used in other statistical tests of significance. The *t* distribution, compared to the normal *z* distribution, may be more appropriate for (small) samples and it provides a more conservative estimate in test statistics. This is due in part to the reduction in the degrees of freedom, which is calculated with a process similar to the one seen in Figure 8.6, where the value is reduced based upon the number of variables (commonly referred to as parameters in this instance), plus the y-intercept. This reduction will result in an increase in the critical value of *t*, by which statistical significance is determined, and a wider confidence interval will be calculated.

CONFIDENCE INTERVAL

The fourth test statistic that is provided in the results of a regression analysis, regardless of the statistical software used, is the confidence interval. As previously defined, a confidence interval is a range of values, based on a specific degree of certainty, where the population value is located. When presented in the results of a regression analysis, the confidence interval refers to the range of values where the population value of the *b* coefficient is located. Like the symbolic representation of the *p* value, the title for the confidence interval varies based on the statistical software used by the data analyst, though some programs (e.g., SAS and *R*) require additional commands for them to appear. Results of a regression analysis conducted in STATA provide two values under the same heading, "[95% Conf. Interval]," representing the level of confidence, and complimentary alpha value (.05), by which most test statistics are estimated. SPSS provides a similar title, "95.0% Confidence Interval for B," though a subheading indicates the "Lower Bound" and "Upper Bound." Excel is similar, with two columns of *"Lower 95.0%"* and *"Upper 95.0%."*

Confidence intervals are relatively younger in their application and development than other test statistics (Stigler, 1999), though variants were seen in the 19th century (Stigler, 1986). Later, Fisher had discussed a similar concept, but confidence intervals, or "limits," as we know them today, were not developed until the 1930s by Jerzy Neyman (1934:1935:1937). However, it would not be another decade until the confidence interval saw its inclusion in statistical manuals and textbooks. It was first introduced to a broad audience by George Snedecor in his 1946 textbook. Once it was introduced, the use and calculation of confidence intervals became pervasive across many disciplines. Snedecor's (1946) textbook was so popular that it became the most frequently cited statistical book by its fourth edition (Cochran, 1977).

The formula to calculate confidence intervals for the partial slope coefficients of a regression is:

$$C.I. = b \pm t(\text{Std. Error})$$

Figure 8.7 Coefficient Confidence Interval Equation

where t = the critical value of t determined by df and the two-tailed level of confidence $(1 - \frac{\alpha}{2})$

$df = n - p - 1$

p = the number of parameters in the regression.

COEFFICIENT OF DETERMINATION:
A value that represents the proportion of the variation of a dependent variable explained by the independent variable(s) under study.

R^2

The fifth, and usually final, common test statistic that is provided in the results of a regression analysis, regardless of the statistical software used, is the R^2 value. The R^2 value is referred to as the coefficient of determination, originally referred to as the "coefficient of double correlation" by Yule (1897, p. 833) when he examined partial correlation coefficients involving a third variable. The coefficient of determination represents the proportion of the variation of the dependent variable that is explained, or correctly predicted, by the independent variable(s) included in the analysis. In a correlation, the value is simply the square of the r correlation value. Though the interpretation is similar, in a regression analysis, the calculation is different.

The formula to calculate the coefficient of determination in regression analysis is:

$$r^2 = \frac{SST - SSE}{SST} = \frac{SSR}{SST}$$

Figure 8.8 Coefficient of Determination Equation

The regression sum of squares (SSR) is calculated by summing the squared differences of the predicted values of the dependent variable ($\bar{y}$), which is the actual line of best fit, and a horizontal regression line. The horizontal line represents an R^2 value of 0 and the mean value of the dependent variable ($\bar{y}$). The greater the value of SSR, the greater the R^2 value and the predictive ability of the variables. The error sum of squares (SSE) is calculated by summing the squared differences of the observed values (y) and the predicted values of the dependent variable ($\bar{y}$). This represents the residual: the difference or distance between the values in the dataset and the values predicted by the regression model, demonstrated by the line of best fit. Finally, the total sum of squares (SST) is calculated by summing the squared differences of the observed values (y) and the mean value of the dependent variable ($\bar{y}$). This represents the difference or distance between the values in the dataset and the horizontal regression line.

As a proportion, the R^2 value can range from 0.0, in which there is no relationship between the dependent variable and the independent variable(s)—thus, they correctly predict 0% of the dependent variable's values, and the line of best fit would be perfectly horizontal—to 1.0, in which the dependent variable is perfectly related to the independent variable(s)—thus they correctly predict 100% of the dependent variable's values, and the line of best fit would be plotted at a 45-degree angle. When plotted, an R^2 of 1.0 would show all data points plotted perfectly on the line of best fit.

Coefficient of Determination	Required	Explains
Correlation	X, Y values; observed	Proportion of variation in one variable explained by the other
Regression	X, Y, intercept, error; observed and predicted	Proportion of variation in dependent variable explained by all independent variables

Figure 8.9 Coefficients of Determination Comparison

SUMMARY

As we have progressed throughout the chapters, we have discussed how different statistical tests require different assumptions and requirements. Regression analysis, due to its increased complexity, has many more assumptions and requirements that need to be met than any other type of statistical test covered thus far. If the assumptions and requirements are not met, the results and conclusions derived from those results will not be valid. Research in the social sciences, particularly criminal justice and criminology, already have several threats to validity (Maxfield & Babbie, 2018). The data analyst can take certain steps to ensure the analysis stage of the research cycle does not contribute any more.

In an effort to approach the methodological rigor of the physical sciences, social scientists conduct studies that can provide support for the existence of a causal relationship. However, due to the criteria needed for a causal relationship to exist, social sciences, like criminal justice and criminology, can never determine such existence with complete certainty. The determination that a statistically significant relationship exists between two variables is easy to be made. By this point in the text, you have the ability to do that. The determination that the perceived causal factor (e.g., the independent variable) preceded the outcome (e.g., the dependent variable) is also easy to make. Often, however, the measurement and data collection procedures preclude this requirement from being confirmed, such as in cross-sectional research. The third criterion, determining if the observed relationship is not spurious, is impossible to meet. Criminal justice and criminological research does not occur in a lab under completely controlled conditions. As a result, many factors are often omitted from study mistakenly or because the data are unmeasurable. Thus, only *support for a causal relationship* can be found in a social science study.

The many assumptions of regression will be further exemplified and explained in the following chapter. Diagnostic tests will be conducted and various approaches to rectifying the violation of the regression assumptions will be discussed. Some of the assumptions of regression analysis are specific to the type of regression conducted, and others can be relaxed. This is similar to the thresholds discussed in Chapter 5. If a measure of variability and dispersion such as skew and kurtosis is not equal to 0, there technically exists skew or kurtosis. However, there are predetermined values by which exceptions can be made when a distribution is technically skewed or kurtotic. Exceptions can also be made, based on the results of various diagnostic tests that measure the degree to which an assumption is violated. When assumptions hold true and data are analyzed, the results can be quite informative. Generally, these results explain the strength of the impact of the independent variable(s), the accuracy of that estimate, if the independent variable is significantly related to the dependent variable, the range of values the effect would be found in the population, and an assessment of how accurately the independent variable(s) predict the values of the dependent variable.

CHAPTER REVIEW QUESTIONS

1. Explain why social sciences, unlike physical sciences, can never determine causation.

2. Explain two of the assumptions of regression analysis. How can their violation impact findings?

3. What is the difference between partial correlation and linear regression?

4. Discuss the two concepts *residuals* and *line of best fit* and how they are related.

5. Explain the meaning of the y-intercept in a regression analysis.

CHAPTER REVIEW EXERCISES

1. Visit the F.B.I.'s *Variables Affecting Crime* page:

https://ucr.fbi.gov/nibrs/2012/resources/variables-affecting-crime

View the section on the second page, *Make valid assessments of crime*. The FBI provides a bulleted list of 13 factors that are known to affect the amount of crime committed in the United States, the types of crime committed, and the geographical differences therein. By themselves, each factor (if measured continuously) along with a crime-related variable represents a correlation. Choose one factor, and explain how the correlative relationship could reach causative status. How might a study find support for a causal relationship?

2. Using the data you collected in Chapter 7 Review Exercise #2, determine if any of the assumptions of simple linear regression are violated. Explain.

3. Discuss the difference between the b coefficient and the beta (β) coefficient.

4. Develop a criminal justice or criminological research question that could be answered using simple linear regression. Explain the variables of interest and the theoretical reason(s) for choosing them.

5. Using your institution's library resources, find a peer-reviewed journal article that is of interest to you that analyzes data using linear regression. Discuss the article, the research question, why the variables were selected, and what the researchers found.

REFERENCES

Adrain, R. (1808). Research concerning the probabilities of the errors which happen in making observations. *The Analyst, IV*, 93–109.

Berry, W.D. (1993). *Understanding regression assumption: Quantitative applications in the social sciences, volume 92.* London, UK: Sage.

Cantor, N. (1932). The search for causes of crime. *Journal of Criminal Law and Criminology, 22*(6), 854–863.

Chaflin, A., & McCrary, J. (2012). The effect of police on crime: New evidence from U.S. cities, 1960–2010. *NBER Working Paper* #18815. Cambridge, MA: National Bureau of Economic Research.

Cochran, W.C. (1977). Statistical methods. *Current Contents, 19*, 10.

David, H.A. (1995). First (?) occurrence of common terms in mathematical statistics. *The American Statistician, 49*(2), 121–133.

Finney, D.J. (1996). A note on the history of regression. *Journal of Applied Statistics, 23*(5), 555–558.

Galton, F. (1877). Typical laws of heredity. *Nature, 15,* 492–495; 512–514; 532–533.

Galton, F. (1885). Presidential address before the anthropological section of the British Association for the Advancement of Science, Aberdeen. *British Association Reports for 1885.*

Galton, F. (1886). Regression towards mediocrity in hereditary stature. *Journal of the Anthropological Institute, XV,* 246–263.

Galton, F. (1888). Co-relations and their measurement, chiefly from anthropometric data. *Proceedings of the Royal Society of London, 45,* 135–145.

Gauss, C. (1809). *Theoria motus corporum coelestium in sectionibus conicis solem abientium.* Hamburg, Germany: Perthes et Besser.

Legendre, A.M. (1805). *Nouvelles méthodes pour la determination des orbites des cométes.* Paris, France: Courcier.

Lin, W., Cochran, J.K., & Mieczkowski, T. (2011). Direct and vicarious violent victimization and juvenile delinquency: An application of general strain theory. *Sociological Inquiry, 81*(2), 195–222.

Maxfield, M.G., & Babbie, E. (2018). Research methods for criminal justice and criminology (3rd Ed.). Stamford, CT: Cengage Learning.

Merriman, M. (1877). On the history of the method of least squares. *The Analyst, IV*(2), 33–36.

Miller, S.J. (2017). Supplemental chapters and materials: *The methods of least squares* in "The probability lifesaver: All the tools you need to understand chance." Princeton, NJ: Princeton University Press.

Neyman, J. (1934). On the two different aspects of the representative method. *Journal of the Royal Statistical Society Series A, 97,* 558–625.

Neyman, J. (1935). On the problem of confidence intervals. *The Annals of Mathematical Statistics, 6,* 111–116.

Neyman, J. (1937). Outline of a theory of statistical estimation based on the classical theory of probability. *Philosophical Transactions of the Royal Society of London. Series A, Mathematical and Physical Sciences, 236*(767), 333–380.

Pearson, K. (1905). One the general theory of skew correlation and nonlinear regression. *Drapers' Company Research Memoirs.* Biometric Series I.

Pigou, A.C. (1910). Memorandum on some economic aspect and effects of poor relief. In *Royal Commission on the Poor Laws and Relief of Distress* (pp. 918–1000). London, UK: His Majesty's Stationary Office.

Rosenfeld, R., & Levin, A. (2016). Acquisitive crime and inflation in the United States: 1960–2012. *Journal of Quantitative Criminology, 32,* 427–447.

Smith, D.E. (1929). *A source book in mathematics.* New York, NY: McGraw-Hill Book Company, Inc.

Snedecor, G.W. (1946). *Statistical methods applied to experiments in agriculture and biology.* Ames, Iowa: Iowa State University Press.

Stanton, J.M. (2001). Galton, Pearson, and the peas: A brief history of linear regression for statistics instructors. *Journal of Statistics Education, 9*(3).

Stigler, S.M. (1986). *The history of statistics: The measurement of uncertainty before 1900.* Cambridge, MA: Harvard University Press.

Stigler, S.M. (1999). *Statistics on the table: The history of statistical concepts and methods.* Cambridge, MA: Harvard University Press.

Valavanis, S. (1959). *Econometrics.* New York, NY: McGraw-Hill.

Walfied, S.M., Socia, K.M., & Powers, R.A., (2017). Religious motivated hate crimes: Reporting to law enforcement and case outcomes. *American Journal of Criminal Justice, 42*(1), 148–169.

Weisburd, D., Wooditch, A., Weisburd, S., & Yang, S. (2016). Do stop, question, and frisk practices deter crime? Evidence at microunits of space and time. *Criminology and Public Policy, 15*(1), 31–56.

Wold, H. (1938). *A Study in the Analysis of Stationary Time Series*. Stockholm, Sweden: Almqvist and Wiksell.

Yule, G.U. (1897). On the theory of correlation. *Journal of the Royal Statistical Society, 60*, 812–854.

Yule, G.U. (1899). An investigation into the causes of changes in pauperism in England, chiefly during the last two intercensal decades (Part I.). *Journal of the Royal Statistical Society, 62*(2), 249–295.

Yule, G.U. (1907). On the theory of correlation for any number of variables, Treated by a New System of Notation. *Proceedings of the Royal Society A: Mathematical, Physical and Engineering Sciences, 79*(520), 182–193.

MULTIPLE LINEAR REGRESSION

INTRODUCTION: SORTING IT ALL OUT

The literature on the topic of criminality reveals a great diversity of factors which have been shown to correlate statistically with this phenomenon. There is, however, no generally accepted conceptual system of crime causation. What would seem most urgently needed, therefore, in this field is the discovery of a few common denominators which will comprise as many of the isolated yet relevant factors as possible. (Dollard, Doob, Miller, Mowrer, & Sears, 1939, p. 110)

Dollard et al. were psychologists who, early in their respective careers, proposed a theory to attempt to explain the causal factor(s) of criminal behavior. As they noted in their highly influential text, *Frustration and Aggression*, there are numerous factors, circumstances, and characteristics that have been shown to be related to criminality. Like today, there existed no consensus on if and how those factors may be causally related to crime. During the 1930s, there were several foci of sociological and criminological research, particularly that of Merton (1938), Sutherland (1939), and the Chicago School (Reckless, 1933; Reckless & Smith, 1932; Shaw, 1930). While their respective approaches and perspectives differed, all of the aforementioned scholars acknowledged that several factors may be at work simultaneously, either directly or indirectly. The development of regression analysis corresponded with, and allowed for, the development of criminological theory. Consider the following:

1. Is the amount of money embezzled related to an offender's sentence length, accounting for his/her age, gender, and race or ethnicity?

2. Is the number of hours a child plays violent video games related to misconduct in school, accounting for the level of parental supervision, mental health status, and the age at which they began to play them?

3. Are crime rates related to the size of the population, accounting for employment rates, geographic location, and levels of police staffing?

These questions should seem familiar, as they are extensions of the questions considered in the Chapter 8 Introduction. Those questions, for the purpose of explaining regression, involved a dependent variable and two independent variables—one of primary interest and a second to control for the effects of that condition. Regression analysis, however, is nearly always conducted in a manner in which there are several independent variables: the presumed causal variable and multiple control variables. Multiple regression analysis provides the data analyst the opportunity to account for the many factors, circumstances, conditions, and characteristics that are present simultaneously, with the purpose of reducing the likelihood an observed relationship is spurious. This chapter examines the determination, interpretation, and explanation of multiple linear regression analysis—an advanced example of ordinary least squares (OLS).

LEARNING OBJECTIVES

By the end of this chapter, students will be able to:

1: Identify the consequences of violating regression assumptions

2: Discuss the processes by which a regression analysis is performed

3: Explain the importance of various diagnostic tests

4: Evaluate the results of a diagnostic test

5: Estimate the value of a dependent variable from a regression equation

KEY TERMS

CONTROL VARIABLE

CURVILINEAR

IMPUTATION

INTERPOLATION

LISTWISE DELETION

MAR

MCAR

MNAR

QUADRATIC TERM

VARIANCE INFLATION FACTOR

PRACTICAL APPLICATIONS OF REGRESSION

Regression analysis, as defined in Chapter 8, is a class of statistical techniques that examine the simultaneous effects of multiple independent variables on one dependent variable. In the social world, individuals, groups, neighborhoods, cities, and even countries are being influenced and affected by an immeasurable number of conditions at the same time. As a result, in order for one to accurately understand, measure, and then predict the consequences of those conditions, they must account for as many of them that are substantively and statistically relevant. Stated differently, regression analysis, like other techniques, can be viewed as a statistical tool "aimed at quantifying relationships among variables that either measure the end result of some process or are likely to affect that process" (Rawlings,

CONTROL VARIABLE:
In data analysis, an independent variable that is held constant to isolate the effect of the primary independent variable of interest.

Pantula, & Dickey, 1998, p. ix). In the fields of criminal justice and criminology, the variables that measure the end result are often connoted negatively. To this end, as we learned in Box 1.1: WHAT WE'VE LEARNED: Uniform Crime Reports, there are several variables that have been shown to affect the crime rate. These variables are also connoted negatively, as the specific values of these variables include high population density, high residential mobility, distressed economic conditions, and single-parent households—just to name a few.

THEORY TESTING

Applying regression techniques to criminal justice and criminological research questions allows a researcher to simultaneously estimate the effects of multiple independent variables on a dependent variable. When a researcher utilizes a regression technique to analyze data they do so in order to statistically account for as many complementary and/or competing variables as possible within the confines of the research. When a condition is statistically accounted for it is referred to as a control variable. The condition is "controlled" by holding it constant in the regression model. This results in the isolation of the effect of the primary independent variable of interest. These techniques are perfectly suited for criminal justice and criminological theory testing, as well as program and policy evaluation.

Criminological theory, for example, offers a variety of explanations for the genesis, continuation, and cessation of criminal behavior. There are many theories that attempt to explain criminal behavior and many ways by which the concepts therein are operationalized in a research study. Furthermore, there are many approaches to testing a criminological theory. One such approach is to include variables of a competing theoretical explanation. This practice would allow a researcher to compare and examine simultaneously occurring conditions while controlling for the others. It is possible, using this approach, to compare two competing theoretical perspectives to see which *better* predicts or explains criminal behavior. Another approach is to include variables that are substantively and/or statistically related to the variables of greatest interest: the dependent variable and the primary independent variable. Pratt (2016) refers to this as "controlling for a bunch of other stuff" (p. 46), as it has long been done out of tradition and convenience, providing little explanation about *why* a relationship may exist. As discussed in Chapter 8, the introduction of, and controlling for, additional conditions would provide support for the findings of an apparent causal relationship—assuming an appropriate research design is utilized. By controlling for additional factors in a multiple regression model, the third criterion of causation—that the relationship between the supposed "cause" and the "effect" is non-spuriousness—can be approached.

Box 9.1: WHAT WE'VE LEARNED: Practical Applications of Regression with Theory Testing

Professors D'Alessio and Stolzenberg (2010) tested two competing theories that attempt to explain male-on-female intimate partner violence. The first theory has its origins in evolutionary psychology. It suggests that when there are more men than women in the population, and increasingly, sexual jealousy occurs, which results in intimate partner violence. Opposing this view is the Guttentag and Secord thesis, which suggests that an increase in the sex ratio makes women more valued and respected by men. Using data from the National Incident-Based Reporting System (NIBRS), the researchers examined incidents of violence in which the two individuals involved were romantically linked. The dependent variable was the male-on-female intimate partner violent crime rate across 134 cities. The primary independent variable was the sex ratio. Control variables included female labor force participation, median income for males, male-to-female median income ratio, economic inequality, population density, geographic location, and city disadvantage. Results showed support for the evolutionary psychology perspective. The higher the sex ratio, the higher the male-on-female intimate partner violent crime rate. This relationship was stronger in cities with higher rates of female labor participation, indicating that violence increases as males and females interact more. It is worth noting that although the sex ratio was significantly related to the crime rate in both models in which it was entered, some control variables evinced stronger relationships.

PREDICTION

Revisit the regression equation discussion in Chapter 8.

$$y = b_0 + b_1 x_1 ... + e_1$$

Figure 9.1 Linear Regression Equation

where y = the value of the dependent variable

b_0 = the y-intercept

b_1 = the slope of the line (i.e., coefficients)

x_1 = the value of the independent variable

e_1 = the value of error term.

In Chapter 8, the regression equation was explained. The left side of the equation is the value of the dependent variable that is estimated based on the values estimated on the right side of the equation. The right side of the equation contains the y-intercept value, values of the independent variables (i.e., the coefficients), and—theoretically—the error term. After a regression model is estimated, the coefficients that represent the effects of the independent variables, as well as the y-intercept value, can be used to estimate the value of the dependent variable based on the input conditions. Not only are the coefficients needed, but so too are the independent variable values of the case whose dependent variable value is being predicted. The variable values of the case are multiplied by their respective coefficients, then added to the value of the y-intercept. This is only done for coefficients, e.g., relationships, that are found to be statistically significant.

Box 9.2: Example: Practical Applications of Regression with Prediction

	b	t
Constant (Intercept)	478.636	2.218
City Disadvantage	249.712*	10.168
Southern City	141.457*	4.152
Racial Segregation	-3.470*	-2.360
Economic Inequality	-916.246*	-2.419
Sex Ratio	.750*	2.045

Dependent Variable = Intimate Partner Crime Rate
*= statistical significance
From: D'Alessio & Stolzenberg (2010)

Figure 9.2: D'Alessio & Stolzenberg (2010) Results

Using the results from D'Alessio & Stolzenberg's (2010) study, we can estimate the male-on-female intimate partner violent crime rate. In Model 2, there were five variables, including the sex ratio, that were found to be significantly related to the male-on-female intimate partner violent crime rate. Thus, the following equation can be used:

$$\text{Intimate Partner Crime Rate} = 249.712(x_1) + 141.457(x_2) - 3.470(x_3) - 916.246(x_4) + .750(x_5)$$

Figure 9.3: D'Alessio & Stolzenberg (2010) Equation

Suppose your city had a sex ratio value that was slightly greater than the mean at a value of 280. Similarly, suppose your city's measure of economic inequality (the Gini coefficient) indicated less variation in the distribution of household income, at a value of 0.10. Similar to the more even distribution of household income, your city has greater integration than the sample mean, at a value of 20. Living in the northwest, the southern city coefficient remains at its null value. Finally, your city has slightly more disadvantage than the sample mean, at a value of 0.20. The y-intercept, sometimes referred to as the constant in a results table, has a value of 478.636. All values above, along with their respective coefficients, can be input into the equation as follows:

$$\text{Intimate Partner Crime Rate} = 249.712(.20) + 141.457(0) - 3.470(20) - 916.246(.10) + .750(280) = 98.92$$

Figure 9.4: D'Alessio & Stolzenberg (2010) Example

Based on the D'Alessio & Stolzenberg (2010) study, your city is estimated to have a male-on-female intimate partner violent crime rate of 98.92, which is considerably lower than the mean value of the 134 cities the researchers analyzed in their study.

In regression analysis, the null hypothesis of a test of significance for b coefficients is that $b = 0$. Thus, a test of significance is actually testing to see if the b coefficient is not equal to 0. If/when the coefficient does not prove to have a significant relationship with the dependent variable, the null hypothesis is accepted (b is not significantly different from 0). Thus, even if it were included into the regression equation for prediction, the product of the variable value and the null coefficient, 0, would be 0. As a result of its inclusion—just like its exclusion—there would be no effect on the regression equation. See Box 9.2 for an example.

DIAGNOSTIC TESTS

Revisit the Assumptions section of Chapter 8. In this section, we learned about several of the assumptions of regression analysis. Not only are the items in the list in Chapter 8 assumptions, but they can also be considered requirements. Nearly all of the requirements can be examined graphically or statistically. However, for some of the requirements, the examination via graphical displays or statistical calculations may prove difficult, such as: *7. There is measurement without error.* By examining various measures of the data, a researcher can determine if an assumption is violated, to what degree it is violated, and can make a decision about a course of action in the analysis stages. Just like there are several different assumptions that a data analyst could examine, there are also several different methods by which some of the assumptions can be assessed. While Chapter 8 introduced and discussed the general assumptions of linear regression analysis, the most popular and simple with respect to calculation and interpretation will be discussed.

MULTICOLLINEARITY

Recall that multicollinearity refers to the condition of a statistical model that includes independent variables that have built-in linearity or are a linear combination of one another. The example provided described a situation where a variable representing a "total" value was included in the model, as well as variables that—when summed—equaled the "total." Having multicollinearity in a statistical model results in an increase in the variance of the coefficients. In turn, this could result in unexpected (and inaccurate) values for the coefficients, disabling a data analyst from truly knowing if there is an effect, which variable is producing the effect, and the direction and strength of the effect.

The term multicollinearity is often used interchangeably with collinearity, though some conceptualize the two differently. The history of the work on multicollinearity is based in the work of Ragnar Frisch. Ragnar Frisch was an economist from Norway who coined the term multicollinearity in 1929, and would continue his work in the study of linear regression and accurately estimating the effects of independent variables (1934). Frisch was very critical of the results obtained from regression analysis and conclusions made therefrom at the time. In one of his writings on the matter, he stated he "believe(s) that a substantial part of the regression and correlation analysis which have been made on statistical data in recent years is nonsense" (Frisch, 1934, p. 6).

There are two ways in which a data analyst can detect or diagnose multicollinearity in a statistical model. The first way to detect multicollinearity was discussed, indirectly, in Chapter 7. When conducting regression analysis, a researcher should examine the correlations of independent variables prior to their inclusion into a regression analysis. By calculating the correlation values of the independent variables, their associations can be examined. A high correlation indicates that one variable can, relative to the r value, predict the value of another variable. If two independent variables are strongly correlated, they are likely to produce, and be reflecting, multicollinearity when included into a statistical model.

VARIANCE INFLATION FACTOR:
A value that represents the degree to which multicollinearity is present in regression analysis.

	Criminal History (# of prior arrests)	Bail (# of dollars)	Age
Criminal History (# of prior arrests)	1.0		
Bail (# of dollars)	.9	1.0	
Age	.8	.8	1.0

Figure 9.5: Correlation Matrix

When two independent variables share a strong correlation, as seen in Figure 9.5, the optimal approach is to "drop" one of the variables from the analysis. Thus, a data analyst may select just one of the two variables to be included in the regression model. What constitutes a strong relationship may vary from analyst to analyst and, possibly, from discipline to discipline, but *r* values that are at least |0.7| are generally considered to be high, as they prove to be problematic in calculating accurate coefficient values. When deciding which variable to select, the choice can be made based on various criteria. For example, the independent variable that shares a stronger relationship with the dependent variable can be chosen as, at least at the point of correlation, it shows evidence of having more explanatory power. An alternative way of choosing is based on theoretical grounds, e.g., selecting which variable *should* be included based on theory and the current research question.

The second way a researcher can detect or diagnose multicollinearity is by calculating, usually via the use of statistical software, the variance inflation factors (VIFs) of each variable. The VIF is a value that indicates the degree to which multicollinearity exists in a statistical model. The VIF is calculated using the following equation:

$$VIF_j = \frac{1}{1 - R_j^2}$$

Figure 9.6 Variance Inflation Factor Equation

where R_j^2 = the coefficient of determination of a regression model that includes all independent variables except the jth variable.

The VIF value can take on a minimum value of 1. If a variable has a VIF value of 1, that would indicate the variable has no correlation with any of the other predictors. Unlike correlation values, data analysts lack consensus as to what range of VIF values is considered acceptable when carrying out the regression analysis without excluding any variables. Some suggest a VIF of 2.5 should be the threshold, some say it should be 5, and even others say 10. Similar to identifying an alpha value, e.g., a level of significance, in hypothesis testing, the threshold at which a VIF results in the exclusion of a variable from regression analysis should be determined before calculation. The value itself or, more accurately, the difference between the value and the lower bound (1) represents the percentage increase of the variance produced by the variable. When there is no correlation and the VIF is equal to 1, this indicates there is no increase in the variance of a coefficient (1 − 1 = 0). Using the possible values above, a VIF of 2.5 would indicate a 150% increase in the variance of the coefficient compared to the value if there was no multicollinearity (2.5 − 1 = 1.5, multiplied by the percentage metric of 100). A VIF of 5 would indicate a 400% increase (5 − 1 = 4), and a VIF of 10 would indicate a 900% increase (10 − 1 = 9).

Box 9.3: WHAT WE'VE LEARNED: Multicollinearity

In 2005, researchers Tartaro and Lester set out to study the explanatory power of Durkheim's theory of suicide with respect to prison suicide rates in the United States. The team obtained data from the annual Bureau of Justice Statistics report, *Correctional Populations in the United States*, as well as the decennial Census. Finally, suicide rates were calculated based on data gathered from the annual publication of the National Center on Health Statistics. The independent variables of interest included the year the suicide occurred, the birth rate, the marriage rate, the divorce rate, and the unemployment rate. Initially, analysis of the data revealed there were several strong correlations between independent variables. The year was negatively and strongly correlated with the marriage rate ($r = -0.88$), as was the year and the divorce rate ($r = -0.92$), and the marriage rate and the divorce rate were positively and strongly correlated ($r = 0.94$). Continuing the inquiry into the variables' relationships and the impact of those relationships suggested three variables could be excluded. It was determined that exclusion from analysis was required for the following variables: marriage rates, divorce rates, and year. Ultimately, the researchers decided to drop marriage rates and year and keep divorce rates in the model. Upon examination of the prison data, the birth rate was found to be negatively associated with suicide rates and the divorce rate was found to be positively associated with suicide rates. When examining the national suicide data, the same pattern was observed, except the directionality was reversed. The birth rate showed a positive coefficient, while the divorce rate showed a negative coefficient.

LINEARITY

Linearity refers to the characteristic of a relationship, specifically one between an independent and dependent variable, which is linear. A linear relationship is one in which the direction and/or strength of the relationship between variables does not vary across values. However, this pattern is not always observed. An independent variable, such as an individual's age, may not have the same relationship at specific value ranges, e.g., less than 10 years old or more than 70 years, as it relates to criminality. The values between those ages may have different associations, in either direction or strength.

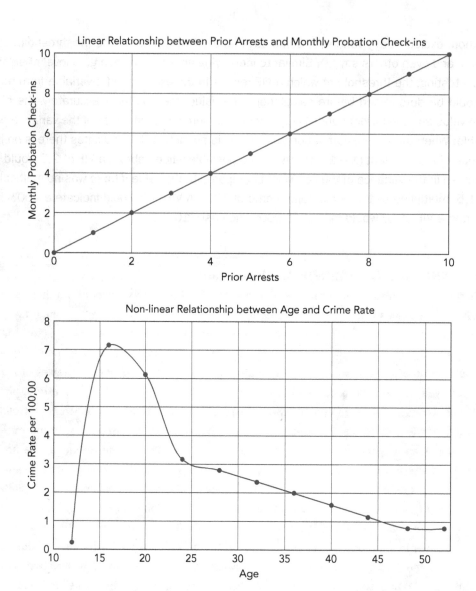

Figure 9.7 Linear vs. Non-linear Relationships

Meeting the assumption of linearity provides the data analyst with accurate descriptions of the relationships within a regression model. A byproduct of this is the estimation of accurate coefficients (Osborne & Waters, 2002). If linearity is assumed but not met, the estimated coefficients, which represent the association between the independent and dependent variables, will be inaccurate. When the coefficients underestimate a relationship, the risk of committing a Type II error is increased. Simultaneously, the risk of committing a Type I error for any variable that covaries with the underestimated variable is increased. Thus, not only can failing to meet the assumption of linearity impact the primary independent variable under study, but there can also be peripheral effects on the other independent variables.

There are three ways in which data analysts commonly examine linearity. The first method to examine linearity is to plot the values of the independent variable against the values of the dependent variable. This is identical to visually examining the data for correlation and can be completed by creating a scatterplot. Linearity can be supported when there is consistent direction and slope of plotted values. The plotted values resemble a straight line.

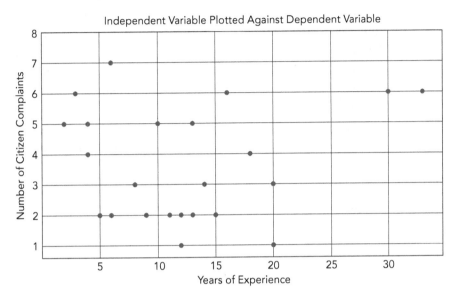

Figure 9.8: Independent Variable Plotted Against Dependent Variable

The second method to examine linearity is to create a residual plot. In a residual plot, the residuals are standardized and plotted by creating a scatterplot. Linearity can be supported when there is consistent direction, location, and/or concentration of residuals.

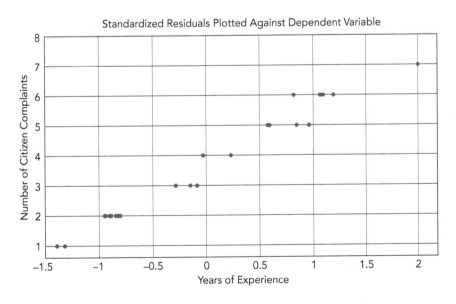

Figure 9.9 Residual Plot

CURVILINEAR:
In data analysis, the characteristic of a relationship (often represented by a line) in which there is inconsistent direction and/or slope.

QUADRATIC:
In data analysis, a term or value that has been squared, e.g., a term to the second power.

The third method to examine linearity is to perform the regression analysis with the inclusion of a transformed independent variable. A curvilinear variable would serve this function. Curvilinear variables include those that are positively exponentiated, which are created by squaring or cubing the variable. A squared variable results in a quadratic term, and a cubed variable results in a cubic term. To support *curvi*linearity, the exponentiated variable, when plotted against the dependent variable, would show a parabolic line or pattern. Statistically, support for curvilinearity would be found with a significant coefficient of the exponentiated variable(s). If the assumption of linearity is found to be violated, a researcher must decide how to proceed with the variable. For example, the variable could be dropped from the analysis, or as is seen more commonly, the researcher can include the exponentiated term in the original statistical model.

Box 9.4: WHAT WE'VE LEARNED: Linearity

Researchers Gostjev and Nielsen (2017) were interested in examining the association between English language fluency and the amount of violent crime reported at the neighborhood level. The team obtained data from the National Neighborhood Crime Study (NNCS) and the decennial census. The NNCS data contained information concerning index crimes, as defined by the Uniform Crime Report, which were recorded in 91 cities. Of particular interest to the researchers were the data concerning homicide and robbery incidents. The primary independent variables of interest, English fluency and bilingualism, were obtained from Census data. The researchers also controlled for neighborhood-specific characteristics, including concentrated disadvantage, residential instability, racial diversity, the percentage of black residents, the percentage of young male residents, and the population. A quadratic term was included for the English fluency (lack of proficiency) variable to see if it had a linear relationship with violence. The results indicated a negative and significant coefficient for the quadratic term, and a positive and significant coefficient for the untransformed term. This indicates that the positive relationship between English fluency and violent crime decreases in strength as there is a greater percentage of residents that lack proficiency of the language in the neighborhood. The authors posit that this may be a byproduct of the formation of ethnic communities brought on by increasing coethnic populations within a neighborhood.

HOMOSCEDASTICITY

Homoscedasticity is another assumption that is easily diagnosed. Recall that homoscedasticity (or homoskedasticity) refers to the condition when the error, e.g., the residual, variance is equal across all values of the independent variable. This indicates that the effect of the independent variable is constant regardless of its value. For example, to be homoscedastic, the association between age and criminality must have the same direction and strength at all values of the variable.

There are ways by which homoscedasticity can be determined by looking at graphical displays of the data. One method involves the visual inspection of a scatterplot, and another method involves the visual inspection of a histogram. The first method requires the residuals to be plotted against fitted values, i.e., predicted values on the line of best fit. If the residuals appear to be approximately the same across all values of the independent variable, the assumption of homoscedasticity has not been violated. If not, it is likely a "fanning" pattern may be observed in the plot and the assumption has been violated.

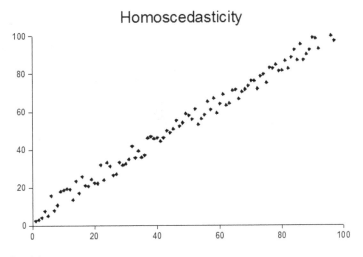

Figure 9.10 Homoscedasticity

The second method to confirm homoscedasticity is to plot the residuals against the independent variable. The same visual pattern must be present in order for the assumption to be met: the residuals must appear to be approximately the same across all values of the independent variable. If there is any unevenness in the residuals, such as larger ones at one end of the range of values, heteroscedasticity is present.

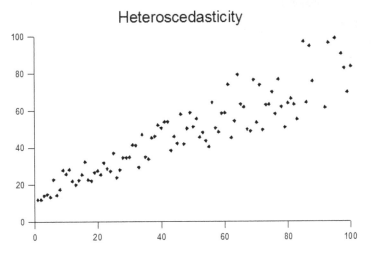

Figure 9.11 Heteroscedasticity

The third method to confirm homoscedasticity is to examine the residuals using a histogram. To meet the assumption, the histogram must show a normal distribution. It should be noted that a non-normal distribution may not necessarily indicate a problematic violation of assumptions. Instead, it may be reflecting another problem in the model, such as the misspecification of variables.

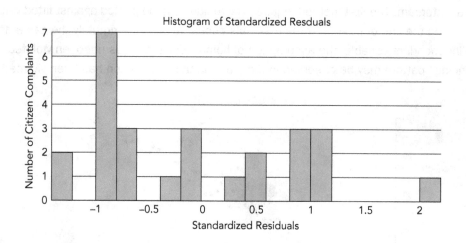

Figure 9.12 Residual Histogram

There are also statistical tests, available in most software, that can quantify heteroscedasticity. These include the Breusch-Pagan (1979) test, the Koenker (1981) test, and the commonly used White's (1980) test. Each of these also tests for statistical significance, utilizing a chi-square distribution.

Homoscedasticity Diagnostic Test	Type
Plotting Residuals Against Fitted Values	Visual Inspection
Plotting Residuals Against Independent Variable	Visual Inspection
Plotting Residuals in a Histogram	Visual Inspection
Significance Tests	Statistical Calculation

Figure 9.13 Homoscedasticity Test Comparison

Box 9.5: WHAT WE'VE LEARNED: Homoscedasticity

Not only are researchers and practitioners interested in what causes crime and what is associated with its increase, but they are also interested, perhaps more importantly, in what may reduce crime. A team of researchers took an interesting approach to examining correlates of crime. Gilstad-Hayden, Wallace, Carroll-Scott, Meyer, Barbo, Murphy-Dunning, and Ickovics (2015) were interested in studying the impact of environmental changes, specifically those concerning neighborhood flora. Conducting the research in New Haven, Connecticut, the group examined the association of tree canopy cover with both violent crime and property crime. The dependent variables in the study were violent crime rate, property crime rate, and total crime rate. The data for the primary independent variable of interest, tree canopy cover, were obtained from the Spatial Analysis Laboratory at the University of Vermont. The data described the percent of the ground that is covered by leaves, branches, and other vegetation from trees if viewed from above. The researchers tested for the violation of a variety of regression assumptions including normality in the error term distribution, absence of multicollinearity, and homoscedasticity. To address the heteroscedasticity that resulted from skewed data, some variables were transformed to produce ones with greater normality. Their findings suggest that a 10% increase in tree canopy cover is associated with a 15% decrease in violent crime and a 14% decrease in property crime.

NORMALLY DISTRIBUTED ERRORS

The errors, or residuals, of a statistical model must be normally distributed. If not, the coefficients estimated by the model, along with their corresponding confidence intervals, will be inaccurate. If the purpose of the research is simply to estimate the coefficients from and of the data analyzed, then a non-normal distribution of errors is not necessarily an issue. However, if the purpose is to generalize, then the accuracy of the coefficients from which to infer is important. Similar to other violated assumptions, a non-normal distribution of errors may be indicative of another issue in the statistical model.

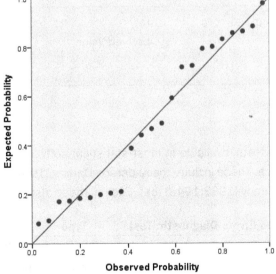

Normal P-P Plot of Standardized Residuals

Figure 9.14 Normal P-P Plot

There are two ways by which a data analyst can visually inspect the data for confirmation of a normally distributed error term. The first method is the creation and examination of a normal probability plot. Proposed by Chambers, Cleveland, Kleiner, and Tukey (1983), the normal probability plot, also known the normal P-P plot, plots the data values against theoretical values that are normally distributed. Normally distributed errors will result in a normal P-P plot that contains a straight line. As the errors become less normal, the line in the normal P-P plot becomes less straight.

The second method used to visually inspect data for confirmation of a normally distributed error term is the creation and examination of a quantile-quantile or normal quantile plot. This plot is also known as a normal Q-Q plot. The normal Q-Q plot functions, and is interpreted in a way, similar to the normal P-P plot. The Q-Q plot, however, plots quantiles of a dataset against the quantiles of another—one that is normal.

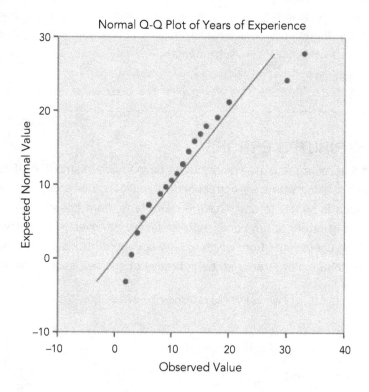

Figure 9.15 Normal Q-Q Plot

There are also statistical tests, available in most statistical software, that can quantify normality of errors and test for significance. These include the Anderson-Darling (1952) test, the Shapiro-Wilk (1965) test, and the Kolmogorov-Smirnov (1933;1948) test. Each of these also tests for statistical significance.

Normally Distributed Errors Diagnostic Test	Type	Metric Used
Normal P-P Plot	Visual Inspection	Data Values
Normal Q-Q Plot	Visual Inspection	Quantiles

Figure 9.16 Normal Errors Test Comparisons

Box 9.6: WHAT WE'VE LEARNED: Normally Distributed Errors

Professors Johnson and Crews (2013) examined the website RateMyProfessors.com to see what characteristics of instructors are related to ratings provided on the website and to see what characteristics listed by those posting on the website are related to ratings of instructors. The authors examined the correlates of five different independent variables: easiness rating, helpfulness rating, clarity rating, overall quality rating, and hotness rating. The first four were measured on a scale from 1 to 5 and the final, hotness rating, was measured on a scale of 0 to 1, indicating an instructor was or was not "hot." Before regression analysis was performed, all variables (dependent and independent) were examined via a correlation matrix. The strongest relationships were between the clarity rating and helpfulness rating ($r = 0.89$), the overall quality rating and helpfulness rating ($r = 0.95$) and the overall quality rating and clarity rating ($r = 0.96$). The researchers used the Shapiro-Wilk's test and found that two independent variables, average number of publications per year and number of ratings, were skewed. These were transformed to allow for accurate estimation in the regression models. Results showed practical experience and employment at a top-level research institution were positively associated with easiness, while years of teaching showed a negative association. The average annual number of publications and practitioner experience were positively associated with helpfulness, while teaching experience and whether or not the instructor had a terminal degree showed a negative association. Interestingly, being white and male were positively associated with clarity. Being white was also associated with overall quality. There were no significant associations with hotness.

AUTOCORRELATION

Autocorrelation in a regression model exists when the residuals are not independent across cases. This is seen most often in time-series data where the residual from a case is related to its residual when measured at a subsequent time period. Similarly, spatial autocorrelation may exist. This occurs when the residual from a case is related to another, adjacent case. In this sense, the term "adjacent" is meant in the literal sense. Spatial analysis examines data based on location, and it is possible, and oft-seen, that adjacent cases (streets, neighborhoods, etc.) have similar values, thus showing significant correlations of raw values and resultant residuals.

The discussion and redress of autocorrelation has been in practice for nearly 100 years. Eugen Slutzky was a Russian economist who wrote a "classic in the field of time-series analysis" (Slutzky, 1937), as he himself described. Slutsky's (1927) paper stimulated the statistics field to address the issue or correlated residuals within or across cases. Interestingly, he referred to the issue by referencing the intended outcome as an "auto-non-correlated" series of data (1937, p. 105). It was not until the work of Wold (1938) that the term autocorrelation, to describe the issue, was used (David, 1998). Autocorrelation can be the result of a variety of things, such as non-random sampling, omitted variable bias, or the use of an incorrect/inappropriate form of analysis (Wehr, 1999). This can result in a loss of reliability in both *t* and *F* tests. Further, the coefficients that are estimated are inaccurate.

There are several ways to detect autocorrelation. One method is to examine the data visually, using a graphical display of data. The second method is to calculate a test statistic, from which a determination regarding the presence and/or level of autocorrelation can be made. One way to examine the data visually is to plot the residuals against time or, perhaps more commonly performed, to plot the residuals against its adjacent case. This is most appropriate with time-series data. See Figure 9.17.

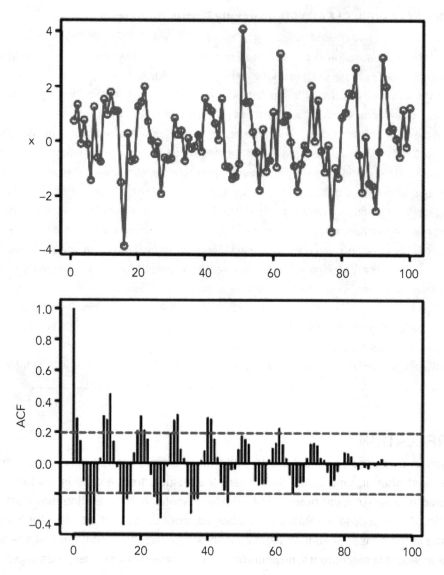

Figure 9.17 Autocorrelation Function (ACF) Plot

The second way of detecting autocorrelation is via the calculation of a test statistic. The most common test statistic used is derived from the Durbin-Watson test. Statisticians James Durbin and Geoffrey Watson (1950:1951) developed this test in two parts, with one article written to discuss "the theory on which the test is based" and the second article written to describe "the test procedures in detail and give(s) tables of bounds to the significance points of the test criterion adopted" (1950, p. 409). Interpretation of the Durbin-Watson statistic, which is produced by most statistical software, requires knowledge of which values indicate the presence of autocorrelation. If there is no autocorrelation, and the regression assumption is met, the Watson test statistic will be between 1.5 and 2.5. Others (such as Field, 2009) give a more relaxed range of 1 and 3. The test statistic can range from 0.0 to 4.0. Thus, either range used represents a middle group of acceptable values, where extreme values indicate autocorrelation. Should autocorrelation exist, inclusion of an important independent variable may remedy the problem should omitted variable bias be the cause. Otherwise, transformation of the variable(s) is suggested.

Durbin-Watson Statistic	Interpretation
0 to < 1.5	Indicates autocorrelation
1.5 to < 2.5	No autocorrelation
2.5 to 4.0	Indicates autocorrelation

Figure 9.18 Durbin-Watson Statistic Interpretation

Box 9.7: WHAT WE'VE LEARNED: Autocorrelation

A promising outcome related to the passing of the Second Chance Act of 2007 is the reduction of recidivism. The Second Chance Act focuses on job training, substance abuse and mental health treatment, familial support, and mentoring to improve the chances of prosocial and productive behavior of those reentering society. Professors Amasa-Annang and Scutelnicu (2016) examined data of young adult male offenders in Alabama, Georgia, and Mississippi. Offenders were between the ages of 18 and 39. Using linear (OLS) regression, the researchers estimated the association of several independent variables with the number of new sentences for black offenders and white offenders. The strongest predictor of new sentences was the number of imprisoned males that were black (for black offenders) and the number of imprisoned males that were white (for white offenders). The second strongest predictor of new sentences was the median household income of the respective state. In order to account for the possibility of autocorrelation among cases, the researchers implemented a specialized form of regression to account for the time-series nature of the model. For each statistical model, the Durbin-Watson test statistic was within the acceptable limits (Model 1, 1.60 and Model 2, 1.75). This indicated autocorrelation was not present in the models.

OUTLIER DETECTION

Another common, and perhaps simpler, condition to test for is the presence and effects of outliers. Outliers can impact the estimation of coefficients, leading to inaccurate and, thus, incorrect results. Some describe outliers as observations or values that are noticeably different from other observations in a dataset (Barnett & Lewis, 1994; Johnson, 1992). Others describe outliers differently, suggesting these observations are in fact noticeably different from other observations, but so much so that they should be cause for concern, statistically, as their inclusion and possible impact on analysis may result in false substantive conclusions (Hawkins, 1980).

Just as the aforementioned diagnostic tests utilize both graphical displays of data and statistical tests, the detection of outliers can come as a result from both methods as well. The first method of detecting outliers is the visual inspection of one of several graphical displays of data. Box plots, when constructed correctly, depict the minimum and maximum values of a variable. A value that is uncharacteristic of the rest of the data, e.g., an extreme value, would be represented by the upper or lower bound being greatly distanced, relatively, from the "box", or distanced from the bound itself. Depending on the variable, outliers may be negative or positive. However, in criminal justice and criminology, variables rarely have negative values, unless transformed or standardized. Thus, attention should be paid to the values used in constructing the box plot and their relation to and distance from one another, not their negative or positive sign.

A second way of detecting outliers by way of visual inspection of a graphical display of data is the use of a histogram. Outliers, inherently, must be measured at the interval or ratio scale. "Extreme" values, generally, do not exist with categorical data. When continuous data are graphed, a histogram is most appropriate. Any "bar" that is substantially different, and distanced, from the other values indicates an outlying value is present in the data. Additional plots can also be used, including variants of normal Q-Q plots.

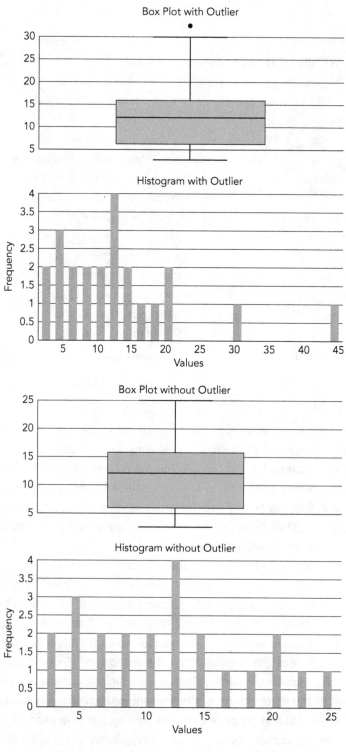

Figure 9.19: Regular Box Plot and Histogram and Outlier Box Plot and Histogram

The second method of detecting outliers involves the calculation of various statistics to quantify the magnitude of the value's extremity. The determination of a value being an outlier, and potentially impacting results, is based on its comparison to another value—similar to a test of significance. One way to do this is to calculate the extreme value's z score. This would represent the number of standard deviations it (the extreme value) is distanced from the mean. The threshold by which an outlier is determined varies, but a common z score to use is $|3|$. Any value with a z score having an absolute value greater than 3 would, in this case, be considered an outlier.

A second way to detect outliers by way of quantifying the magnitude of a value's extremity is to use the variable's inter-quartile range (IQR). Many statistical software programs utilize this approach and offer its calculation, as well as other more sophisticated statistical tests. It is not uncommon to see detection followed by the removal of the outlying cases. Values are considered outliers if they are:

< 25th percentile − 1.5(IQR)   and   > 75th percentile + 1.5(IQR)

or

≤ 25th percentile − 1.5(IQR)   and   ≥ 75th percentile + 1.5(IQR)

Data Values	Descriptive Statistics
2, 2, 4, 6, 8, 8, 8, 10, 10, 12, 12, 12,	Min. = 2
14, 16, 16, 24	Q1 = 7
	Q2 (Median) = 10
	Q3 = 13
	Max. = 24
	IQR = 6

Is 2 < 7 − 1.5(6)? = 2 < 7 − 9 = 2 < −2 = No, 2 is not an outlier.

Is 24 > 13 + 1.5(6)? = 24 > 13 + 9 = 24 > 22 = Yes, 24 is an outlier.

Figure 9.20 Outlier Calculation from IQR

Box 9.8: WHAT WE'VE LEARNED: Outlier Detection

Recently, a group of researchers was interested in seeing if there was a noticeable effect of the incident(s) in Ferguson, Missouri, on crime rates, specifically effects of the 2014 shooting of Michael Brown and the police-citizen interactions thereafter. Pyrooz, Decker, Wolfe, and Shjarback (2016) compared pre-August 2014 and post-August 2014 data to see if there was indeed a "Ferguson Effect." Discussion of this effect is the result of speculation that police-involved shootings, specifically when the officer is white and the shooting victim is black, have led to an increase in crime. The authors were able to gather data from 81 large United States cities via the Uniform Crime Reports. The research team examined the supposed effect on total crime rate, as well as the individual crime rates for all Part I offenses: homicide, rape, robbery, aggravated assault, burglary, larceny, and motor vehicle theft. To confirm the assumptions of regression were met, several diagnostic tests were performed. Outliers were defined by the authors as a case with a value +4 standard deviations from the mean. This led to the authors adopting a variant of regression analysis to account for the presence of these values. Pyrooz et al. analyzed data from the 12 months following the Ferguson shooting. From the examination of pre-Ferguson crime rates and post-Ferguson crime rates, the authors found there was no significant change in crime trends in the 81 large United States cities under study. There was no "Ferguson Effect".

MISSING DATA

The research article discussed in Box 9.8: WHAT WE'VE LEARNED: Outlier Detection included the examination of various crime rates in 81 large cities in the United States. The authors, Pyrooz et al. (2016), stated that these represented 81 of the largest 105 cities in the United States. From those cities, some were excluded from analysis as a result of missing data, e.g., the crime data were not reported/available. Of the seven regression analyses they performed (see Table 2 of their article), only the examination of homicide used data from all 81 cities. The examination of rape used data from the fewest number of cities: 76. When data are unavailable or "missing," it can cause several problems and prompt a researcher to make several considerations with respect to the research question, the variables examined, the analysis performed, and the resultant conclusions that can be made.

Missing data is one of the most pervasive issues in data preparation and subsequent analysis in criminal justice and criminological research. There are several possible reasons for missing data. First, a human or coding error can result in incorrect (or in this case, missing) information. Second, information from particular cases or items of particular variables may be unavailable to those collecting the information. For example, in victimization surveys, or in any data collection instrument, voluntary participation is required. The respondents are free to provide, or not provide, the requested information as they choose. This can be seen when data are missing from the National Crime Victimization Survey (NCVS). Third, information may be unavailable to those analyzing it. This was exemplified in the Pyrooz et al. (2016) article, in which some jurisdictions were excluded due to only providing four months of data. Thus, missing data may be a result of coding error, being unknown, or willful omission.

TYPES OF MISSING DATA

There are several different types of missing data. Each type of missing data has different implications with respect to an analyst's treatment of the data and the subsequent analysis. The pattern of missing data is usually more important than the amount of missing data. Missing values found randomly throughout a dataset pose few problems for a researcher. Missing values that are found nonrandomly are much more problematic. This is often the case, regardless of how few the missing values are, as the nonrandom nature impacts the generalizability of the results.

There are three types of missing data. They are often referred to by their abbreviations. The first type of missing data is data that are missing completely at random (MCAR). Data that are missing completely at random pose few problems, if any, for the data analyst—particularly in large datasets. It is very unlikely that excluding cases on the basis of missing data will impact findings, as there is unlikely to be a significant difference between the group of cases that are

MCAR:
Abbreviating missing completely at random, this type of missing data is rarely problematic, as there are no patterns by which values in a dataset are missing.

MAR:
Abbreviating missing at random, this type of missing data may be problematic, as there is a pattern by which values in a dataset are missing in accordance with values of the other independent variables.

MNAR:
Abbreviating missing not at random, this type of missing data is nearly always problematic, as there is a pattern by which values in a dataset are missing in accordance with values of the dependent variable.

included in the analysis and the group of cases that are excluded in the analysis. The missing values are not related to any other variable, independent or dependent.

The second type of missing data is data that are missing at random (MAR). Data that are missing at random may pose some problems for the data analyst. These missing data usually exhibit a pattern that is predictable, thus methods of estimation can be used. Estimation of these missing values can be done based on prior knowledge or estimation can be done based on the values of other cases and variables in the dataset. The missing values are related to at least one other independent variable, but not the dependent variable. Most statistical software can perform this estimation. Using data that is known would help inform and produce an estimate of what would, or could, be the value that is missing.

The third type of missing data is data that are missing not at random (MNAR). Data that are missing not at random pose the most problems for the data analyst. When this pattern exists, the data that are available are likely an artifact of selection bias. There is often a reason, related to the dependent variable, that the value is missing. For example, suppose a self-report survey was administered to examine victimization and offending. Suppose further that there were many cases in which the data values for the question(s) concerning offending were missing. Analysis of the data that were present suggested there was a low offending rate of the respondents. However, it is possible that the results do not reflect reality if the excluded cases contained missing values related to their offending. It is possible that cases with missing information concerning offending have high offending rates. Thus, there would be a significant difference, substantively and likely statistically, between the group that provided data and that which did not. This would greatly impact the generalizability of any results, as they are not representative of the larger group, e.g., the population.

Missing Data Type	Characteristic	Impact
Missing Completely at Random (MCAR)	Missingness unrelated to IV/ DV	No pattern, no problem
Missing at Random (MAR)	Missingness related to IV	Some pattern, some problem
Missing Not at Random (MNAR)	Missingness related to DV	Pattern, problem

Figure 9.21 Missing Data Comparison

ADDRESSING MISSING DATA

Just as there are several types of missing data, there are also several ways in which a data analyst can determine the severity of the "problem," e.g., the impact of the missingness, and address it with respect to analysis. The methods of redress are based on the type of missingness, specifically whether or not it is patterned at random (e.g., MCAR or MAR) or not at random (e.g., MNAR). The actions an analyst takes in data preparation and analysis are also based on elements such as the intent of the research and the ability to perform certain actions. This latter element is often dependent on the availability of functions within statistical software.

The most common method to address the problem of missing data is, technically, not addressing it all. By default, when analysis is performed with statistical software, the program "drops" cases in which there are missing values for variables included in the analysis. For example, if a regression analysis was examining the impact of an individual's income on the number of crimes they commit and an individual did not provide information for the income variable, that case would be excluded from analysis automatically. This is referred to as listwise deletion. Unfortunately, if there are many missing values for a variable, and many variables in the analysis, there exists great potential for the exclusion of many cases from analysis. This is not usually a problem with data that are MCAR, but for MAR data and MNAR data listwise deletion may not be an option. Generalizability of results decreases and if/when many cases are excluded from analysis, the risk of committing a Type II error increases.

Another common method to address the problem of missing data is to estimate the values that are missing based on data that are available. These data come from other values of the same case in the dataset. This practice is referred to as interpolation. This is often seen in time-series research. For example, suppose crime rates are being examined for a 10-year period (e.g., 2000–2009), yet one year, 2006, is missing. One option is to interpolate the missing value. This could be done by finding the value precisely between the two surrounding values: the crime rate in 2005 and the crime rate in 2007. This would be referred to as linear interpolation as it is being assumed the

---

Box 9.9: WHAT WE'VE LEARNED: Addressing Missing Data—Interpolation

A recent study conducted by Pincham, Bryce, and Fearon (2015) examined the emotion processing of juvenile offenders. The research team recruited 122 male adolescents from an inner-city region of London. All of the subjects were between the ages of 13 and 17 and came from areas with a high level of socioeconomic disadvantage, operationalized as the proportion of households living in poverty. Poverty was based on median income. The estimates of poverty were produced as a result of triangulation, where multiple data sources are used. In this case, surveys, the census, and administrative data provided information from which to estimate poverty. The youth were compared based on a grouping variable that separated them on account of whether or not they reported committing a qualifying offense. Thus, the research sought to compare emotion processing of juvenile offenders and non-offenders. Using EEGs and interpolated data, elements of brain activity were recorded. Initial results showed no differences in emotion processing across groups. Further inquiry suggested that juvenile offenders are "hypo-reactive to unpleasant emotional images at the neural level" (p. 1000). The researchers concluded that antisocial behavior is likely to be enhanced and/or sustained based upon a youth's neural and physiological response. Treatment programs focused on emotion processing and subsequent responses were suggested.

changes over time are linear. If the value that is missing is a boundary measure, e.g., 2000 or 2009, one way to interpolate would be to calculate and use the difference between adjacent measures, e.g., 2001 and 2002 or 2007 and 2008, to obtain the missing value. This would also assume linearity, at least for those three values. Similar methods involve using longer time periods. Again, suppose the crime rate for 2006 is missing. Instead of using the two adjacent measures, from 2005 and 2007, the entire range of data may be used—2000 through 2009. The distance between these values can be averaged across the number of measurements (e.g., years) and used to estimate the missing value(s). Thus, there are several ways in which a data analyst can interpolate missing values.

Another way of estimating the values that are missing based on data that are available is by way of imputation. This practice involves estimating missing data values based on known data values from other observations or cases. There are several ways this estimation can be carried out. For example, single imputation may involve the estimation of a missing value from a known value derived from the random selection of a similar case. Another way to impute data is to calculate and use the mean value of a variable from all cases in the

IMPUTATION:
In data analysis, the estimation of missing data values based on known data values from other observations.

Box 9.10: WHAT WE'VE LEARNED: Addressing Missing Data—Imputation

While the National Incident-Based Reporting System (NIBRS) offers the opportunity to analyze a wealth of information related to a criminal incident, including offense, victim, property, and arrestee characteristics, one of its unfortunate weaknesses is the abundance of missing data. With advanced technology, by way of increased computing power and sophisticated statistical software, missing data from NIBRS are more often imputed today than it was in the past. Lyons and Roberts (2014) exemplify that point. In their recent study of crime clearance, they compared the time to clearance between hate and non-hate crimes. NIBRS data, however, proved problematic. Using data from the years 2005–2010, the researchers identified an inordinate number of cases that were missing information and would have been listwise deleted. A total of 18.4% of their cases would have met this fate (p. 276). Using multiple imputation, in which imputation was performed to create several datasets, i.e., possible values, averages were calculated. This allowed for the inclusion of the aforementioned 18.4%. From their analysis, they found that non-hate crimes were more likely to be cleared than hate crimes, and they were generally cleared in a shorter amount of time. Unsurprisingly, incident characteristics such as weapon type, victim-offender relationship, and victim injury—among others—were also related to crime clearance and time to clearance.

dataset. In larger datasets for which a categorical variable is being imputed, the means would represent a proportion of the cases that would have each category imputed. Thus, different values would be distributed across cases with missing data proportionally. A more sophisticated approach extends this by incorporating available data from multiple independent variables. Imputation may cause inaccuracies in the results obtained from an analysis of "complete" data. The standard errors may be underestimated, which, ultimately, would overestimate the associated test statistic, e.g., z, t, or F. Thus, imputation may result in an increased chance of Type I error (Allison, 2001).

INTERPRETING RESULTS

The interpretation of the results of regression analysis is consistent across disciplines, whether it be across sciences, e.g., physical to social, or within sciences, e.g., sociology to criminal justice and criminology. The same F values are computed (coefficients and standard errors), tested for significance (using t and p values), and estimated allowing for error based on a predetermined level of significance (confidence intervals). The values are explained the same way. The only difference resides in the content, i.e., *what* is being interpreted and explained.

As we saw in Chapter 8, there are several values and measures that are provided in the results of a regression analysis, including a measure that quantifies the explanatory power of the model. The coefficient of determination, or the R^2 value, is a summary measure calculated to describe how well the data "fit." This value can be used to compare different models using the same data or models from different data to see which combination of independent variables or which data best explain the dependent variable. This is not the only summary measure available to researchers that are attempting to quantify the predictive or explanatory power of a statistical model, or to compare models with one another. In addition to the coefficient of determination (R^2), an F test is also performed.

F TEST

In a regression model, regardless of the variant employed, an F test is conducted, most often by default, and its results are provided with the other aforementioned values and measures. An F test compares two models, the model that was analyzed and what is known as an "intercept-only" model. In essence, the F test is testing to see if the model analyzed, e.g., the model with the independent variables you selected, is a significantly better predictor of the dependent variable than a model with no independent variables. Thus, unlike the t test that evaluates coefficients individually, the F test evaluates all coefficients simultaneously.

	Sum of Squares	DF	Mean Square	F	Sig.
Regression	2.085	2	1.043	.285	.755
Residual	73.132	20	3.657		
Total	75.217	22			

Figure 9.22: Linear Regression F-test Example

The utility of an F test is considered, by some, rather limited. A significant F test, as evidenced by an associated p value of less than 0.05, indicates that the model analyzed provides a better fit, or better predicts or explains the dependent variable, than if no independent variables were input into the regression. More often than not, this will also be reflected in the significance of the model's coefficients. If any coefficient evidences statistical significance, so too will the F test. If at least one variable significantly predicts or explains the dependent variable, this would indicate the model's explanatory power, evidenced by the proportion of the variance of the dependent variable explained, is significantly different from 0. This is analogous to a significant F test: the model explains a proportion of the variance of the dependent variable that is significantly different from 0. As a result, if the F test is significant, the R^2 can be interpreted as being statistically significant. There are times, though rare, when an F test is significant, but none of the individual coefficients are. This would indicate that while no single independent variable significantly predicts or explains the dependent variable, a combination of them does. This may be a cause for concern, as this could occur if independent variables are highly correlated or additive, providing evidence of multicollinearity. Thus, some diagnostic tests can be performed before and—in a sense—after a regression is conducted.

SUMMARY

In order to test theory, or the effect(iveness) of a program or policy, researchers attempt to account for any substantively or statistically relevant condition when conducting regression analysis. The account for, and inclusion of, additional variables beyond the primary independent variable of interest allows the researcher and data analyst to control for the additional variables' effects. This further clarifies the relationship between the primary independent variable of interest and the dependent variable. Control variables are included in regression analysis for many reasons. These variables represent characteristics or conditions that may, by themselves, have been proven to be associated with the dependent variable under study. Related, they may have also been proven to be associated with the primary independent variable. Controlling for these effects supports the validity of findings, as the inclusion of multiple independent variables provides support for the third requirement of causality—the observed association is non-spurious.

Linear (OLS) regression, like all variants of regression analysis, has its own set of assumptions and requirements. This chapter was focused on what may be referred to as the primary assumptions—those that should be met at minimum for results to be considered valid, assuming an appropriate research design was utilized. These assumptions, generally, concern the values and relationships of and between the independent variables. For claims of significant relationships between the dependent and independent variable(s) to be valid, at least to the levels of certainty data analysis in criminal justice and criminology allow, the assumptions of OLS must not be violated. OLS assumptions are easily defined and perhaps more easily detected. Independent variables must not be strongly correlated with one another, independent variables must have a linear relationship with the dependent variable, the independent variables must have an equal variance across all values, the errors (residuals) of the independent variables must be normally distributed, and the errors (residuals) of the independent variables must not be correlated with one another. In addition to these considerations, and the other assumptions of OLS, further inspection and preparation of data should be performed. Outliers should be detected and, if they are too "extreme" or their impact too large, removed and excluded from analysis, as they may result in inaccurate findings.

Inaccurate findings may also be a byproduct of excluding cases on the basis of missing data. When data are missing, further inspection is required to determine what type of missingness is present. This determination will impact the subsequent steps taken by the researcher. In some cases, such as with data MCAR, listwise deletion is an appropriate action. In other cases, such as with data MAR and data

MNAR, several methods by which the missing values can be estimated are available. If data from the same observation or case are available for estimation, interpolation is most appropriate. If data from other observations or cases are available for estimation, imputation is most appropriate. Inspection and correspondingly appropriate treatment of data is necessary prior to any analysis of data. Without the examination and confirmation of regression assumptions, ultimately, the results will be inaccurate, and the conclusions will be invalid.

CHAPTER REVIEW QUESTIONS

1. Explain how regression results can be used for prediction.

2. Explain two of the diagnostic tests for assumptions of regression analysis. Explain if/how they can be conducted using graphical displays of data and statistical tests.

3. What is the difference between MCAR and MAR data?

4. Discuss the two regression summary measures, R^2 and the F test, and how they are related.

5. Explain the difference between interpolation and imputation.

CHAPTER REVIEW EXERCISES

1. Visit the National Institute of Justice's Crime Prevention page: https://www.nij.gov/topics/crime/Pages/delinquency-to-adult-offending.aspx
From the list of topics, select *From Juvenile Delinquency to Young Adult Offending*. View the image of the age-crime curve. Based on the shape of the curve, if age was used as an independent variable in a time-series research design, what regression assumptions might be violated? Explain.

2. Using the data you collected in Chapter 7 Review Exercise #2, determine if any of the assumptions of linear (OLS) regression are violated. Explain.

3. Explain how, by interpolation, a missing value for the annual number of incarcerated persons can be estimated.

4. Using your institution's library resources, find a peer-reviewed journal article that is of interest to you that discusses one of the diagnostic tests discussed in this chapter. Discuss the article, the diagnostic test, and what the researcher(s) found.

5. Using your institution's library resources, find a peer-reviewed journal article that is of interest to you that utilizes linear (OLS) regression to answer a research question. Based on the results, specifically the y-intercept and coefficient values, estimate a case's value based on various conditions, e.g., variable values, you select. Explain the results. See Box 9.2: Example: Practical Applications of Regression with Prediction for an example.

REFERENCES

Allison P. (2001). *Missing data—Quantitative applications in the social sciences.* Thousand Oaks, CA: Sage.

Amasa-Annang, J., & Scutelnicu, G. (2016). How promising is the second chance act in reducing recidivism among male ex-offenders in Alabama, Georgia and Mississippi? *Journal of Public Management & Social Policy, 23*(2), 22–37.

Anderson, T.W., & Darling, D.A. (1952). Theory of certain "goodness-of-fit" criteria based on stochastic processes. *Annals of Mathematical Statistics, 23,* 193–212.

Barnett, V., & Lewis, T. (1994). *Outliers in statistical data.* New York, NY: John Wiley & Sons.

Breusch, T.S., & Pagan, A.R. (1979). A simple test for heteroscedasticity and random coefficient variation. *Econometrica, 47*(5), 1287–1294.

Chambers, J., Cleveland, W., Kleiner, B., & Tukey, P. (1983). *Graphical methods for data analysis.* Boston, MA: Duxbury Press.

D'Alessio, S.J., & Stolzenberg, L. (2010). The sex ratio and male-on-female intimate partner violence. *Journal of Criminal Justice, 38,* 555–561.

David, H.A. (1998). First (?) occurrence of common terms in probability and statistics—A second list, with corrections. *The American Statistician, 52*(1), 36–40.

Dollard, J., Doob, L.W., Miller, N.E., Mowrer, O.H., & Sears, R.R. (1939). *Frustration and aggression.* New Haven, CT: Yale University Press.

Durbin, J., & Watson, G. (1950). Testing for serial correlation in least squares regression, I. *Biometrika, 37*(1–4), 409–428.

Durbin, J., & Watson, G. (1951). Testing for serial correlation in least squares regression, II. *Biometrika, 38*(1–2), 159–179.

Field, A.P. (2009). *Discovering statistics using SPSS: And sex and drugs and rock 'n' Roll* (3rd edition). London, UK: Sage.

Frisch, R. (1929). Correlation and scatter in statistical variables. *Nordic Statistical Journal, 8,* 36–102.

Frisch, R. (1934). Statistical confluence analysis by means of complete regression systems. Publikasjon no. 5. Oslo: Universtetets Økonomisk Institutt.

Gilstad-Hayden, K., Wallace, L.R., Carroll-Scott, A. Meyer, S.R., Barbo, S., Murphy-Dunning, C., & Ickovics, J.R. (2015). Research note: Greater tree canopy cover is associated with lower rates of both violent and property crime in New Haven, CT. *Landscape and Urban Planning, 143,* 248–253.

Gostjev, F.A., & Nielsen, A.L. (2017). Speaking the same language? English language fluency and violent crime at the neighborhood level. *The Sociological Quarterly, 58*(1), 111–139.

Hawkins, D. (1980). *Identification of outliers.* London, UK: Chapman and Hall.

Johnson, R. (1992). *Applied multivariate statistical analysis.* Upper Saddle River, NJ: Prentice Hall.

Johnson, R.R., & Crews, A.D. (2013). My professor is hot! Correlates of RateMyProfessors.com ratings for criminal justice and criminology faculty members. *American Journal of Criminal Justice, 38*(4), 639–656.

Koenker, R. (1981). A note on studentizing a test for heteroskedasticity. *Journal of Econometrics, 17,* 107–112.

Kolmogorov, A.N. (1933). Sulla determinazione empirica di une legge di distribuzione. *Giorn. dell'Instit. degli att., 4,* 83–91.

Lyons, C.L., & Roberts. (2014). The difference "hate" makes in clearing crime: An event history analysis of incident factors. *Journal of Contemporary Criminal Justice, 30*(3), 268–289.

Merton, R. (1938). Social structure and anomie. *American Sociological Review, 3*(5), 672–682.

Osborne, J.W., & Waters, E. (2002). Four assumptions of multiple regression that researchers should always test. *Practical Assessment, Research, & Evaluation, 8*(2), 1–5.

Pincham, H.L., Bryce, D., & Pasco Fearon, R.M. (2015). The neural correlates of emotion processing juvenile offenders. *Developmental Science, 18*(6), 994–1005.

Pratt, T.C. (2016). Theory testing in criminology. In Alex R. Piquero (Ed.) *The handbook of criminological theory* (pp. 37–49). Malden, MA: Wiley-Blackwell.

Pyrooz, D.C., Decker, S.H., Wolfe, S.E., Shjarback, J.A. (2016). Was there a Ferguson effect on crime rates in large U.S. Cities? *Journal of Criminal Justice, 46*, 1–8.

Rawlings, J.O., Pantual, S.G., & Dickey, D. A. (1998). *Applied regression analysis: A research tool* (2nd edition). New York, NY: Springer.

Reckless, W.C. (1933). *Vice in Chicago*. Chicago, IL: University of Chicago Press.

Reckless, W.C., & Smith, M. (1932). *Juvenile delinquency*. New York, NY: McGraw-Hill Book Company, Inc.

Shapiro, S.S., & Wilk, M.B. (1965). An analysis of variance test for normality (complete samples). *Biometrika, 52*(3–4), 591–611.

Shaw, C. (1930). *The Jack-Roller: A delinquent boy's own story*. Chicago, IL: University of Chicago Press.

Slutzky, E. (1927). Slozhenie sluchainykh prichin, kak istochnik tsiklicheskikh protsessov. *Voprosy kon"yunktury, 3*, 34–64.

Slutzky, E. (1937). The summation of random causes as the source of cyclic processes. *Econometrica, 5*(2), 105–146.

Smirnov, N.V. (1948). Table for estimating the goodness of fit of empirical distributions. *Annals of Mathematical Statistics, 19*, 279–281.

Sutherland, E. (1939). *Principles of criminology* (3rd Ed.). Philadelphia, PA: Lippincott.

Tartaro, C., & Lester, D. (2005). An application of Durkheim's Theory of Suicide to prison suicide rates in the United States. *Death Studies, 29*, 413–422.

Wehr, R. E. (1999). *Diagnosing model problems*. Retrieved from http://wweb.uta.edu/economics/facpages/wehr/scan/3328/DiagonisingModelProblems.pdf

White, H. (1980). A heteroscedasticity-consistent covariance matrix estimator and a direct test for heteroscedasticity. *Econometrica, 48*, 817–838.

Wold, H. (1938). *A study in the analysis of stationary time series*. Stockholm, Sweden: Almqvist and Wiksell.

IMAGE CREDITS

LOGISTIC REGRESSION

10

INTRODUCTION: PREDICTING THIS OR THAT

The scientific examination of offenders has become an accepted procedure in the administration of Anglo-American justice. The most usual types of examinations employed are medical, social, psychological, and psychiatric. ... For the most part, these examinations are made on a selective basis in those cases where more exact knowledge is required. The usual aims of these examinations are to demonstrate any social and personal factors which may have influenced the offender in making his decision to commit crime. (Smith, 1962, p. 6)

Dr. Charles E. Smith (1962), physician for the Federal Bureau of Prisons, provides a wonderfully succinct and accurate description of research in criminal justice and criminology, which is still applicable to this day. Contrary to popular belief, the overwhelming majority of individuals do not commit crime. Thus, since crime is such a relatively rare phenomenon, the study of its genesis and society's subsequent response has long been of interest—and of interest to individuals across a variety of disciplines, such as: sociology, psychology, physiology, and philosophy. As a result, the analysis of crime and the criminal has been observed for hundreds of years (Jeffery, 1959). As Smith states, perhaps of most interest to those involved in criminal justice and criminological research is the study of dichotomous outcomes, exemplified by his reference to the decision to commit crime. Consider the following:

1. What individual characteristics are associated with the decision to commit crime?

2. What factors are associated with the likelihood a criminal incident will be cleared?

3. What characteristics of a criminal victimization are associated with it being reported to law enforcement?

These questions may seem quite similar to the Introduction questions presented in Chapter 8 and Chapter 9. In fact, they are quite similar. Like the questions posed previously, the questions presented here are also structured to examine associations, or relationships, between several independent variables and a dependent variable. Thus, these questions may also be answered using regression analysis. However, this is where the questions here depart from those in the previous chapters. These questions reflect an element of Smith's quote—the dichotomous outcome. Just as different graphical displays of data, measures of central tendency, measures of variability and dispersion, tests of equality, and tests of association are made, calculated, or conducted on data of specific levels of measurement, so too are different forms of regression analysis. Like linear, or ordinary least squares (OLS), regression, logistic regression analysis provides the data analyst the opportunity to account for the many individual, social, and structural factors, circumstances, conditions, and characteristics that are presented simultaneously. The purpose of their inclusion is the reduction in the likelihood an observed relationship is spurious. This chapter examines the determination to use and the interpretation and explanation of logistic regression analysis.

LEARNING OBJECTIVES

By the end of this chapter, students will be able to:

1: Identify the different model summary measures of logistic regression

2: Discuss the difference(s) between linear and logistic regression

3: Explain the results of a logistic regression analysis

4: Evaluate the pseudo-R^2 summary measure

5: Interpret the results of a dummy variable

KEY TERMS

AKAIKE INFORMATION CRITERION (AIC)

BAYESIAN INFORMATION CRITERION (BIC)

BINARY

DUMMY VARIABLE

GENERALIZED LINEAR MODEL

ODDS

ODDS RATIO

PSEUDO R-SQUARED

PURPOSE OF LOGISTIC REGRESSION

Logistic regression provides the data analyst the opportunity to account for the many factors, circumstances, conditions, and characteristics that are presented simultaneously, with the intent of reducing the likelihood an observed relationship is spurious. The utility of logistic regression, like the other variants of this form of analysis, lies in its distinct requirements and resultant specialized purpose.

Logistic regression does not have the same requirements as linear (OLS) regression. Thus, the data used for logistic regression analysis are not the same—just as the results that are calculated and the way(s) in which they are interpreted are not the same. The term logistic refers to the function used in the estimation of probabilities associated with the regression analysis. Linear (OLS) regression examines a change in the value of a dependent variable, while logistic regression examines a change in the likelihood of observing a value in a dependent variable. Early versions of the function were developed during the 19th century (Verhulst, 1838,1845), when the term logistic was first used (David, 1995). Originally, the logistic function was used to describe the growth of populations. Despite its early popularity in academic circles, it would be another 80 years until the topic received consistent attention once again by mathematicians and statisticians. During the interim, however, the logistic function was frequently used in chemistry (Cramer, 2002). As the 20th century progressed, others in the field of statistics began to expand upon the early ideas and applications of the logistic function. During the 1950s and 1960s, logistic regression as we generally understand and use it today was developed (Cox, 1958: 1969).

Logistic regression attempts to provide the same conclusions that linear regression does: specific conditions result in, e.g., *cause*, a specific outcome. Logistic regression, as a form of multiple regression, examines the impact of at least two conditions on an outcome. These conditions are independent variables that are examined to see if they are significantly associated with an outcome—a dependent variable. The same criteria for causation in the Purpose of Regression section in Chapter 8 apply to logistic regression. In fact, they apply to all variants of regression. The inclusion of, and control for, multiple independent variables, e.g., conditions, is done for the purpose of meeting the criteria for causality, specifically the third—and impossible—criterion: non-spuriousness. As we will see, the explanation of the dependent variable in logistic regression is done with much lower accuracy, generally, than in a linear (OLS) regression analysis.

Box 10.1 WHAT WE'VE LEARNED: OLS and Logistic Regression

While the majority of researchers and data analysts opt to use one type of regression in a study, it is sometimes appropriate to use more than one. This is just what Roche, Pickett, and Gertz (2016) did when they set out to study whether Internet news consumption is related to anxiety about crime and support for social controls. Other forms of media have indicated the relationships between news consumption and anxiety, and support for social controls are positively related. Roche et al. used data from four surveys: one administered by Oppenheim Research, one administered by The Research Network, a Web-based survey, and the Cooperative Campaign Analysis Project (CCAP). Since the data were measured differently across the surveys, it was necessary to conduct both linear (OLS) and logistic regression. The first three surveys utilized linear regression, and the fourth survey used logistic regression. The results of their study suggested that Internet news consumption is not positively associated with anxiety about crime or support for social control. In sum, the first three regression models contained 116 different coefficients, none of which were statistically significant. The final regression model, examining the dichotomous dependent variable, showed evidence of a negative association between 16 of the 18 independent variables included in the analysis. The two variables found to not have significant associations were: if the individual was a born-again Christian or self-identified as politically Conservative. When these conditions were present, controlling for the other independent variables, there was no effect on the outcome (favoring the death penalty).

VARIABLES

In logistic regression analysis, there are some assumptions of the variables included in the statistical models(s). These assumptions, or characteristics, of the variables included in the models are different for logistic regression than those of linear regression analysis. As discussed in Chapter 8, the decision to use logistic regression instead of linear regression, or some other variant, is made based on levels of measurement. Logistic regression is appropriate when the dependent variable is measured at the nominal level.

DEPENDENT VARIABLE

Not only must the dependent variable of a logistic regression be nominal, but it must have only two values. This is referred to as a discrete and dichotomous, or binary, variable. These variables are categorical and can take on only two possible values, labeled as "0" or "1." Thus, the logistic regression model examines the impact of predictors on the probability an outcome, labeled as "1," will occur. As Aldrich and Nelson (1984) note, while linear regression measures the effects of independent variables on the average value of the dependent variable, logistic regression measures the effects of a change in the independent variables on the probability that the dependent variable is equal to 1 (p. 40–42). To this end, logistic regression can be thought of as an analysis of factors related to group membership (Tabachnick & Fidell, 2007). These groups are represented by the aforementioned labels: 0 and 1.

INDEPENDENT VARIABLE(S)

There are no requirements for the levels of measurement of the independent variables examined in a logistic regression model. In this specific type of a generalized linear model, they can be continuous, e.g., interval or ratio; count data; or categorical, e.g., nominal or ordinal (Aldrich & Nelson, 1984). A generalized linear model is one in which a link function allows for the modeling of a nonlinear dependent variable as a linear function of independent variables. Like dependent variables that are nominal, independent variables that are binary are labeled as "0" or "1," representing the two variable values or groups. When a variable has just two values, it is referred to as a dummy variable. This indicates the absence or presence of a condition. For example, if criminal history was operationalized with the nominal level of measurement, it could be coded/scored as "no criminal record = 0, criminal record = 1." The interpretation of dummy variables will be explained later in the Interpreting Results section.

A benefit of logistic regression is the relaxed assumptions, or requirements, of the independent variables included in the analysis. In logistic regression, the independent variables' errors do not need to be normally distributed. The independent variables are not required to have equal variances across all variables: they need not be homoscedastic. Finally, the independent variables are not required to be linearly related to the dependent variable. In fact, that is impossible due to the inherent nature of the logistic function, which can be represented graphically with the family of sigmoid functions. The sigmoid function is used in the probabilistic examination of an event occurring or a condition being present. Probabilistic examination refers to the determination of the odds (or probability) of an event occurring or a condition being present.

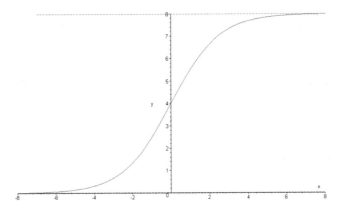

Figure 10.1 Sigmoid Logistic Curve

As discussed above, linear regression measures the effects of independent variables on the average value of the dependent variable. As seen in Figure 10.1, it does not "make sense" to examine or predict the average value of a dichotomous or binary variable. With values of 0 and 1, representing different outcomes, any average value that is calculated will be nonsensical: a case can't have membership "between" two groups. This necessitates the use of the sigmoid function, or s-curve, and logit link. This process transforms the dependent variable's predicted scores into a version of probability. This allows, subsequently, for the calculation of odds.

THE REGRESSION EQUATION

The equation for logistic regression is:

$$\ln\left(\frac{\hat{p}}{1-\hat{p}}\right) = \beta_0 + \beta_1 X_1 \ldots + \varepsilon_1$$

Figure 10.2 Logistic Regression Equation

where ln = the natural logarithm

$\hat{p}$ = the probability that $Y = 1$.

$$\hat{p} = \frac{e^{\beta_0 + \beta_1 X_1 \ldots}}{1 + e^{\beta_0 + \beta_1 X_1 \ldots}}$$

ODDS RATIO:
The value obtained when a coefficient is exponentiated in logistic regression analysis, representing the proportional or percentage differences, or changes, observed in the dependent variable based on a change in or condition of the independent variable.

This equation is a bit more complex than the equation for linear regression. Figure 10.3 below (the probability) value being calculated from its own equation:

Fortunately, statistical software perform all calculations and transformations. The natural logarithm is used due to its resultant interpretability. The coefficients calculated therefrom are interpretable as proportional differences, or changes (Gelman & Hill, 2007). Thus, the natural logarithm's opposite, the exponent function, is used to compute odds ratios. This transformation via the exponent is required, as the values derived from the equation in Figure 10.2 are not based on the same assumptions and requirements that data meet in linear regression. The values that are exponentiated (the odds ratios) are very easily interpreted. These will be discussed further in the Interpreting Results section.

Box 10.2: Example: Practical Applications of Regression with Prediction II

	b	SE	OR	90% CI
Constant (Intercept)	−.005	.454	.99	[.47, 2.11]
Juvenile	−1.501*	.586	.22	[.26, .56]
College Degree	−.753*	.345	.47	[.26, .83]
Multiple Incidents	−.677*	.339	.51	[.29, .88]

Dependent Variable = Reporting to Law Enforcement
*= statistical significance
From: Walfield, Socia, & Powers (2017)

Figure 10.4 Walfield, Socia, & Powers (2017) Results

Revisit Box 8.2: WHAT WE'VE LEARNED: Multicollinearity. Walfield, Socia, and Powers (2017) examined the characteristics of victims, offenders, and incidents that were related to the likelihood that a hate crime was reported to police and the likelihood that a crime resulted in an arrest. Using the results from their study, we can estimate the probability a criminal incident is reported to police (from Table 3 of the article) and results in arrest (from

Table 5). In Table 3, there were two variables, with a total of three characteristics, which were found to be significantly related to the likelihood a violent crime is reported to police (see Model 1). In Table 5, there were four variables, with a total of six characteristics, which were found to be significantly related to the likelihood a crime results in arrest. Thus, the following equations can be used:

$$\ln\left(\frac{\hat{p}}{1-\hat{p}}\right) = -.005(0) - 1.501(X_1) - .753(X_2) - .677(X_3)$$

Figure 10.5 Walfield, Socia, & Powers (2017) Equation

$$\ln\left(\frac{\hat{p}}{1-\hat{p}}\right) = -1.741 + .579(X_1) + .525(X_2) + .558(X_3) - 1.320(X_4) + .868(X_5) + 1.288(X_6) + .690(X_7)$$

Figure 10.6 Walfield, Socia, & Powers (2017) Equation #2

In reviewing the significant coefficients, we see there are two victim characteristics that are unlikely to be present simultaneously. Negatively related to the likelihood of crime reporting are the characteristics of being a juvenile and having a college degree. Since most juveniles have not yet earned a college degree, at least one of these coefficients will be equal to zero as a result of that variable value being "0" (the condition being absent). Thus, suppose the victim of the hate crime was a juvenile and a similar offense occurred within the past six months (represented as a "1" for *multiple incidents*). Since the constant, e.g., the y-intercept, is not significant, it has a coefficient that is equal to zero. The values above (each coded as "1"), along with their respective coefficients, can be input into the equation as follows:

$$\ln\left(\frac{\hat{p}}{1-\hat{p}}\right) = 0 - 1.501(1) - .753(0) - .677(1) = -2.178$$

Figure 10.7 Walfield, Socia, & Powers (2017) Example

The data provided by the National Incident-Based Reporting System (NIBRS) in Table 5 provide more variables for consideration. Like the example above, there are two characteristics, which are values of one variable, which would not be input simultaneously into the equation for estimation. If an injury is present, it is coded as being either minor or major. When there are more than two variable values, the same coding pattern applies. A reference category is coded as "0." This is a value of the variable to which the other values are compared. Based on the tests of significance, suppose the incident involved anti-Christian bias, had multiple victims, occurred at a religious institution in a Western state, and resulted in a minor injury. Due to the number of categories, the religious institution value of the location variable is coded as a "1," and the West value of the region variable is coded "1." In this model, the constant, e.g., the y-intercept, is significant and has a coefficient that is not equal to zero. Thus, it would be included in estimation. All other values (each coded as "1"), along with their respective coefficients, can be input into the equation as follows:

$$\ln\left(\frac{\hat{p}}{1-\hat{p}}\right) = -1.741 + .579(1) + .525(1) + .558(1) - 1320(1) + .868(1) + 1.288(0) + .690(1) = .159$$

Figure 10.8 Walfield, Socia, & Powers (2017) Example #2

Based on the Walfield, Socia, and Powers (2017) data in Table 3, your incident is estimated to have a log-odds of -2.178. Recall this must be transformed for greater interpretability. The odds can be calculated by exponentiating the log-odds ($e^{log\text{-}odds}$). The resultant value is approximately 0.11. This odds value can further be converted to a probability by using the following formula: probability $= \left(\frac{odds}{1+odds}\right)$. The resultant value is approximately 0.10. If this probability was explained using a different metric, such as percentage that has a base of 100, the results can be interpreted as follows: A hate crime with a juvenile victim who has experienced multiple incidents within the last six months has a 10% probability of being reported to police.

Based on the data in Table 5, your incident is estimated to have a log-odds of .159. When transformed for greater interpretability, the exponentiated value is represented as the odds. This odds value is approximately 0.60. This odds value can further be converted to a probability using the equation in the preceding paragraph. The resultant value is approximately 0.54. Using the percentage metric that has a base of 100, the results can be interpreted as follows: An anti-Christian hate crime that occurred at a religious institution in the West with multiple victims who sustained minor injuries has a 54% of probability of resulting in arrest.

Box 10.3: WHAT WE'VE LEARNED: Logistic Regression

A topic that that has drawn considerable interest recently is police–citizen relations. Related, the documentation of police–citizen interactions by way of body worn cameras (BWCs) or on-officer video cameras (OVCs) has garnered the attention of the federal government. Research solicitations, along with corresponding funding opportunities, have seen more criminal justice and criminology scholars examine the use of BWCs/OVCs. Drs. Ready and Young (2015) recently conducted an experiment concerning the issue in Arizona. The researchers conducted a 10-month long evaluation of 100 officers in the Mesa Police Department. The group of officers was divided into two 50-officer groups: one group was the treatment group that wore the BWCs/OVCs, while the other group was the control group that did not. As a result of using logistic regression, odds ratios were calculated in addition to the traditional regression values. There were several significant findings. Officers were 42% more likely to arrest an individual during the discretionary period than when the use of the BWC/OVC was considered mandatory. Officers wearing the device were 85% more likely to write a citation than officers in the control group, yet 55% less likely to stop and frisk. Officers wearing the device were also 77% more likely to have initiated the encounter than officers in the control group. Officers that volunteered to wear the BWC/OVC were 2.23 times as likely to write a citation as officers than those that were assigned to wear the BWC/OVC.

ASSUMPTIONS

As previously stated, the assumptions of regression that are observed when the dependent variable is measured continuously (OLS/linear regression) are substantially relaxed, if not absent, when the dependent variable is measured dichotomously. As a form of analysis with a categorical and limited dependent variable, logistic regression does not require variables have particular characteristics that linear regression does (Long, 1997). As a result, the following regression assumptions do not apply to logistic regression:

1. The error terms are normally distributed

2. The dependent variable is normally distributed

3. There is homoscedasticity

4. The independent variables and dependent variables are linearly related

Assumption	Linear Requirement	Logistic Requirement
Absence of multicollinearity	X	X
Error term uncorrelated with IVs	X	
Mean of error term is 0	X	
Error term is normally distributed	X	
Absence of autocorrelation	X	X
Measurement without error	X	X
Linearity	X	

Figure 10.9 Linear and Logistic Regression Assumptions Comparison

Figure 10.9 provides a comparison between a linear regression model and a logistic regression model. The comparison shows the four aforementioned assumptions that do not apply to logistic regression. There are some assumptions that remain important in logistic regression, as well as some that are generally restricted to discussion of regression analysis with categorical and limited dependent variables. First, the error terms must be independent. Second, there must be an absence of multicollinearity. Third, the relationship between the independent variables and the log odds, e.g., the left side of the logistic regression equality, must be linearly related. This is why the logit link is so important—it is required to transform the dichotomous measure to a linearly relatable value. Fourth, logistic regression requires a large sample size. The method by which the analysis is performed has less power than the ordinary least squares method. Rule of thumb states that 10 cases are needed for each independent variable included in the analysis. This rule has been extended, by some, to 20 and, by others, to 30. Thus, the greater the number of cases, the greater the probability of correctly rejecting the null hypotheses in the significance tests. Linear regression requires fewer cases per variable; about half of what logistic regression requires, though this rule of thumb varies too.

Box 10.4: WHAT WE'VE LEARNED: Multicollinearity II

Despite the fact that many of the assumptions, or requirements, of regression are relaxed or absent in logistic regression, some do still remain. One of the most common issues in logistic regression analysis is multicollinearity. Many variables are closely related to one another. For example, weapon use is often related to injury or seriousness of offense. Detecting multicollinearity and appropriately responding to it increases the validity of the regression analysis results. Matejkowski, Lee, and Han (2014) detected multicollinearity in their analysis of criminal history and mental health treatment among people with a serious mental disease. Evidenced by a variance inflation factor (VIF) of greater than 4, an interaction term was excluded from their analysis. An interaction term is when one variable is multiplied by another, suggesting the effect of one is dependent on, or changes based on, the value of another. These researchers had reason to believe that individuals with bipolar disorder would be more likely than others to use mental health services. While this was correct, due to multicollinearity, the interaction term of bipolar by age was excluded from analysis. A significant coefficient here would have suggested that the likelihood of using mental health services by those with bipolar disorder significantly varies based on one's age.

INTERPRETING RESULTS

When conducting a logistic regression analysis, there are several important calculations from which one may interpret the results. Statistical software programs used in data analysis vary in how they report results and what results they report. The format differs, as well as the metrics provided when statistics are outputted. Consideration must also be made to the software program's default settings when conducting the regression, specifically with respect to independent variables and their corresponding results. For example, by default, R sorts categorical independent variable values alphabetically and then uses the "lowest" or "first" value as the reference category, e.g., the one whose first letter comes first in the alphabet. Reference categories will be explained in the next subsection: Coefficients. In SPSS, the "highest" or "last" value of a variable is used as the reference category. However, for some other programs, there is no change in ordering of the values unless commanded by the data analyst. Thus, data inspection and preparation is suggested regardless of the statistical software employed or the analysis conducted.

Variable	B	S.E.	Wald	df	Sig.	Exp(B)	95% Lower	95% Higher
Constant (Intercept)	−10.851	6.403	2.872	1	.090	.000		
Complaints	1.396	.578	5.837	1	.016	4.039	1.301	12.536
Salary ($1,000)	.156	.116	1.804	1	.179	1.169	.931	1.469
Dependent Variable = Voting for a Union								

Figure 10.10 Logistic Regression Results

COEFFICIENTS

Regardless of what variant of regression analysis is conducted, the first test statistic provided in the results is the coefficient. This partial slope coefficient, or *b* value, represents the effect of an independent variable on a dependent variable: specifically, the average change in the dependent variable as a result of a one-unit increase in the independent variable, controlling for the other independent variables. In the discussion of coefficients in Chapter 8, the coefficients provided in the output were explained as being unstandardized. That condition remains. Thus, they are presented in their original units. It is not uncommon, then, to see *b* values that are substantially different from one another. This is a byproduct of the independent variables being measured by different metrics. For example, an individual's college debt may have *b* representing an effect of changes in the thousands, while the *b* value for sex may be less than one, because the range of possible values is so limited due to the variable's categorical nature. Some suggest standardized *b* values are less interpretable than the unstandardized *b* values, particularly in logistic regression. Thus, they are often left unreported, unless commanded by the data analyst.

Variable	B
Constant (Intercept)	–10.851
Complaints	1.396
Salary ($1,000)	.156

Figure 10.11 Estimated Coefficients

Figure 10.11 provides the coefficients that can be found in the logistic regression results table in Figure 10.10. These results are from a logistic regression analysis that examines the hypothetical citizen complaint data used throughout this text. Additional variables, and their respective values, were added to the dataset for the purposes of this chapter. This regression examines and estimates the effects of an officer's salary and their respective number of complaints on a new dependent variable: whether or not they voted for the establishment of a union.

It may be hypothesized that increases in salary are associated with favorability toward unions to secure one's income level. Conversely, it may be hypothesized that decreases in salary are associated with favorability toward unions, which can influence labor agreements, such as those involving salary minimums and annual increases. Further, it may be hypothesized that increases in the number of citizen complaints an officer receives is associated with favorability toward unions, as labor agreements may afford and define strict processes by which complaints are addressed and provide additional protections to union members.

Since the coefficients are unstandardized, they can be interpreted and explained in their respective metrics. The *complaints* variable is a continuous variable that is operationalized using integers, e.g., count data. Thus, the *b* value can be interpreted as a representation of the effect of an increase of one citizen complaint on the log-odds of voting for the union. Since the *b* value represents the effect of a change in the variable in its own metric, it would not be surprising to see a seemingly absent effect of salary on the likelihood of voting for the union. The range of salary is so great compared to the metric being used. As a continuous variable, the smallest change in the variable *salary* is, technically, one (dollar). Thus, the coefficient would explain the effect of an increase of one dollar on the log-odds of voting for the union. With continuous variables with high values, it is advisable to transform the variable. In this case, we created a new variable by dividing *salary* by 1,000. Thus, we examined the effect that a $1,000 increase has on the likelihood of voting for the union. The *b* value in this case would be 0.156, indicating a positive effect on the log-odds of voting for the union. Of course, this can only be stated if the association is found to be statistically significant. Remember, at this point, the value of the dependent variable is still in log-odds form, requiring the steps found in Box 10.2: Example: Practical Applications of Regression with Prediction II to have a value of greater interpretability.

STANDARD ERROR

Variable	S.E.
Constant (Intercept)	6.403
Complaints	.578
Salary ($1,000)	.116

Figure 10.12 Estimated Standard Errors

The standard error has no discernable difference when comparing its presentation and interpretation in a logistic regression to a linear regression analysis. There are, however, some things to be cautious of. Generally, standard errors in regression analysis, regardless of the variant, can indicate potential problems in the model. These problems are related to, and may reflect, violations of regression assumptions. For example, standard errors that are large may indicate the presence of multicollinearity. It may also indicate misspecification of the model. It is important to note that it is not uncommon for standard errors to be relatively larger in logistic regression results than in linear regression results. This is specifically the case for the constant, e.g., y-intercept, and categorical variables, such as dummy variables. Recall the standard error reflects the precision of the coefficient estimate. When data are measured categorically, there are few possible values; thus, the precision by which an individual variable, or value, estimates the value of the dependent variable is reduced. The larger the standard error, the lower the chance of finding statistical significance of the coefficient. In Figure 10.12, the standard errors for the y-intercept and *complaints*, at this point, may warrant some caution. The standard error for *salary* may not.

SIGNIFICANCE

Variable	Sig.
Constant (Intercept)	.090
Complaints	.016
Salary ($1,000)	.179

Figure 10.13 Test of Significance

To determine if there are significant associations between the independent variables and the dependent variable, one must only view the results outputted by the statistical software. The presentation of the values needed differs across software platforms. As discussed previously in Chapter 8, "some programs will explicitly title the values as 'P values' (e.g., Excel); some will refer to them as the indicator of significance, such as 'Sig.' (e.g., SPSS); and others title the values with reference to both the p value and the distribution from which it is calculated, such as 'P > |t|' (e.g., SAS, STATA, and R)." The interpretation is the same regardless of the statistical software used or presentation of the outputted results. These p values are compared to the preselected threshold, e.g., the alpha value, by which statistical significance is determined. In criminal justice and criminology research, the least stringent threshold typically used is the 0.05 alpha value. Some (see Walfield, Socia, & Powers, 2017 for an example) also denote significance based on the 0.10 alpha value. This may be done, because the variable is of particular substantive or theoretical importance or because the p value is approaching but not quite lower than 0.05. Thus, it is plausible that a different sample—one of different or one of more cases—may evidence statistical significance.

In Figure 10.13, the p value for *complaints* is less than 0.05, while the p value for *salary* is not. This indicates that, when controlling for the effects of the officer's salary, the number of complaints an officer has is significantly related to the log-odds of voting for the union. Similarly, when controlling for the effects of the number of complaints an officer has, the officer's salary is not significantly related to the log-odds of voting for the union. Most interpretations do not follow this format, e.g., referencing the log-odds, since transformations are performed subsequently. Thus, the same aforementioned statements of the existence and absence of the two relationships, respectively, can be made without the inclusion of "the log-odds of."

$$\text{Wald Statistic} = \left(\frac{B}{S.E.} \right)^2$$

Figure 10.14 Wald Statistic Equation

$$\text{Wald Statistic (Complaints)} = \left(\frac{B}{S.E.} \right)^2 = \left(\frac{1.396}{.578} \right)^2 = 5.83$$

Figure 10.15 Wald Statistic Example

Another, albeit less common, method used to determine significance is by examination of the Wald statistic. Abraham Wald (1943) developed a way to test for significance using test statistics that are already presented in regression output: a coefficient and a standard error. The Wald statistic is calculated by squaring the quotient of the coefficient and the standard error. The coefficient is divided by the standard error; then, this value is squared. Recall the discussion of chi-square in Chapter 7. The Wald statistic is a chi-square statistic: its critical value is the square of the critical value for z at the same level of significance, with one degree of freedom. The critical value for z, at the 0.05 level of significance is 1.96. The value of 1.96 squared is 3.841—identical to the critical chi-square value at the 0.05 level of significance, with one degree of freedom. Interpreted similarly to the chi-square tests of Chapter 7, determinations of significance can then be made. Since the calculated value (Wald statistic) is larger than the critical value, the null hypothesis would be rejected. This indicates that the coefficient, at the .05 level of significance, is significantly different from 0. Thus, it has a significant association with the dependent variable—the likelihood of voting for the union. It should be noted, however, that some suggest the Wald test is not appropriate for small samples and that it can be affected by large coefficients and, in turn, standard errors, thus increasing the likelihood of committing a Type II error (Agresti 1996; Menard, 1995). Another way to interpret the outputted results of a logistic regression analysis to determine significance will be discussed in the Confidence Interval section.

ODDS RATIO

Variable	Exp(B)
Constant (Intercept)	.000
Complaints	4.039
Salary ($1,000)	1.169

Figure 10.16 Estimated Odds Ratios

Logistic regression, despite some of its limitations, provides the opportunity to discuss results in terms and measures that are conceptually easy to understand by, and are likely familiar to, a study's audience. Some statistical software provide these measures by default in the results of a logistic regression (such as SPSS), while others require additional commands (such as R). The measure commonly associated with logistic regression is the odds ratio. Defined, the odds ratio is the value obtained when a coefficient is exponentiated in logistic regression analysis, representing the proportional or percentage differences, or changes, observed in the dependent variable based on a change in or condition of the independent variable. Stated differently, the odds ratio provides a way to estimate and compare the probability or likelihood of an outcome occurring (when the dependent variable = "1") based on the values of the independent variables. The term odds ratio was used first by Dr. J.J. Gart (1962) to describe the relative risk of an outcome occurring. Odds ratios are interpreted based on their value relative to 1.0. Assuming significance, an odds ratio that is greater than 1 suggests the variable, or value of the variable, is positively associated with the outcome (when the dependent variable = "1"). Conversely, an odds ratio that is less than 1 suggests the variable, or value of the variable, is negatively associated with the outcome. The null hypothesis states that the odds ratio is equal to one. The value one, then, represents an equal probability of the outcome occurring.

Our example in Figure 10.10 shows the only significant odds ratio is that of the *complaints* variable. When examining odds ratios, the value describes the relative change in likelihood that the outcome will occur. With our data, the odds ratio is greater than one, indicating a positive association with (the log-odds of) whether or not an officer votes for the union. With an odds ratio of 4.039, this can be interpreted using the following statement: A one-unit increase in the number of citizen complaints is associated with a 303.9% increase in the likelihood they vote for the union. Using the term "increase" implies difference. As a result, the percentage was calculated by computing the difference between the odds ratio and one, and multiplying by the percentage metric with a base of 100 (4.039 − 1.0 x 100). The odds ratio can also be described in relation to a previous value using the following statement: the odds of voting for the union is 4.039 times higher for every one-unit increase in the number of citizen complaints. See Box 10.3 WHAT WE'VE LEARNED: Logistic Regression for a practical example.

Interpreting odds ratios is slightly different when the value is less than 1.0. If the odds ratio is less than 1.0, this would indicate a negative association with the (log-odds of) dependent variable. While the explanations of these instances of being "less likely" or having "lower odds" are often used, the interpretation is less clear than when a variable has an odds ratio greater than 1.0. As a result, it is not uncommon for a data analyst to recode or reorder variable values to produce an odds ratio greater than 1.0 when applicable.

Similarly, interpreting odds ratios is slightly different when the independent variable is categorical. If the categorical variable is a dummy variable, where there are only two options—not having the condition or having the condition—the odds ratio is interpreted as the increase/decrease or change in odds when the value is "1" compared to when the value is "0." For example, if the *gender* variable was coded "0" for female and "1" for male in a logistic regression analysis examining the likelihood of voting for the union, and it yielded, hypothetically, an odds ratio of 1.5, the result could be interpreted with the following statement: being male is associated with a 50% increase in the likelihood of voting for the union compared to being female. This was calculated using the same steps previously described. The difference between the odds ratio and one is calculated (1.5 − 1), and the resultant value is multiplied by the percentage metric of 100 (0.5 x 100). The results could also be explained using the following statement: the odds of voting for the union is 1.5 times higher for males compared to females. For some, the use of this explanation may be preferable to the first version. Both forms of explanation are correct, and which is used is often the result of personal preference.

Box 10.5: WHAT WE'VE LEARNED: Odds Ratio

In a recent study conducted by Monahan, VanDerhei, Bechtold, and Cauffman (2014), the forced absence from school by way of a disciplinary suspension or expulsion and a willful absence from school by way of truancy were examined. Of specific interest were the relationships between these factors and the likelihood of being arrested. The researchers obtained data from the Pathways to Desistance study, which collected data from Philadelphia and Phoenix area youth from 2000 to 2006. Most youth were of lower socioeconomic status and/or a racial or ethnic minority. The data for the dependent variable, like that for the independent variables, were gathered from interviews. Of those that provided data, approximately half (47%) reported at least one arrest, and approximately one quarter of the cases reported being truant (26%) or suspended or expelled from school (24%). To analyze the data, the authors employed a variant of logistic regression. Several analyses were conducted by incorporating different control variables, such as the presence of peer delinquency, parental monitoring, and school commitment. Consistent across all four models, being suspended or expelled was positively associated with the odds of being arrested. The odds ratios ranged across the four models from 2.10 to 3.51. The next strongest association was found between peer delinquency and the odds of being arrested, with an odds ratio of 3.02. Interestingly, none of the parental monitoring variables were significant.

Categorical variables that are not binary are interpreted in a slightly different way than dummy variables where there are only two possible values. When there is a categorical variable with multiple possible values, one value is defined as the reference category. The odds ratio of the remaining values reflects the change in odds when that condition is present compared to the reference category. For example, if the *shift* variable was included in the regression analysis, the reference category would be determined by a default setting of the software (either the first value as coded or based on the first value according to alphabetical order) or by a setting determined by the data analyst. Suppose the first value for *shift*, "first shift," was the reference category. If, when examining the likelihood of voting for the union, the regression yielded, hypothetically, an odds ratio of 2.1 for "second" and 1.1 for "third," the results could be interpreted with the following statement: the odds of voting for the union is 2.1 times higher for officers on second shift, and 1.1 times higher for officers on third shift, compared to officers on first shift. Thus, each odds ratio represents the change in odds of the outcome occurring if the respective value was present compared to if the value of the reference category was present.

CONFIDENCE INTERVAL

Variable	95% Lower	95% Higher
Constant (Intercept)		
Complaints	1.301	12.536
Salary ($1,000)	.931	1.469

Figure 10.17 Odds Ratio Confidence Intervals

As previously mentioned in the Significance section, there is a method by which statistical significance of a coefficient can be determined based on the outputted results of a logistic regression analysis. This is done by examining the values of the confidence intervals. The confidence intervals provided in the results of a logistic regression analysis are not like those outputted in the results of a linear (OLS) regression analysis. In the results of an OLS regression, the confidence interval provides a range of values, based on a specific degree of certainty (α), e.g., the level of significance, where the population value of the coefficient is located. In essence, a range of values in which the actual value of the coefficient is located is calculated.

Like in OLS regression, the confidence intervals provided in the results of a logistic regression analysis do provide a range of values in which the actual value is located. However, in logistic regression, the range that is calculated does not refer to the location of the coefficient. Instead, the range refers to the location of the odds ratio. The confidence interval can be interpreted for statistical significance very easily. If the value 1.0 is located in the range of values produced by the confidence interval, the odds ratio and the respective coefficient are not statistically significant. Recall an odds ratio of 1.0 indicates there is an equal probability of the outcome occurring. If the value 1.0 is located within the range, it would suggest the possibility that the variable, and the condition it represents, does not impact the probability of the outcome occurring. In both Figure 10.10 and Figure 10.17, the confidence interval for the variable *complaints* does not include the value 1.0. This is one of the several indicators of statistical significance. By examining the second independent variable, *salary*, we see that the confidence interval does include the value 1.0. This would also be the case if the variable was not transformed based on a metric of 1,000, such as was described in the Coefficients section.

SUMMARY MEASURES

Cox & Snell R^2	Nagelkerke R^2
.449	.618

Figure 10.18 Model Summaries

PSEUDO-R^2:
A regression summary measure, based upon the coefficient of determination, that measures the dependent variable variation accounted for in a logistic regression.

Linear regression (OLS) provides the summary measure R^2. Called the coefficient of determination, this value represents the proportion of the variation of a dependent variable explained by the independent variable(s) in the study. In essence, R^2 quantifies how well the values of the independent variable(s) in the study predict the value of the dependent variable. While this summary measure is helpful and informative in regression models with continuous dependent variables, it has much less utility in regression models with categorical dependent variables. This is due to the inherent nature of categorical variables. They are not defined by a unit or measured on a scale from which variation can be calculated. An alternative measure, referred to as the pseudo-R^2, is usually measured on the same scale (0 to 1.0) as the coefficient of determination (see Mittlbock & Schemper, 1996 for a review).

Though there are many different pseudo-R^2s (Mittlbock & Schempher, 1996, discussed 12), the most commonly provided measures by statistical software are the McFadden (1974), Cox and Snell (1989), and the Nagelkerke (1991) pseudo-R^2. Some software require the data analyst to explicitly define which value is desired (e.g., R and STATA), while others provide at least one with the outputted results (e.g., SPSS). In Figure 10.18, model summary measures from the logistic regression analysis that examined the effects of the number of officer complaints and salary on the likelihood an officer votes for the union are provided. The first model summary measure provided is the Cox and Snell pseudo-R^2, which has a value of 0.449. A "perfect" model for this version of the statistic, theoretically, cannot reach a value of one. The second model summary measure provided is the Nagelkerke pseudo-R^2, which has a value of 0.618. This indicates a much better fit of the data or, in other words, there is greater explanation of the variation of the dependent variable. The Nagelkerke pseudo-R^2 is based on the Cox and Snell pseudo-R^2, providing a statistical adjustment to the scale in order for the possible values to range from 0 to 1.0. So, it may be expected that this value is larger.

There are two other very common summary measures that are used and presented in criminal justice and criminological research and that most statistical software provide. These are the Akaike Information Criterion (AIC) and the Bayesian Information Criterion (BIC). The AIC is named after its developer,

Hirotugu Akaike (1973), a Japanese statistician. Interestingly, since the papers in which he developed and discussed this measure were written only in Japanese, it would be some time before his work became well-known. The AIC, as a model summary measure, was developed as a way to compare different models on a given outcome (Snipes & Taylor, 2014). For example, if researchers conducted several logistic regression analyses on the same dataset, but with different independent variables, they could see which model explains the data the best, i.e., which group of independent variables explains the most variation of the dependent variable. Unlike the R^2 values, it is desirable to have as low an AIC value as possible. A low AIC value indicates a good model fit: the independent variables explain much of the variation of the dependent variable.

Closely related to the AIC is the BIC. The BIC was developed just a few short years after the AIC was discussed in Akaike's paper. In 1978, Gideon Schwarz published his seminal paper. Schwarz was a statistician whose work paralleled that of Akaike, both temporally and conceptually. Like with the AIC, it is desirable to have as low a BIC value as possible. A low BIC value indicates a good model fit: the independent variables explain much of the variation of the dependent variable. Many comparisons have been made between the two measures (see Burnham & Anderson, 2002, 2004; Vrieze, 2012). Some suggest that the use of the AIC is preferable when a Type II error is considered worse than a Type I error, and the use of the BIC is preferable when a Type I error is considered worse than a Type II error (PSU, n.d.). Related, some suggest that using the AIC is preferable with regression (Yang, 2005). This is likely a byproduct of its calculation, in which the BIC penalizes for additional variables, resulting in an equation that is different from the AIC by one value— the number of predictors.

SUMMARY

This chapter, like the preceding chapters, introduced new and fairly advanced material for the beginning data analyst. In this chapter, we expanded our knowledge and skill set with respect to regression analysis. Many of the requirements and purposes of regression from the discussion of linear (OLS) regression are also found in logistic regression. The primary difference between the two types of regression lies in the dependent variable. In OLS regression, the dependent variable must be measured at a continuous level. In logistic regression, the dependent variable must be measured at the categorical—specifically nominal—level and have only two possible variable values. A byproduct of this difference is the relaxation or elimination of assumptions of the independent variables. In logistic regression, the error terms are not required to be normally distributed, homoscedasticity is not required, and the independent variables are not required to be linearly related to the dependent variable.

There are many similarities, or commonalities, between OLS and logistic regression. First, the intent or purpose of the research is the same. Regression is a group of analytic techniques that identifies one measured outcome and seeks to predict or explain it. All regression variants simultaneously analyze the effects of multiple factors. With proper research design, data collection, and analysis, two of the three criteria for causality can be met. The third can be approached. Thus, regression allows for the provision of support for theoretical assumptions, as well as for the evaluation of interventions and treatments, such as programs, policies, and laws. Further, OLS and logistic regression share the requirements that there must be an absence of multicollinearity and autocorrelation, measurement must be without error, and a sufficient number of cases must be, and have data, available for analysis.

While logistic regression may suffer from disadvantages, such as the inability to produce an easily interpreted summary measure by which to evaluate a model's explanatory power, the reason for it—the categorical dependent variable—allows for ease in interpretation of the results. The examination and interpretation of coefficients, standard errors, and p values are no different in logistic regression from OLS. What is different are the confidence intervals and the estimated values they reflect, which provide a way to compare the effect of different variable values more directly than OLS. Odds ratios allow for the data analyst, or a consumer of the results, to see the relative impact of changing conditions on a single "either/or" or "yes/no" outcome. The results of OLS, having a dependent variable on a continuous scale, cannot be interpreted that way.

Through 10 chapters and dozens of questions and exercises, you learned: the history of many of the most commonly used techniques of data analysis, when to use these various techniques, how to evaluate the techniques themselves by way of strengths and weaknesses, and how to interpret the results from these many forms of analysis. Now, as a data analyst, you are equipped to conduct research, disseminate findings, and—with great hope—positively impact the fields of criminal justice and criminology and all of those involved.

CHAPTER REVIEW QUESTIONS

1. Explain why the assumptions of linear regression do not apply to logistic regression.

2. Interpret a significant odds ratio of 1.45 when the "1" value for the independent variable is *owning a car* and the "1" value for the dependent variable is *getting a DUI*.

3. What level(s) of measurement must a dummy variable be?

4. Discuss the meaning of an odds ratio that is less than one and an odds ratio that is greater than one.

5. Explain the significance of a variable when the confidence interval of its odds ratio is between .6 and 1.

CHAPTER REVIEW EXERCISES

1. Visit the BJS page: https://www.bjs.gov/

In the search bar, search the phrase *Profile of Intimate Partner Cases*. The first result is the report on the Profile of Intimate Partner Violence Cases in Large Urban Counties. Find Table 14 on page 7.

Based on this table, how would you describe the effects of the case characteristics on the probability of conviction? Explain each odds ratio.

2. Suppose you input coefficients into a logistic regression equation. What would the value on the left side of the equation represent? How does that differ from the value from the same location in a linear regression?

3. Why is logistic regression referred to as a generalized linear model? How is it "generalized?"

4. Develop a criminal justice or criminological research question that can utilize both linear regression and logistic regression to answer it. See Box 10.1 WHAT WE'VE LEARNED: OLS and Logistic Regression for an example.

5. Using your institution's library resources, find a peer-reviewed journal article that is of interest to you that conducts analysis using logistic regression. Discuss the article, the operationalization of the dependent variable, the largest odds ratio(s), and what the researcher(s) found.

REFERENCES

Agresti, A. (1996). *An introduction to categorical data analysis.* Hoboken, NJ: John Wiley & Sons.

Akaike, H. (1974). A new look at the statistical model identification. *IEEE Transactions on Automatic Control AC, 19,* 716–723.

Burnham, K.P. & Anderson, D.R. (2002) *Model selection and multimodel inference: A practical information-theoretic approach* (2nd Ed). New York, NY: Springer-Verlag.

Burnham, K.P. & Anderson, D.R. (2004). Multimodel inference: Understanding AIC and BIC in model selection. *Sociological Methods & Research, 33,* 261–304

Aldrich, J.H. & Nelson, F.D. (1984). *Linear probability, logit, and probit models.* Thousand Oaks, CA: Sage.

Cox, D.R. (1969). *Analysis of binary data.* London, UK: Chapman and Hall.

Cox, D.R., & Snell, E.J. (1989). *Analysis of binary data* (2nd Edition). London, UK: Chapman and Hall.

Cramer, J.S. (2002). *The origins of logistic regression.* Tinbergen Institute Working Paper No. 2002–119/4.

David, H.A. (1995). First (?) occurrence of common terms in mathematical statistics. *The American Statistician, 49*(2), 121–133.

Jeffery, C.R. (1959). The historical development of criminology. *Journal of Criminal Law and Criminology, 50*(1), 3–19.

Gart, J.J. (1962). Approximate confidence limits for the relative risk. *Journal of the Royal Statistical Society, Series B, 24,* 454–463.

Gelman, A., & Hill, J. (2007). *Data analysis using regression and multilevel/hierarchical models.* Cambridge: Cambridge University Press.

Long, J.S. (1997). *Regression models for categorical and limited dependent variables. Advanced quantitative techniques in the social sciences, number 7.* Thousand Oaks, CA: Sage Publications.

Matejkowski, J., Lee, S., & Han, W. (2014). The association between criminal history and mental health service among people with serious mental illness. *Psychiatric Quarterly, 85,* 9–24.

McFadden, D. (1974). Conditional logit analysis of qualitative choice behavior. In P. Zarembka (Ed.), *Frontiers in econometrics* (pp. 105–142). New York, NY: Academic Press.

Menard, S. (1995). *Applied logistic regression analysis*. Thousand Oaks, CA: Sage.

Mittlbock, M., & Schemper, M. (1996). Explained variation in logistic regression. *Statistics in Medicine, 15*, 1987–1997.

Monaha, K.C., VanDerhei, S., Bechtold, J., & Cauffman, E. (2014). From the school yard to the squad car: School discipline, truancy, and arrest. *Journal of Youth and Adolescence, 43*(7), 1110–1122.

Nagelkerke, N.J.D. (1991). A note on the general definition of the coefficient of determination. *Biometrika, 78*, 691–692.

PennState. (n.d.). AIC vs. BIC. *Ask a methodologist*. The Methodology Center. Retrieved from https://methodology.psu.edu/AIC-vs-BIC

Ready, J.T., & Young. J.T.N. (2015). The impact of on-officer video cameras on police-citizen contacts: Findings from a controlled experiment in Mesa, AZ. *Journal of Experimental Criminology, 11*(3), 445–458.

Roche, S.P., Pickett, J.T., & Gertz, M. (2016). The scary world of online news? Internet news exposure and public attitudes toward crime and justice. *Journal of Quantitative Criminology, 32*(2), 215–236.

Schwarz, G.E. (1978). Estimating the dimension of a model. *Annals of Statistics, 6*(2), 461–464.

Smith, C.E. (1962). Observation and study of defendants prior to sentence. *Federal Probation, 26*(6), 6–10.

Snipes, M., & Taylor, D.C. (2014). Model selection and Akaike Information Criteria: An example from wine ratings and prices. *Wine Economics and Policy, 3*(1), 3–9.

Tabachnick, B.G., & Fidell, L.S. (2007). *Using multivariate statistics* (5th edition). Boston, MA: Pearson.

Verhulst, P.F. (1838). Notice sur la loi que la population suit dans son accroissement. *Correspondance mathématique et Physique, publiée par A. Quetelet, 10*, 113–120

Verhulst, P.F. (1845). Recherches mathématiques sur la loi d'accroissment de la population. *Nouveaux Mémoires de l'Académie Royale des Sciences, des Lettres et des Beaux-Arts de Belgique, 18*, 1–38.

Vrieze, S.I. (2012). Model selection and psychological theory: A discussion of the differences between the Akaike Information Criterion (AIC) and the Bayesian Information Criterion (BIC). *Psychological Methods, 17*, 228–243.

Wald, A. (1943). Tests of statistical hypotheses concerning several parameters when the number of observations is large. *Transactions of the American Mathematical Society, 54*, 426–482.

Walfied, S.M., Socia, K.M., & Powers, R.A., (2017). Religious motivated hate crimes: Reporting to law enforcement and case outcomes. *American Journal of Criminal Justice, 42*(1), 148–169.

Yang, Y. (2005). Can the strengths of AIC and BIC be shared? *Biometrika, 92*, 937–950.

IMAGE CREDIT

- Fig. 10.1: Source: https://commons.wikimedia.org/wiki/File:Logistic.png.

DISTRIBUTION TABLES

Z table

	Area under the curve and left of z									
z	.00	.01	.02	.03	.04	.05	.06	.07	.08	.09
−3.60	.0002	.0002	.0001	.0001	.0001	.0001	.0001	.0001	.0001	.0001
−3.50	.0002	.0002	.0002	.0002	.0002	.0002	.0002	.0002	.0002	.0002
−3.40	.0003	.0003	.0003	.0003	.0003	.0003	.0003	.0003	.0003	.0002
−3.30	.0005	.0005	.0005	.0004	.0004	.0004	.0004	.0004	.0004	.0003
−3.20	.0007	.0007	.0006	.0006	.0006	.0006	.0006	.0005	.0005	.0005
−3.10	.0010	.0009	.0009	.0009	.0008	.0008	.0008	.0008	.0007	.0007
−3.00	.0013	.0013	.0013	.0012	.0012	.0011	.0011	.0011	.0010	.0010
−2.90	.0019	.0018	.0018	.0017	.0016	.0016	.0015	.0015	.0014	.0014
−2.80	.0026	.0025	.0024	.0023	.0023	.0022	.0021	.0021	.0020	.0019
−2.70	.0035	.0034	.0033	.0032	.0031	.0030	.0029	.0028	.0027	.0026
−2.60	.0047	.0045	.0044	.0043	.0041	.0040	.0039	.0038	.0037	.0036
−2.50	.0062	.0060	.0059	.0057	.0055	.0054	.0052	.0051	.0049	.0048
−2.40	.0082	.0080	.0078	.0075	.0073	.0071	.0069	.0068	.0066	.0064
−2.30	.0107	.0104	.0102	.0099	.0096	.0094	.0091	.0089	.0087	.0084
−2.20	.0139	.0136	.0132	.0129	.0125	.0122	.0119	.0116	.0113	.0110
−2.10	.0179	.0174	.0170	.0166	.0162	.0158	.0154	.0150	.0146	.0143
−2.00	.0228	.0222	.0217	.0212	.0207	.0202	.0197	.0192	.0188	.0183
−1.90	.0287	.0281	.0274	.0268	.0262	.0256	.0250	.0244	.0239	.0233
−1.80	.0359	.0351	.0344	.0336	.0329	.0322	.0314	.0307	.0301	.0294
−1.70	.0446	.0436	.0427	.0418	.0409	.0401	.0392	.0384	.0375	.0367
−1.60	.0548	.0537	.0526	.0516	.0505	.0495	.0485	.0475	.0465	.0455
−1.50	.0668	.0655	.0643	.0630	.0618	.0606	.0594	.0582	.0571	.0559
−1.40	.0808	.0793	.0778	.0764	.0749	.0735	.0721	.0708	.0694	.0681
−1.30	.0968	.0951	.0934	.0918	.0901	.0885	.0869	.0853	.0838	.0823
−1.20	.1151	.1131	.1112	.1093	.1075	.1056	.1038	.1020	.1003	.0985
−1.10	.1357	.1335	.1314	.1292	.1271	.1251	.1230	.1210	.1190	.1170
−1.00	.1587	.1562	.1539	.1515	.1492	.1469	.1446	.1423	.1401	.1379

Source: R. A. Fisher and F. Yates, Statistical Tables for Biological, Agricultural and Medical Research. Oliver and Boyd, 1957.

−0.90	.1841	.1814	.1788	.1762	.1736	.1711	.1685	.1660	.1635	.1611
−0.80	.2119	.2090	.2061	.2033	.2005	.1977	.1949	.1922	.1894	.1867
−0.70	.2420	.2389	.2358	.2327	.2296	.2266	.2236	.2206	.2177	.2148
−0.60	.2743	.2709	.2676	.2643	.2611	.2578	.2546	.2514	.2483	.2451
−0.50	.3085	.3050	.3015	.2981	.2946	.2912	.2877	.2843	.2810	.2776
−0.40	.3446	.3409	.3372	.3336	.3300	.3264	.3228	.3192	.3156	.3121
−0.30	.3821	.3783	.3745	.3707	.3669	.3632	.3594	.3557	.3520	.3483
−0.20	.4207	.4168	.4129	.4090	.4052	.4013	.3974	.3936	.3897	.3859
−0.10	.4602	.4562	.4522	.4483	.4443	.4404	.4364	.4325	.4286	.4247
0.00	.5000	.4960	.4920	.4880	.4840	.4801	.4761	.4721	.4681	.4641
0.00	.5000	.5040	.5080	.5120	.5160	.5199	.5239	.5279	.5319	.5359
0.10	.5398	.5438	.5478	.5517	.5557	.5596	.5636	.5675	.5714	.5753
0.20	.5793	.5832	.5871	.5910	.5948	.5987	.6026	.6064	.6103	.6141
0.30	.6179	.6217	.6255	.6293	.6331	.6368	.6406	.6443	.6480	.6517
0.40	.6554	.6591	.6628	.6664	.6700	.6736	.6772	.6808	.6844	.6879
0.50	.6915	.6950	.6985	.7019	.7054	.7088	.7123	.7157	.7190	.7224
0.60	.7257	.7291	.7324	.7357	.7389	.7422	.7454	.7486	.7517	.7549
0.70	.7580	.7611	.7642	.7673	.7704	.7734	.7764	.7794	.7823	.7852
0.80	.7881	.7910	.7939	.7967	.7995	.8023	.8051	.8078	.8106	.8133
0.90	.8159	.8186	.8212	.8238	.8264	.8289	.8315	.8340	.8365	.8389
1.00	.8413	.8438	.8461	.8485	.8508	.8531	.8554	.8577	.8599	.8621
1.10	.8643	.8665	.8686	.8708	.8729	.8749	.8770	.8790	.8810	.8830
1.20	.8849	.8869	.8888	.8907	.8925	.8944	.8962	.8980	.8997	.9015
1.30	.9032	.9049	.9066	.9082	.9099	.9115	.9131	.9147	.9162	.9177
1.40	.9192	.9207	.9222	.9236	.9251	.9265	.9279	.9292	.9306	.9319
1.50	.9332	.9345	.9357	.9370	.9382	.9394	.9406	.9418	.9429	.9441
1.60	.9452	.9463	.9474	.9484	.9495	.9505	.9515	.9525	.9535	.9545
1.70	.9554	.9564	.9573	.9582	.9591	.9599	.9608	.9616	.9625	.9633
1.80	.9641	.9649	.9656	.9664	.9671	.9678	.9686	.9693	.9699	.9706
1.90	.9713	.9719	.9726	.9732	.9738	.9744	.9750	.9756	.9761	.9767
2.00	.9772	.9778	.9783	.9788	.9793	.9798	.9803	.9808	.9812	.9817
2.10	.9821	.9826	.9830	.9834	.9838	.9842	.9846	.9850	.9854	.9857
2.20	.9861	.9864	.9868	.9871	.9875	.9878	.9881	.9884	.9887	.9890
2.30	.9893	.9896	.9898	.9901	.9904	.9906	.9909	.9911	.9913	.9916
2.40	.9918	.9920	.9922	.9925	.9927	.9929	.9931	.9932	.9934	.9936
2.50	.9938	.9940	.9941	.9943	.9945	.9946	.9948	.9949	.9951	.9952
2.60	.9953	.9955	.9956	.9957	.9959	.9960	.9961	.9962	.9963	.9964
2.70	.9965	.9966	.9967	.9968	.9969	.9970	.9971	.9972	.9973	.9974
2.80	.9974	.9975	.9976	.9977	.9977	.9978	.9979	.9979	.9980	.9981
2.90	.9981	.9982	.9982	.9983	.9984	.9984	.9985	.9985	.9986	.9986
3.00	.9987	.9987	.9987	.9988	.9988	.9989	.9989	.9989	.9990	.9990
3.10	.9990	.9991	.9991	.9991	.9992	.9992	.9992	.9992	.9993	.9993
3.20	.9993	.9993	.9994	.9994	.9994	.9994	.9994	.9995	.9995	.9995
3.30	.9995	.9995	.9995	.9996	.9996	.9996	.9996	.9996	.9996	.9997
3.40	.9997	.9997	.9997	.9997	.9997	.9997	.9997	.9997	.9997	.9998
3.50	.9998	.9998	.9998	.9998	.9998	.9998	.9998	.9998	.9998	.9998
3.60	.9998	.9998	.9999	.9999	.9999	.9999	.9999	.9999	.9999	.9999

T Table

df/α	0.05	0.01
	Critical values (two–tailed)	
1	12.076	63.657
2	4.303	9.925
3	3.182	5.841
4	2.776	4.604
5	2.571	4.032
6	2.447	3.707
7	2.365	3.499
8	2.306	3.355
9	2.262	3.250
10	2.228	3.169
11	2.201	3.106
12	2.179	3.055
13	2.160	3.012
14	2.145	2.977
15	2.131	2.947
16	2.120	2.921
17	2.110	2.898
18	2.101	2.878
19	2.093	2.861
20	2.086	2.845
21	2.080	2.831
22	2.074	2.819
23	2.069	2.807
24	2.064	2.797
25	2.060	2.787
26	2.056	2.779
27	2.052	2.771
28	2.048	2.763
29	2.045	2.756
30	2.042	2.750
40	2.021	2.704
60	2.000	2.660
120	1.980	2.617
∞	1.960	2.576

Source: R. A. Fisher and F. Yates, Statistical Tables for Biological, Agricultural and Medical Research. Oliver and Boyd, 1957.

F table

						Critical values (α= .05 two tailed)						
df1/df2	1	2	3	4	5	6	7	8	9	10	15	20
1	647.8	799.5	864.2	899.6	921.8	937.1	948.2	956.6	963.3	968.6	984.9	993.1
2	38.51	39.00	39.17	39.25	39.30	39.33	39.36	39.37	39.39	39.40	39.43	39.45
3	17.44	16.04	15.44	15.10	14.88	14.73	14.62	14.54	14.47	14.42	14.25	14.17
4	12.22	10.65	9.98	9.60	9.36	9.20	9.07	8.98	8.90	8.84	8.66	8.56
5	10.01	8.43	7.76	7.39	7.15	6.98	6.85	6.76	6.68	6.62	6.43	6.33
6	8.81	7.26	6.60	6.23	5.99	5.82	5.70	5.60	5.52	5.46	5.27	5.17
7	8.07	6.54	5.89	5.52	5.29	5.12	4.99	4.90	4.82	4.76	4.57	4.47
8	7.57	6.06	5.42	5.05	4.82	4.65	4.53	4.43	4.36	4.30	4.10	4.00
9	7.21	5.71	5.08	4.72	4.48	4.32	4.20	4.10	4.03	3.96	3.77	3.67
10	6.94	5.46	4.83	4.47	4.24	4.07	3.95	3.85	3.78	3.72	3.52	3.42
11	6.72	5.26	4.63	4.28	4.04	3.88	3.76	3.66	3.59	3.53	3.33	3.23
12	6.55	5.10	4.47	4.12	3.89	3.73	3.61	3.51	3.44	3.37	3.18	3.07
13	6.41	4.97	4.35	4.00	3.77	3.60	3.48	3.39	3.31	3.25	3.05	2.95
14	6.30	4.86	4.24	3.89	3.66	3.50	3.38	3.29	3.21	3.15	2.95	2.84
15	6.20	4.77	4.15	3.80	3.58	3.41	3.29	3.20	3.12	3.06	2.86	2.76
16	6.12	4.69	4.08	3.73	3.50	3.34	3.22	3.12	3.05	2.99	2.79	2.68
17	6.04	4.62	4.01	3.66	3.44	3.28	3.16	3.06	2.98	2.92	2.72	2.62
18	5.98	4.56	3.95	3.61	3.38	3.22	3.10	3.01	2.93	2.87	2.67	2.56
19	5.92	4.51	3.90	3.56	3.33	3.17	3.05	2.96	2.88	2.82	2.62	2.51
20	5.87	4.46	3.86	3.51	3.29	3.13	3.01	2.91	2.84	2.77	2.57	2.46

Source: R. A. Fisher and F. Yates, Statistical Tables for Biological, Agricultural and Medical Research. Oliver and Boyd, 1957.

Chi–square table

	Critical values	
df/α	0.05	0.01
1	3.841	6.635
2	5.991	9.210
3	7.815	11.345
4	9.488	13.277
5	11.070	15.086
6	12.592	16.812
7	14.067	18.475
8	15.507	20.090
9	16.919	21.666
10	18.307	23.209
11	19.675	24.725
12	21.026	26.217
13	22.362	27.688
14	23.685	29.141
15	24.996	30.578
16	26.296	32.000
17	27.587	33.409
18	28.869	34.805
19	30.144	36.191
20	31.410	37.566

Source: R. A. Fisher and F. Yates, Statistical Tables for Biological, Agricultural and Medical Research. Oliver and Boyd, 1957.

U table

									Critical values ($\alpha = .05$)										
n_1/n_2	1	2	3	4	5	6	7	8	9	10	11	12	13	14	15	16	17	18	19	20
1	–	–	–	–	–	–	–	–	–	–	–	–	–	–	–	–	–	–	–	–
2	–	–	–	–	–	–	–	0	0	0	0	1	1	1	1	1	2	2	2	2
3	–	–	–	–	0	1	1	2	2	3	3	4	4	5	5	6	6	7	7	8
4	–	–	–	0	1	2	3	4	4	5	6	7	8	9	10	11	11	12	13	13
5	–	–	0	1	2	3	5	6	7	8	9	11	12	13	14	15	17	18	19	20
6	–	–	1	2	3	5	6	8	10	11	13	14	16	17	19	21	22	24	25	27
7	–	–	1	3	5	6	8	10	12	14	16	18	20	22	24	26	28	30	32	34
8	–	0	2	4	6	8	10	13	15	17	19	22	24	26	29	31	34	36	38	41
9	–	0	2	4	7	10	12	15	17	20	23	26	28	31	34	37	39	42	45	48
10	–	0	3	5	8	11	14	17	20	23	26	29	33	36	39	42	45	48	52	55
11	–	0	3	6	9	13	16	19	23	26	30	33	37	40	44	47	51	55	58	62
12	–	1	4	7	11	14	18	22	26	29	33	37	41	45	49	53	57	61	65	69
13	–	1	4	8	12	16	20	24	28	33	37	41	45	50	54	59	63	67	72	76
14	–	1	5	9	13	17	22	26	31	36	40	45	50	55	59	64	67	74	78	83
15	–	1	5	10	14	19	24	29	34	39	44	49	54	59	64	70	75	80	85	90
16	–	1	6	11	15	21	26	31	37	42	47	53	59	64	70	75	81	86	92	98
17	–	2	6	11	17	22	28	34	39	45	51	57	63	67	75	81	87	93	99	105
18	–	2	7	12	18	24	30	36	42	48	55	61	67	74	80	86	93	99	106	112
19	–	2	7	13	19	25	32	38	45	52	58	65	72	78	85	92	99	106	113	119
20	–	2	8	13	20	27	34	41	48	55	62	69	76	83	90	98	105	112	119	127

Source: Roy C. Milton, "An Extended Table of Critical Values for the Mann-Whitney (Wilcoxon) Two-Sample Statistic," Journal of the American Statistical Association, vol. 59, no. 307. American Statistical Association, 1964.

W table

Critical values (paired sample)		
n/α	.05	.01
5	–	–
6	0	–
7	2	–
8	3	0
9	5	1
10	8	3
11	10	5
12	13	7
13	17	9
14	21	12
15	25	15
16	29	19
17	34	23
18	40	27

Source: Frank Wilcoxon and Roberta A. Wilcox, Some Rapid Approximate Statistical Procedures. Lederle Laboratories, 1964.

19	46	32
20	52	37
21	58	42
22	65	48
23	73	54
24	81	61
25	89	68
26	98	75
27	107	83
28	116	91
29	126	100
30	137	109

H table

Critical values (3 groups)		
Groups n/α	**.05**	**.01**
2,2,1	–	–
2,2,2	4.5714	–
3,2,1	–	–
3,2,2	4.5000	–
3,3,1	–	–
3,3,2	5.1389	6.2500
3,3,3	5.6000	6.4889
4,2,1	4.8214	–
4,2,2	5.1250	6.0000
4,3,1	5.4000	–
4,3,2	5.4000	6.3000
4,3,3	5.7273	6.7455
4,4,1	4.8667	6.1667
4,4,2	5.2364	6.8727
4,4,3	5.5758	7.1364
4,4,4	5.6538	7.5385
5,1,1	–	–
5,2,1	4.4500	–
5,2,2	5.0400	6.1333
5,3,1	4.8711	6.4000
5,3,2	5.1055	6.8218
5,3,3	5.5152	6.9818
5,4,1	4.8600	6.8400
5,4,2	5.2682	7.1182
5,4,3	5.6308	7.3949
5,4,4	5.6176	7.7440
5,5,1	4.9091	6.8364
5,5,2	5.2462	7.2692
5,5,3	5.6264	7.5429
5,5,4	5.6429	7.7914

Source: J. Patrick Meyer and Michael A. Seaman, "Expanded Table of the Kruskal-Wallis Statistic." 2008.

H table *(Continued)*

Critical values (3 groups)		
Groups n/α	.05	.01
5,5,5	5.6600	7.9800
6,1,1	–	–
6,2,1	4.6222	–
6,2,2	5.0182	6.5455
6,3,1	4.8545	6.5818
6,3,2	5.2273	6.7273
6,3,3	5.5513	7.1923
6,4,1	4.9242	7.0833
6,4,2	5.2628	7.2115
6,4,3	5.6044	7.4670
6,4,4	5.6667	7.7238
6,5,1	4.8359	6.9974
6,5,2	5.3187	7.2989
6,5,3	5.6000	7.5600
6,5,4	5.6558	7.8958
6,5,5	5.6985	8.0118
6,6,1	4.8571	7.0659
6,6,2	5.3524	7.4095
6,6,3	5.6000	7.6833
6,6,4	5.7206	7.9890
6,6,5	5.7516	8.1190
6,6,6	5.7193	8.1871

DECISION CHART

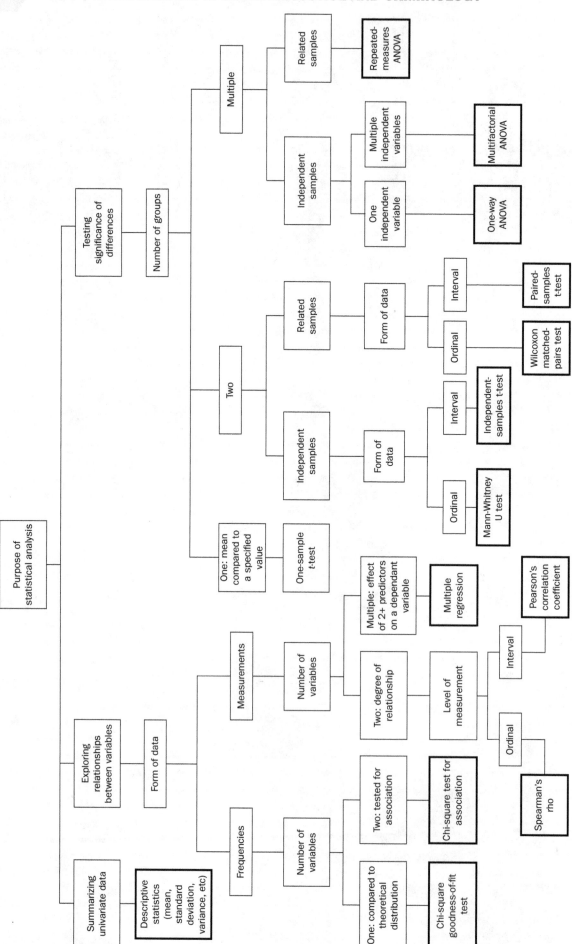

Figure 9. Choosing an appropriate statistical procedure

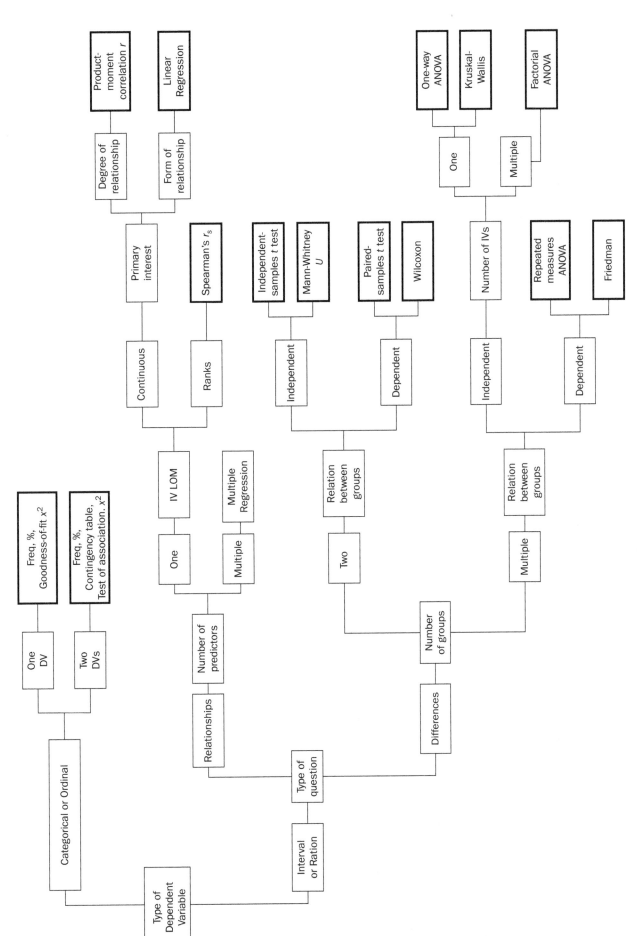

Adapted by James Neill, 2008, from: Howell, D. C. (2008). *Fundamental statistics for the behavioral sciences* (6th ed.). Belmont, CA: Wadsworth (back inside cover).

INDEX

A

Absolute value, 117, 141, 146
Administrative data, 19
Aggregate, 19
Akaike information criterion, 252
Alpha value, 137, 213, 247
Analysis of variance, 157
Annual survey of jails, 20
Asymmetrical, 118
Asymptotic, 78
Attribute, 42
Autocorrelation, 194, 221

B

Bar chart, 49
Bayesian information criterion, 252
Beta, 203
Bimodal, 80
Binary, 238
Box plot, 63

C

Cambridge study in delinquent development, 18
Categorical variables, 45, 79, 99, 139, 164, 196, 249, 251
Causation, 185
Census of jails, 20
Census of state and local law enforcement agencies, 19
Central tendency, 94
Chicago School, 54

Chi-square, 142, 165, 247
Class intervals, 57
Coefficient, 196, 211, 244, 245
Coefficient of determination, 200, 230
Cohort studies, 17
Collinearity, 211
Column percent, 48
Concentric zone model, 54
Concept, 195
Conceptualization, 31
Confidence interval, 194, 199, 250
Contingency coefficient, 169
Contingency table, 58
Continuity, 61
Continuous variables, 56, 86, 103, 151, 174, 190, 246
Control, 237
Control variable, 208
Correlation, 175, 188, 221
Correlation coefficient, 176
Count data, 36
Crime map, 52, 66
Critical value, 156, 178, 247
Cross-tab, 142
Cross-tabulation, 58, 169
Cubic, 216
Cumulative frequency, 46
Curvilinear, 216

D

Dark figure of crime, 12
Deductive research, 42

CPSIA information can be obtained
at www.ICGtesting.com
Printed in the USA
LVHW05194522O819
628613LV00009B/135/P